Lexical Input Processing and Vocabulary Learning

Language Learning & Language Teaching (LL&LT)
ISSN 1569-9471

The LL&LT monograph series publishes monographs, edited volumes and text books on applied and methodological issues in the field of language pedagogy. The focus of the series is on subjects such as classroom discourse and interaction; language diversity in educational settings; bilingual education; language testing and language assessment; teaching methods and teaching performance; learning trajectories in second language acquisition; and written language learning in educational settings.

For an overview of all books published in this series, please see
http://benjamins.com/catalog/lllt

Editors

Nina Spada
Ontario Institute for Studies in Education
University of Toronto

Nelleke Van Deusen-Scholl
Center for Language Study
Yale University

Volume 43

Lexical Input Processing and Vocabulary Learning
by Joe Barcroft

Lexical Input Processing and Vocabulary Learning

Joe Barcroft
Washington University in St. Louis

John Benjamins Publishing Company
Amsterdam / Philadelphia

The paper used in this publication meets the minimum requirements of the American National Standard for Information Sciences – Permanence of Paper for Printed Library Materials, ANSI z39.48-1984.

DOI 10.1075/lllt.43

Cataloging-in-Publication Data available from Library of Congress:
LCCN 2015025310 (PRINT) / 2015028285 (E-BOOK)

ISBN 978 90 272 1328 0 (HB)
ISBN 978 90 272 1329 7 (PB)
ISBN 978 90 272 6805 1 (E-BOOK)

© 2015 – John Benjamins B.V.
No part of this book may be reproduced in any form, by print, photoprint, microfilm, or any other means, without written permission from the publisher.

John Benjamins Publishing Co. · https://benjamins.com

Table of contents

Acknowledgments　　XI

CHAPTER 1
Introduction　　1
Research on lexical input processing　2
Goals of the book　3
    Subprocesses in lex-IP for different subcomponents
    of vocabulary learning　3
    Task-based effects　4
    Input-based effects　4
    Lex-IP at the intersection of SLA and psychology　5
    Implications of lex-IP theory and research for vocabulary instruction　5
Intended audience of the book　6
Organization of the book　6

Unit 1. Understanding lex-IP

CHAPTER 2
Multiple levels of input processing and language learning　　11
Different levels and types of input processing　12
Lex-IP and vocabulary learning　14
A new dimension in input processing　15
Different types of input processing yield different types of memory
    and learning　18
Examples of processing resource allocation in multilevel
    input processing　19
Input processing for different types of form-meaning relationships　21
The construct of "intake" in lex-IP　23
The central role of lex-IP in linguistic development　24
Differences in the meaning of "direct teaching" for morphosyntax
    versus lexis　25
Incidental and intentional vocabulary learning　25
Methodological issues in research on lex-IP and vocabulary learning　26

CHAPTER 3
Three key components of learning a word: Form, meaning, mapping   29
What is a word?   29
What does it mean to know a word?   31
What are the limits of the conceptual and semantic space of lexical items?   33
How do we learn new words? Necessary ingredients
      and basic mechanisms   34
The incremental nature of vocabulary learning   35

CHAPTER 4
Contexts of lexical input processing: L1/L2 and incidental/intentional   39
Lex-IP in L1 and L2 vocabulary learning   39
Similarities between L1 and L2 vocabulary learning   39
Differences between L1 and L2 vocabulary learning   40
L1, L2, and the "learning burden" in vocabulary learning   41
The case of learning new words and new meanings for the first time in L2   42
Lex-IP in both intentional and incidental learning contexts   42
What are the parameters of a lex-IP study?   43
Distinguishing between research on lex-IP and research
      on lexical processing   43
"Incidental" versus "incidentally oriented" vocabulary learning:
      A clarification   44
The incidental-intentional continuum in vocabulary learning   45
Six areas of research on L2 vocabulary across the incidental-intentional
      continuum   45
Four other areas of research related to L2 vocabulary   49
Research on lex-IP and *intentional* L2 vocabulary learning   51
Research on lex-IP and *incidental* L2 vocabulary learning   52

Unit 2. Task-based effects

CHAPTER 5
Specificity in type of processing and learning: The TOPRA model   57
Processing resource allocation   58
Specificity in type of processing   59
Semantic elaboration, LOP, and vocabulary learning   60
Impacts of LOP on ideas about semantic processing
      and vocabulary learning   61
Transfer appropriate processing   62
The type of processing – Resource allocation (TOPRA) model   62
A pivotal study on TOPRA and intentional L2 vocabulary learning   64
Specificity in type of processing and type of human memory and learning   67

CHAPTER 6
Effects of tasks involving semantic and structural elaboration   69
Studies on intentional vocabulary learning   70
    What is the effect of sentence writing?   71
    What is the effect of questions about word meaning?   77
    What is the effect of different types of instructions regarding focus on word meaning and word form?   78
    What is the effect of referent token variability?   79
    What is the effect of pleasantness ratings and letter counting on mapping?   80
    The Keyword Method, mnemonics, and the TOPRA model   81
Studies on incidental vocabulary learning   82
    What is the effect of synonym generation?   83
    What is the effect of pleasantness ratings and letter counting?   85
    What are the effects of type (semantic, structural) and amount of processing?   86
    The involvement load hypothesis, the TOPRA model, and lex-IP   87
Summary and analysis   89
    Instructional implications   91

CHAPTER 7
Effects of output with and without access to meaning   93
Research on output *without* access to meaning and L2 vocabulary learning   94
    What are the effects of copying target words?   94
    What are the effects of copying target words and word fragments?   95
    What are the effects of choral repetition?   96
    What are the effects of spoken output on learning novel L2 phonemic contrasts?   97
Research on output *with* access to meaning and L2 vocabulary learning   98
    Output *with* access to meaning and L2 vocabulary: A study by Royer (1973)   99
Summary and analysis   100

CHAPTER 8
Effects of opportunities for target word retrieval   103
Retrieval opportunities and research on human memory   104
Retrieval opportunities and intentional L2 vocabulary learning   107
Do benefits of retrieval opportunities extend to incidental vocabulary learning?   109
Summary and implications   111

Unit 3. Input-based effects

CHAPTER 9
Privileging and patterns in partial word form learning　115
Is the "receptive-productive" distinction an artefact of partial word
　　form knowledge?　116
Research on the bathtub effect　119
Research on partial word form learning　119
Bathtub versus recliner effects　121
Summary and implications　122

CHAPTER 10
Effects of increased and spaced exposure　125
Time of exposure and the meaning of effectiveness　125
Length of exposure interval and number of exposures (repetitions)　126
The spacing effect in L2 vocabulary learning　127
Expanding rehearsal and L2 vocabulary learning　129
Summary and implications　130

CHAPTER 11
Effects of semantic versus thematic sets　133
Arguments in favor of semantic clustering　133
Arguments against semantic clustering　134
Research on semantic and thematic clustering　134
Lexical networks, semantic relatedness, and lex-IP　136
Summary and implications　137

CHAPTER 12
Effects of input enhancement　139
What counts as input enhancement for L2 vocabulary learning?　139
Why might input enhancement lead to better L2 vocabulary learning?　140
Research on input enhancement and L2 vocabulary learning　142
The relationship between input enhancement and lex-IP　145
Summary and implications　146

CHAPTER 13
Effects of acoustically varied input　149
Acoustic variability and L1 speech processing　150
Acoustic variability and learning L2 phonemic contrasts　152
Acoustic variability and vocabulary learning　152
Summary of research findings in support of EPRH　156
A visual model of the effects of acoustic variability across the lifespan　157
Acoustic variability, vocabulary learning, and lex-IP　160
Acoustic variability and vocabulary instruction　161

Unit 4. Conclusions and future research

CHAPTER 14
Summary of theoretical and instructional implications 165
Summary of theoretical implications   165
    Thirty observations about lex-IP and vocabulary learning   166
Summary of instructional implications   171

CHAPTER 15
Directions for future research 173
Understanding multilevel input processing   173
Quantifying predictions of the TOPRA model   174
Assessing tasks in incidental contexts   175
Advancing our understanding of dissociable types of processing   175
Evaluating different input-retrieval patterns   176
Isolating benefits of input enhancement   177
Appraising the qualitative effects of acoustic variability   177
Concluding remarks   178

References	179
Appendix A	191
Appendix B	192
Index	193

Acknowledgments

I would like to thank Kees Vaes, Nina Spada, Nelleke van Deusen-Scholl and Patricia Leplae for their assistance during the preparation of this book. I also extend my appreciation to Muriel Barcroft and Paul Mandell for their helpful revision suggestions.

CHAPTER 1

Introduction

Research on *lexical input processing* (lex-IP) concerns how learners allocate their limited attentional and cognitive processing resources when they are exposed to a new word or lexical phrase as *input*, or samples of the target language. The purpose of this book is to provide an integrated account of research and theoretical advances in the study of lex-IP to date and to clarify how future research in this area can advance our understanding of vocabulary learning and language acquisition in general. The book is designed to clarify what constitutes research on lex-IP, to identify the boundaries of different subareas of research related to lex-IP, and to survey key theoretical and methodological issues being addressed within each of the subareas. As such, it is hoped that the book not only informs but also serves a springboard for researchers interested in conducting future research within this developing and expanding area of inquiry. Before focusing on specific issues related to lex-IP and the organization of the book, we begin by situating lex-IP as it relates to language acquisition in general and, more specifically, to the study of input processing across multiple levels of linguistic analysis.

Input refers to samples of a language to which a learner is exposed. It is what drives language acquisition. Without input, children would never acquire their first language (L1) nor would anyone acquire any language, including adults attempting to learn a second language (L2). It was therefore a fortunate turn of events when the field of second language acquisition (SLA) turned a substantial amount of its attention to the role of input in acquisition some four decades ago. Krashen's (1981, 1982, 1985) contributions drew attention to the central role that input plays in acquisition, the type of input that is well suited to promote acquisition, and the extreme limits of explicit learning that results from studying grammatical rules as compared to implicit learning that results from attending to input.

Input processing refers to the process of deriving *intake*, which is the subset of input that becomes available as linguistic evidence or data available to the learner's developing linguistic system (VanPatten, 1996, p. 10). Consequently, input processing is also a central and necessary component of successful language acquisition. If learners do not process the input to which they are exposed, they cannot obtain the linguistic data that they need to move forward in their acquisition of any given target language. More specifically, input processing leads to intake, which is the type of data that a learner's developing linguistic system needs to restructure itself. Learners then make use of their linguistic system to produce *output*, or language produced by the learner by means of activating their developing linguistic system and engaging in *output processing*. The basic information-processing model being described here is the following:

> INPUT > INPUT PROCESSING > INTAKE > DEVELOPING SYSTEM (RESTRUCTURING) > OUTPUT PROCESSING > OUTPUT.

Over time, the processing of input leads to changes in learners' developing linguistic systems that allow them to produce increasingly native-like output, although not always in a linear manner. This increasingly native-like output is the result of input processing and restructuring of the linguistic system, not output practice. Practice in producing output may be helpful in achieving more fluency, but it is not the primary cause or driving force in acquisition or the ability to produce increasingly native-like output. Without sufficient exposure to input and sufficient (successful) input processing, output of this nature would never be possible because learners rely on the current version of their developing linguistic system to produce output, at least when they are attempting to do so for communicative purposes.

To date, SLA research on the input-processing component of this model of SLA has focused mostly on sentence-level input processing and its relation to attention to and acquisition of (morpho)syntactic features of different L2s. This focus on sentence-level input has led to research findings with a number of important theoretical and pedagogical implications, such as the finding that learners preferentially process (a) lexical items more than grammatical items and (b) more meaningful morphology more than less or nonmeaningful morphology (see VanPatten, 1996). Focus on input processing at the sentence level alone does not capture, however, the more complete nature of what input processing is and the various types of linguistic competence that input processing underlies and affects. We need to investigate how L2 development is affected by input processing at other levels of linguistic competence, such as at the phonetic-phonemic, lexical, and discourse levels.

Research on lexical input processing

In recent years, new research and theoretical advances have begun to address this issue, particularly at the level of lexis (note also the large number of studies on the relationship between input and the acquisition of L2 phonology in the 2009 book *Input Matters in SLA*, edited by Piske & Young-Scholten). Research on *lexical input processing*, which refers to the processes by which learners allocate processing resources when they are exposed to a new word or lexical phrase as input, has led to a number of intriguing findings with important pedagogical implications. Some studies have demonstrated, for example, that increases in semantically oriented processing associated with tasks like attending to questions about word meaning (Barcroft, 2003b) or writing words in original sentences (Barcroft, 2004a) can negatively affect L2 word learning, which runs contrary to some commonly held beliefs about tasks that should be effective for promoting L2 vocabulary learning. Other studies (Barcroft & Sommers, 2005; Sommers & Barcroft, 2007) have demonstrated that systematically increasing certain types of acoustic variability during the presentation of target L2 words as input produces positive effects on L2 vocabulary learning. As a final example, other studies (Barcroft, 2008; Barcroft & Rott, 2010) have demonstrated, based on investigations of partial word form learning during the initial stages of learning L2 words, that processing of word-initial segments of novel word forms is privileged over processing word-medial and word-final segments.

Goals of the book

As mentioned previously, this book is designed to provide an integrated account of current research and theoretical advances related to lex-IP and to clarify how future research can continue to advance our understanding in this area. It also clarifies the type of research that is informative with regard to lex-IP, identifies the boundaries of different subareas of research related to lex-IP, and summarizes key theoretical and methodological issues being addressed within each of the subareas. One way of better understanding the various subareas of research on lex-IP is to consider different subcomponents of vocabulary learning, the types of processing that are needed for these subcomponents to be learned, and how different types of tasks and learning conditions affect each of these subcomponents individually or in combination.

Subprocesses in lex-IP for different subcomponents of vocabulary learning

In order to learn a new word or any type of lexical item (lexical phrase, formulaic expression, and so forth), a learner must always attend to the item as an input string and engage a series of subprocesses specific to lex-IP. At a minimum the learner must (a) encode the form of the new word in memory, (b) activate an appropriate semantic representation for the word, and (c) map the form of the word onto the appropriate semantic representation of the word. These subprocesses must be engaged regardless of whether the lexical item in question is being learned intentionally or incidentally from context. Research on lex-IP has identified how specific *tasks* (such as semantically and structurally oriented tasks) and *learning conditions* related to how target vocabulary is presented as input affect the manner in which learners allocate their limited (cognitive) processing resources towards each of these three subprocesses and how, in turn, these tasks and learning conditions affect L2 vocabulary learning. To date, most research on these issues has focused on intentional L2 vocabulary learning, but some research has begun to focus on incidental L2 vocabulary learning as well.

Task-based effects

To provide some examples related to tasks, consider a series of studies on how output *with* access to meaning based on opportunities for target word retrieval as the specific task (Barcroft, 2007a; McNamara & Healy, 1995; Royer, 1973) and output *without* access to meaning based on word copying as the specific task (Barcroft, 2006) affect intentional L2 vocabulary learning. Interestingly, the combined findings of these studies indicate that only output with access to meaning produced positive effects whereas output without access to meaning produced negative effects as compared to a condition with no additional task. Why this pattern of results? From a lex-IP perspective, it is critical to note that output with access to meaning requires that learners have at least one opportunity to process target words as input because learners cannot attempt to retrieve a target word if they have never been exposed to the word previously. Under these circumstances, learners who attempt to retrieve target words to which they have recently been exposed enjoy the benefits of retrieval opportunities, which have been well established in memory research in psychology and which continue to be a predominant focus of research in recent years (Roediger, 2009). Output without access to meaning does not imply having had an opportunity to retrieve a target word, however, and under these circumstances, the act of simply repeating or "parroting" the input can interfere with successful lex-IP for the target word in question.

Input-based effects

To provide some examples of effects related to how lexical items are presented as input, let us begin by considering studies that have demonstrated that presenting target words in acoustically varied formats (based on variations in talker, speaking style, and speaking rate) can produce positive effects on spoken word-picture based intentional L2 word learning (Barcroft & Sommers; 2005; Sommers & Barcroft, 2007). These positive effects suggest that learners encode not only linguistic information when processing target vocabulary but also *indexical* information (about the talker, the speaking style being used by the talker, and so forth), and when they do so, the indexical information leads to more distributed (robust) developing word-form representations, providing the learner with additional means of accessing the target word form when cued (such as by a picture) to do so. Other research (Sommers & Barcroft, 2013) has revealed, on the other hand, that varying the referent of target words produces increasingly negative effects on spoken word-picture based intentional L2 word learning. Therefore, it is critical to identify the *type* of processing a given type of input variability promotes when predicting learning outcomes. Whereas phonetically relevant acoustic variability increases word form learning by means of more distributed (robust) word-form representations, referent token variability decreases L2 word form learning by utilizing resources in the direction of referent-oriented (semantic, visual) processing and thereby depleting resources that could have been directed toward encoding novel word forms. These combined findings are consistent with Barcroft's (2002a) type of processing – resource allocation (TOPRA) model, as explained later in greater detail.

Lex-IP at the intersection of SLA and psychology

Another goal of this book is to draw attention to and to extrapolate upon important connections between theoretical advances in lex-IP and well-known theoretical frameworks in psychology related to human memory and learning, such as levels of processing (Craik & Lockhart, 1972) and transfer appropriate processing (Morris, Bransford & Franks, 1977). Barcroft's type of processing – resource allocation (TOPRA) model, for example, provides a visual depiction of why we should expect semantically oriented tasks to negatively affect L2 word form learning when processing demands are sufficiently high. It depicts how semantic and structurally oriented processing are dissociable and how, when learners' processing capacities reach a level of exhaustion, tasks that increase semantically oriented processing can decrease learners' abilities to process the formal properties of novel words, leading to less overall word form learning. This model and the research findings that have provided support for it (e.g., Barcroft, 2002a, 2004a, 2006) are consistent with the transfer-appropriate-processing framework but are inconsistent with the levels-of-processing framework when applied to L2 vocabulary learning in absence of some *very* special qualifications, such as the need to distinguish between memory for novel form versus memory for different types of semantic information.

Implications of lex-IP theory and research for vocabulary instruction

Finally, although the primary goals of the book are theoretical and research-oriented in nature, the theory and research in question have important implications regarding the way that instructors teach, or should teach, vocabulary. To provide one consequential example, within the past fifteen years or so, and as mentioned previously, a series of studies by Barcroft (2002a, 2004a, 2008) have demonstrated that semantically elaborative tasks such as writing target words in sentences, addressing questions about the meaning of target words, and generating L1 synonyms for target words *negatively* affect L2 word form learning during the initial stages of learning new words (including, at least in the case of synonym generation, for incidentally oriented L2 vocabulary learning). While such findings may seem counterintuitive upon initial consideration, the theory and research spelled out in this book are designed to provide the reader with opportunities to understand them in a new light, one in which they can become intuitive. The negative effects of semantically oriented tasks become more intuitive, for example, if one considers the critical roles of (a) *specificity* in type of processing (in particular, semantic versus structurally oriented processing), (b) processing *resource allocation*, and (c) the predictions of the *TOPRA* model.

Intended audience of the book

This book was written for SLA researchers, students of SLA, students of language teaching methodology, and L2 instructors interested in lex-IP, a fascinating and continuously developing area of inquiry within SLA. As mentioned above, most research on input processing in SLA to date has focused on sentence-level input processing, but because input processing occurs at all levels of linguistic analysis, including lexical and discourse levels, it needs to be investigated and theorized as such. This book takes an important step in this direction by examining and providing a synthesis of theory and research directly related to lex-IP within the past fifteen years and pertinent work beyond this time period. As such, the book is unique in its origin and content and in the research methodologies it reviews, methodologies that differ substantially from those that have been used to investigate sentence-level input processing.

Organization of the book

The organization of the book reflects the distribution of key research on lex-IP to date. Chapter 1 presents an introduction to lex-IP as an area of inquiry and situates it within the larger field of SLA. It defines key terms and introduces major theoretical issues, such as those related to processing type specificity and output *with* versus *without* access to meaning, which are discussed throughout the rest of the book. Chapters 2–15 are then divided into four key units: UNDERSTANDING

LEX-IP (Chapters 2–4), TASK-BASED EFFECTS (Chapters 5–8), INPUT-BASED EFFECTS (Chapters 9–13), and CONCLUSIONS AND FUTURE RESEARCH (Chapters 14–15).

The first of these three units includes Chapters 2 through 4. Chapter 2 explains how lex-IP is situated with respect to research on other levels of input processing. Chapter 3 identifies and exemplifies the relevance of form, meaning, and mapping as components of vocabulary learning. Chapter 4 discusses key differences between lex-IP in first language (L1) and L2 vocabulary learning and clarifies how lex-IP is pertinent in contexts of both intentional and incidental vocabulary learning.

The second unit, which includes Chapters 5 through 8, focuses on task-based effects in lex-IP theory and research. Chapter 5 reviews theoretical developments and research findings related to the effects of a variety of tasks on vocabulary learning, including the predictions of the type of processing – resource allocation (TOPRA) model. Chapter 6 examines the differential effects of semantically elaborative tasks, such as addressing questions about word meaning, and structurally elaborative tasks, such as letter counting. Chapters 7 and 8 consider, respectively, the negative effects of tasks that involve output *without* access to meaning such as word copying (Chapter 7), and the positive effects of output *with* access to meaning based primarily on studies on opportunities for target word retrieval (Chapter 8).

The third unit, which includes Chapters 9–13, addresses a series of input-based effects in lex-IP research and theory. Chapter 9 focuses on research on particular patterns in partial word form learning, such as primacy effects in learning at the word level. Chapter 10 reviews implications of the positive effects of increased and spaced exposure to target vocabulary. Chapter 11 considers negative effects of learning new words in semantic as opposed to thematic sets due to interference (e.g., Finkbeiner & Nicol, 2003). Chapter 12 explores demonstrations of positive effects of input enhancement. Chapter 13 assesses the implications of an increasingly large body of research on the effects of presenting target words in acoustically varied formats based on multiple talkers, speaking styles, speaking rates, amplitudes, and overall fundamental frequencies.

Finally, the remaining two chapters make up the fourth unit of the book. They provide a summary and look toward the future. Chapter 14 summarizes theoretical and instructional implications of research within the multiple subareas of research related to lex-IP, making specific reference to input-based incremental (IBI) vocabulary instruction (Barcroft, 2012). Chapter 15 then discusses the potential of various possible directions for future research that can help to advance our understanding of lex-IP and the pivotal role of input processing in language acquisition in general.

UNIT 1

Understanding lex-IP

CHAPTER 2

Multiple levels of input processing and language learning

In the study of language acquisition, *input* refers to samples of a target language to which a language learner is exposed. It includes spoken, written, visual, and tactile varieties of extended discourse such as speeches and novels, less extended discourse such as accounts of daily events or short stories, "pre-assembled" multiword lexical phrases such as *hours of operation, on the other hand, out and about, not ready for prime time*, and *brute force*, as well as individual words such as *apricot, buckle, art, retired, exquisitely, blank, sidewalk, gnarly, kitten, supercalifragilisticexpialidocious*, and *bye*. In all of these cases, input conveys meaning (during communication) to the listener(s), reader(s), viewer(s) (as in the case of signed languages), or individual(s) perceiving the input using the sense of touch (as in the case of Braille and tactile signing). As such, all of these segments of input are *meaning-bearing*. The extent to which they are comprehensible is a very different issue, however. Input comprehensibility is determined by a number of factors, including the proficiency level of the individual(s) to which the input is directed, the frequency of the words contained within the input segment, the syntactic complexity of the input, and the speed at which the input is presented.

Within the past four decades or so, many SLA researchers have focused on the critical role of input in L2 development. In the Monitor Model, Krashen (1985) proposed that meaning-bearing comprehensible input is a necessary ingredient for SLA and that $i+1$, or input with structures slightly beyond one's current level of competence, is what increases L2 proficiency over time. Other researchers have expanded on Krashen's work with more fine-grained analyses by considering the roles of input processing, conversion of input to intake, integration, and system change in their models of the developing L2 system (Gass, 1997; VanPatten, 1996). These areas of research continue to apply an *information processing* framework (INPUT > DEVELOPING SYSTEM > OUTPUT) to study the cognitive processes that take place in the mind (and brain) of the L2 learner.

Different levels and types of input processing

Input and input processing can and should be analyzed at multiple levels and with respect to how they affect the acquisition of multiple types of linguistic structures. Imagine, for example, that this intriguing e-mail message (sent by CNN as Breaking News on Oct 15, 2009) were received by or read out loud to a low-intermediate or intermediate-level learner of L2 English:

> A 6-year-old climbed into a balloon-like experimental aircraft built by his parents and floated into the Colorado sky.

Here the learner is being exposed to a string of input with a great deal of information about English as a linguistic system. *Multilevel input processing* proceeds. Beginning at the phonetic-phonemic level, if the input segment is spoken, it provides the learner with a variety of different types of information about consonants and vowels in English, such as the variant pronunciations of the vowels /a/ and /o/ and the conditioned pronunciation of the morpheme *-ed* in different phonetic contexts. At the lexical level, it may provide the learner with opportunities to learn or reinforce a variety of novel or fairly novel words, such as possibly *climb, balloon, aircraft,* and *float*. The learner may already know one or more of these words but may have an opportunity, however limited given the limited context of the single sentence alone (but less so if the learner is also viewing a picture or video of the event being described), to infer the meaning of one or more of the other words. At the level of morphology and morphosyntax, the sentence demonstrates how English permits *X-like* (*balloon-like*) structures to be used as adjectives and how *-ed* conveys pastness. At the level of syntax, the sentence demonstrates the use of compound verbs (*climbed … and floated*), the permissibility of reductions such as *built* from *that was built*, and the use of a noun as an adjective (*Colorado sky*).

In addition to this incomplete list of information being provided at the phonetic-phonemic, lexical, morphological, morphosyntactic, and syntactic levels, the sentence also provides the learner with a somewhat unique opportunity to test reliance on *form* in the face of probable versus improbable *meaning*. The content/meaning of the sentence might seem highly improbable, especially if the learner hearing the input is not also viewing a picture or video of the event being described. The learner may wonder "Am I interpreting this correctly?" When it turns out that the interpretation is indeed correct, the experience may help to strengthen the learner's ability to rely on form in the face of the improbable meaning that the form indeed is intended to convey. Even native speakers of English may be incredulous about the correctness of what they are hearing when exposed to a sentence such as this one.

Input segments involving a large number of sentences can provide information about all linguistic subsystems, including information about language-specific pragmatic functions, organizational patterns, and so forth. Imagine, for example, that a fluent speaker of Mandarin reads a 15-minute-long story to an intermediate-level L2 learner of Mandarin. How the learner processes this input string (the story) can be analyzed at multiple levels. At the phonemic level, the learner may make use of evidence about individual phonemic sequencing patterns in Mandarin, some of which may occur in the learner's L1 and some of which may not. At the lexical level, the learner may make use of the presence of new word forms and infer their meaning from context. At the sentence level, the learner may make use of syntactically oriented data about the Mandarin (morpho)syntactic system. At the discourse level, the learner may make use of information about how stories tend to be organized differently in Mandarin as compared to how stories tend to be organized in the learner's L1. Understanding how input processing works at all of these levels helps to paint a more complete picture of why SLA progresses with regard to multiple types of linguistic competence.

Input segments also need not be so long in order to provide similar types of linguistic data. It is possible for shorter segments of input in any language, such as only 30 seconds of spoken input, to be analyzed with regard to the various types of linguistic information they provide about the language in question. When provided with 30 seconds of spoken input only, a learner often has access to information about most or all of the linguistic subsystems of the language in question, including information about pragmatic and sociocultural features.

As the preceding examples demonstrate, the linguistic data provided by an input segment contains evidence about numerous features of the target language. Given that learners are limited in their capacity to process input, however, it is likely that they will not be able to attend to all of this evidence at once. Only a subset of the information may be attended to and processed. These data become *intake*, the subset of the input that is attended to and made available to the developing linguistic system, regardless of whether it is intake at the sentence level or at another level of linguistic analysis. Therefore, a long-term goal of research on input processing is to investigate the relationship between limited processing capacity, patterns in input processing at multiple levels of linguistic analysis, and the acquisition of linguistic features at all levels of analysis, from the phonetic-phonemic to pragmatics, sociolinguistic features, and beyond. To this end, input segments of varying lengths need to be considered, including individual vocabulary items (isolated lexical items), individual sentences, 30-second input segments, 15-minute input segments (as in the examples provided above), and so forth. Patterns and principles of input processing can be identified and analyzed at all of these different levels (lengths) of input with regard to how the input may provide intake for the acquisition of multiple types of linguistic knowledge.

Lex-IP and vocabulary learning

As mentioned previously, to date, research on SLA has focused more on sentence-level input processing and grammar acquisition (e.g., Gass, 1997; VanPatten, 1996) than on other levels of input processing and other aspects of acquisition. In recent years, however, researchers have become more interested in the role of lexical input processing and the acquisition of different aspects of L2 vocabulary. *Lexical input processing* (lex-IP) refers to the manner in which learners process words and lexical phrases as input, or samples of the target language presented in communicative contexts. The more restrictive term *word-level input processing* refers to how learners process individual words as input. Whereas research on sentence-level input processing focuses on how learners process input at the sentence level, research on lexical input processing focuses on how learners process input at the level of individual words and lexical phrases. Applying the same information-processing approach that has been used previously to investigate input processing at the sentence level, research on lex-IP seeks to identify patterns and principles within the following information-processing flow chart.

> lex-INPUT > lex-INPUT PROCESSING > lex-INTAKE > DEVELOPING LEXICOSEMANTIC SYSTEM > lex-OUTPUT PROCESSING > lex-OUTPUT

Clearly, the information processing system depicted here at the lexical level is integrated with information processing systems at other levels of linguistic analysis, as in the case of phonetic/phonemic input (phon-INPUT) and phonetic/phonemic input processing (phon-IP) at the sublexical level; morphological input (morph-INPUT) and morphological input processing (morph-IP) at the level of lexical combinations; syntactic input (syn-INPUT) and syntactic input processing (syn-IP) at the sentence level; pragmatic input (prag-INPUT) and pragmatic input processing (prag-IP) at the pragmatic level; discourse input (disc-INPUT) and discourse input processing (disc-IP) at the discourse level; and sociolinguistic-oriented input (soc-INPUT) and sociolinguistic input processing (soc-IP) at the sociolinguistic level. One level of IP also often corresponds with part of another level of IP, such as when phon-IP corresponds to a form-oriented subcomponent of lex-IP, morph-IP, syn-IP, and so forth. Additionally, within one type of IP, additional subdivisions can be made in order to specify even further. When focusing on morph-IP, for example, one may wish to distinguish between input related to derivational morphology (d.morph-INPUT) versus input related to inflectional morphology (i.morph-INPUT) and their IP counterparts: derivational morphology input processing (d.morph-IP) and inflectional morphology input processing (i.morph-IP). The former of these two types of IP focuses more on the use of form (e.g., phonemic sequences and their graphemic counterparts) in the formation of new words whereas the latter concerns the inflectional paradigms (e.g., verbal paradigms) that so often have become a major focus in L2 learning and instruction.

We have presented several examples of how such a large segment or stream of input can provide opportunities for phon-IP, lex-IP, morph-IP, and syn-IP levels, and it may be fairly intuitive to understand how input processing can occur at these multiple levels simultaneously or intermittently when a learner attends to an input segment at the sentence level or beyond, but let us consider some concrete examples at the levels of prag-IP, disc-IP and soc-IP. If a learner of L2 English is reading a book or listening to a speech in English, it is easy to see how input can appear and be processed at all of these levels, providing opportunities for input processing at each of these levels to emerge.

For prag-IP, sentences such as *What's up?* and *Why don't you have a seat?* may appear, for example, in a book or in speech. Taken literally, either one of these two sentences could be very confusing, but the context in which they appear can help to confirm to the learner that they mean *How are you?* and *You may sit down* respectively, providing evidence in each case as to how these sentences have a fixed meaning that is different from any literal interpretation of them. These are just two of many examples of how *pragmatic use* (use of language in a social context and the ways in which meanings are derived), in this case in English, is likely to appear in the book or the speech in question, both of which are substantially large input segments. Regarding disc-IP, the manner in which the entire book or speech is organized will provide information about the organization of discourse in English, and if the learner reads the book and listens to the speech, that combination of input will provide evidence about differences in organizational structures of a certain type of speech and a certain type of book in English. Finally, for soc-IP, examples of how social context can affect language use may appear. In the book, the same character may greet other characters in different ways, such as when saying *Hey* to a sibling or a parent, *'Sup, dude?* to a friend, and *Good morning, Mrs. Brown* to a teacher, all of which provide important information about how social context determines the particular linguistic forms we choose to use, however automatically.

A new dimension in input processing

What all of these examples of input and input processing suggest is that we need a new dimension in the study of input processing, one that addresses how processing resources are allocated at each of many *different* levels during input processing, that is, during *multilevel input processing*. Limited processing resources are allocated not only within any one level of input processing; instead, they are allotted among all levels. How does this happen? One reasonable explanation is that a *resource allocator* mechanism, however parallel and distributed in nature it may be, allocates resources in varying degrees to each of the different levels of cognitive/neural processing in question.

Figure 2.1 depicts what this mechanism can accomplish, even though the depiction does not represent how non-modular, parallel, and distributed the mechanism may be. In fact, the resource allocator would be a distributed mental mechanism, one that can be represented in a highly distributed manner, consistent with a connectionist/emergentist perspective, even though it is depicted here as a single circle. This representation of the allocator in this manner is intended to demonstrate its function at a larger level, the critical point being that allocation of resources among the different levels (types) of input processing must take place. Also, the equal size of the circles in the figure should not be interpreted as indicating that an equal amount of processing resources will be needed for each of the different levels of input processing. To the contrary, the amounts needed for each level will necessarily change as opportunities for learning at each level change as the nature of the input being provided and the need for different types of intake progresses over time.

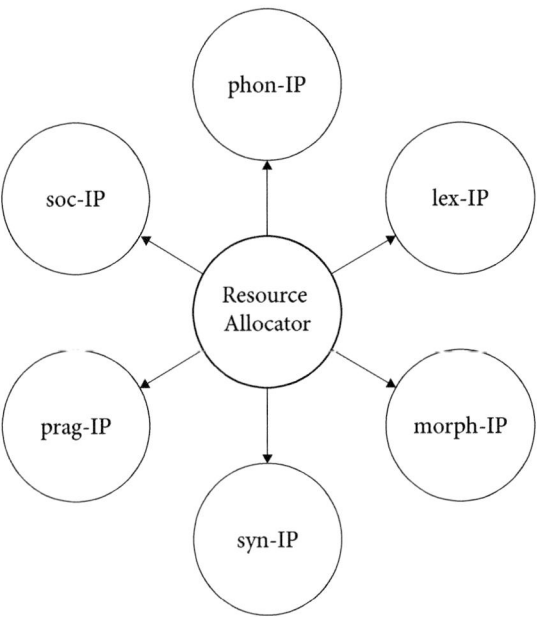

Figure 2.1 Executive control model of allocation of processing resources across multiple levels of input processing.

To date, research on syn-IP has not focused on allocation of processing resources at the level depicted in Figure 2.1. The same holds true for research on lex-IP. In both areas of research, an assumption is made about learners having a maximum amount of processing resources available at any given time, for syn-IP when processing sentence-level input and for lex-IP when processing any new lexical item. This assumption should not preclude keeping the larger picture in mind, however. Learners' processing resources are limited from the beginning, and the demands of attending to input at multiple levels draw upon these resources from the beginning. Therefore, research on syn-IP, lex-IP, and any other level of input processing needs to be understood and interpreted in this light.

The notion of multiple resource pools and allocators may also be pertinent. Wickens (1984), for example, focused on how different tasks affect performance when the tasks in question draw resources from multiple task-specific resource pools as compared to single resource pools. What seems clear, however, is that regardless of how many resource pools and types of processing with which one may be dealing, there are always limits, both within any one pool or across all of the pools combined. Some researchers (DeKeyser, et al., 2002) have argued against this point of view when addressing issues related to syn-IP (and morph/syn-IP) and VanPatten's Processing Instruction. They argue in favor of models in which attentional resource capacity is deemed to be "unlimited," claiming that "[s]uch unlimited-capacity models specify 'mechanisms' causing breakdowns in performance and processing, arguing that increasing the number of stimuli and response alternatives or the similarity between them will sometimes lead to confusion, reducing performance efficiency. This can be caused by 'competition' for the same types of codes during information flow or 'cross-talk' between similar codes" (p. 807), citing Neumann (1996) and Robinson (2008).

Putting aside what "confusion" in this context might mean in more precise terms, note that a substantial part of this book (and in particular, Chapters 5 and 6) focuses on why specificity in type of processing and type of learning is critical to understanding the effects of different tasks on different aspects of vocabulary learning and, for that matter, any type of learning. At first glance, this assertion about the importance of specificity and the research that supports it might be viewed as being consistent with the unlimited-resource multiple-codes interference model discussed by DeKeyser et al. It is not, however, because the assertion of limited resources remains a critical backdrop to all of the various types of processing in which a learner can engage, regardless of total number of resource pools.

The effects discussed in both of the main units of this book are consistent with the idea that there are overall *limits* on processing resources, including both attentional resources and other types of processing resources for which allocation of conscious attention is less involved. The cognitive construct of *processing resource allocation* is also tied to overall limits much more so than the possibility of different types of processing-related interference (see, e.g., all of the research in support of the type of processing – resource allocation model, Barcroft, 2000a, 2002a, discussed in Chapters 5 and 6). Effects that have been attributed to interference, such as the negative effects of grouping target vocabulary in semantic sets (as opposed to, for example, thematic sets), are pointed out as such, but interference-related effects of this nature do not negate the general assertion that processing resources are limited. Very much to the contrary, it is the limited nature of overall processing resources, combined with the critical notion of specificity in type of processing and learning, that allows us to understand the cognitive underpinnings of effects that otherwise might not be understood, might be viewed as counterintuitive, or both.

Different types of input processing yield different types of memory and learning

The study of input processing and language acquisition is tied to the neurobiology of different aspects of language learning and linguistic knowledge. Researchers in this area have distinguished between two types of long-term memory (learning): *declarative* (or explicit) and *procedural* (or implicit) (see Anderson, 2000). The following quote from Mastin (2010) on human memory <http://www.human-memory.net/types_declarative.html> provides a clear explanation of the declarative-procedural distinction:

> Declarative memory ("knowing what") is memory of facts and events, and refers to those memories that can be consciously recalled. It is sometimes called explicit memory, since it consists of information that is explicitly stored and retrieved, although it is more properly a subset of explicit memory. Declarative memory can be further sub-divided into episodic memory and semantic memory.
>
> Procedural memory ("knowing how") is the unconscious memory of skills and how to do things, particularly the use of objects or movements of the body, such as playing a guitar or riding a bike. It is composed of automatic sensorimotor behaviours that are so deeply embedded that we are no longer aware of them, and, once learned, these "body memories" allow us to carry out ordinary motor actions automatically. Procedural memory is sometimes referred to as implicit memory, because previous experiences aid in the performance of a task without explicit and conscious awareness of these previous experiences, although it is more properly a subset of implicit memory.

Mastin also summarizes how brain regions that subserve these two types of long-term memory are also distinct. The hippocampus is commonly involved encoding declarative (explicit) memories, but they are stored in other locations, such as the temporal cortex. Procedural (implicit) memory, in contrast, is encoded without the involvement of the hippocampus in the cerebellum, putamen, caudate nucleus, and motor cortex.

According to Ullman's (e.g., 2001, 2005) declarative-procedural model, the *mental lexicon*, which refers to our entire lexicosemantic system (including all word forms, word meanings, semantic categories, and so forth), exists within the neural systems that underlie *declarative memory* in the temporal lobe. This system is designed to subserve encoding and storage of different types of idiosyncratic information and knowledge. *Syntactic knowledge* (knowledge of the mental "rules" or procedures to follow for language processing, such as procedures for verb movement, question formation, and so forth), on the other hand, is subserved by an independent set of neural systems that underlie *procedural memory* in other areas of the brain (frontal, basal ganglia, parietal, cerebellum). Ullman (2004, 2005) has presented a large body of neuroimaging evidence in support of this proposed independence of lexis and syntax at the level of the brain.

Distinctions such as this one imply that input processing at different levels of linguistic analysis are subserved by processing and storage in different regions of the brain, at least when it comes to the distinction between knowledge of lexis, which involves declarative (explicit) memory stored in one set of regions of the brain, versus knowledge of syntax, which involves procedural (implicit) memory that is stored in another. Similar distinctions hold true for other types of linguistic knowledge, such as phonetic and phonological processing, and the regions of the brain in which they are localized in the brain (see Poeppel & Embick, 2005, for further discussion on the relationship between linguistics and neuroscience, including how different linguistic subsystems correspond to different strata at the level of the brain). What this means in general terms is that different levels of input processing (e.g., phon-IP, lex-IP, morph/syn-IP) should be expected to correspond to and draw on qualitatively different types of memory and learning.

Examples of processing resource allocation in multilevel input processing

Before focusing more on the nature form, meaning, and mapping at different levels of input processing, let us consider a couple of examples of possible patterns of processing resource allocation during multilevel input processing over time. Figure 2.2 presents a hypothetical example that focuses on lex-IP and syn-IP only. The assumption in this figure is that a substantial amount of input processing is being directed toward lexical and syntactic aspects of the input in question given that the total allocation toward all levels of multilevel input processing can never exceed 100%. The input in this case would be at minimum sentence-level (but could be discourse-level) if it is to provide data about syntactic structures that have yet to be acquired by the learner. The input also necessarily would include novel lexical items, even if the lexical items in question make up a small percentage of all of the lexical items and even if one or more of those items have already been partially acquired (e.g., some partial but not complete words have been learned, a new meaning or collocation for a previously acquired word form appears, and so forth). As is clear in the figure, the relative allocation of processing resources to lex-IP and syn-IP can vary substantially over time. Allocation to lex-IP is greatest at Times 3 and 5 and is particularly low at Time 3 whereas allocation to syn-IP is greatest at Time 4 and lowest at Times 3 and 5. Considering how allocation percentages in this example are fairly high and how overall allocation can never exceed 100%, at the times when allocation to lex-IP is particularly high, allocation to syn-IP must decrease in order to accommodate. Similarly, at the time when syn-IP is particularly high (Time 4), allocation to lex-IP must decrease in order to accommodate.

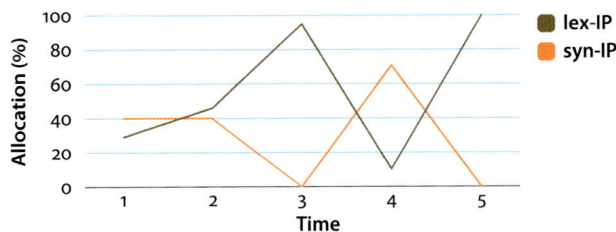

Figure 2.2 Example of allocation of processing resources between lex-IP and syn-IP over time.

Figure 2.3 depicts a somewhat more complex hypothetical example of multilevel input processing. It includes three dissociable types of input processing: (1) d.morph-IP, which focuses on and leads to the acquisition of derivational morphology; (2) i.morph-IP, which focuses on and leads to the acquisition of inflectional morphology; and (3) syn-IP, which focuses on and leads to the acquisition of sentence-level syntactic relationships, such as long-distance dependencies. In this case, note first how both i.morph-IP and syn-IP both increase together at Time 2, which is definitely a possibility when processing certain types of morpho-syntactic structures. Also observe how at Time 3 all three types of IP decrease, perhaps due to a conspicuous increase in another type of IP other than the three depicted here. Lastly, notice how when allocation to syn-IP increases greatly at Time 5, allocation to d.morph-IP and i.morph-IP decrease, potentially in order to accommodate and free up processing resources for whatever the particular focus of syn-IP at Time 5 might be.

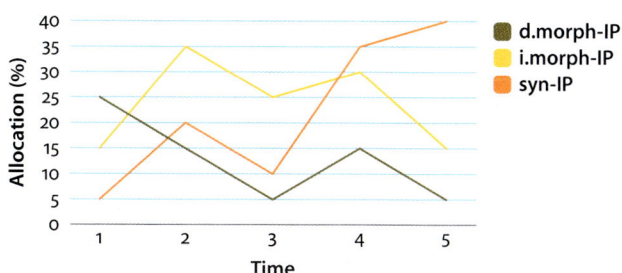

Figure 2.3 Example of allocation of processing resources among multiple levels of IP.

The examples presented here are only two of an infinite number of possible patterns of processing resource allocation in multilevel input processing over time, but they depict how three critical variables – type of IP, amount of allocation (in %), and time – need to be considered in this area of study. There are many other types of IP that could be included and that certainly come into play at different times during the language acquisition process, and the present examples do not tease apart IP dedicated to the formal (phon-IP in spoken language as well as its graphemic counterpart in reading) versus meaning-oriented (including to some extent functional) aspects of the particular types of IP exemplified. This issue is addressed in the next section, however. Additionally, the five times indicated in the examples could refer to a wide variety of possible time intervals, including second-by-second, 10-second intervals over 50 seconds, minute-by-minute over five minutes, or otherwise. Despite this lack of detail, the examples should help to illustrate the larger picture when it comes to multilevel IP and any one particular type of IP. They should also draw attention to the importance of expanding future research in this area, which, although challenging and inherently complex, should lead to a new level of understanding of the complex relationship between input processing and language acquisition.

Input processing for different types of form-meaning relationships

Although lexis, morphology, and syntax are distinct linguistic subsystems that involve distinct types of knowledge, they share commonalities and overlap in important ways. All three concern the need to get meaning from the input and to encode form-meaning relationships, but the form-meaning relationships one must acquire at the levels of inflectional morphology and syntax tend to be much more *form-function* in nature. They involve a one-to-many relationship: one instance of a form (and oftentimes alternate "irregular" forms thereof) in many different contexts while always conveying one central meaning. Well-known cases of morphological markers such as *-ed* as a verb suffix conveying pastness or third-person *-s* as a verb suffix indicating a singular (instead of plural) third-person subject, exemplify this form-function or many-to-one relationship. The same holds true for cases of grammatical words, such as the personal *a* in Spanish, which marks objects in within sentences: *A María le saludó Juan*. 'Juan greeted María.' (literally: "Object-Marker-*a* María greeted Juan"). The Spanish personal *a* will always convey function *the following word is the object* but will do so in numerous (ultimately limitless) different intrasentential contexts, thereby expressing a form-function or one-to-many type of relationship.

Knowledge of lexis (vocabulary), on the other hand, involves a different, more one-to-one type of relationship. Lexical acquisition is about learning novel forms (e.g., the phonological forms and various types of lexical phrases and, possibly, their graphemic counterparts) and mapping those forms onto different meanings. It involves knowledge that is highly idiosyncratic, formulaic, and pattern-sensitive in nature. The relationship between the formal aspect of lexical knowledge and the conceptual/semantic space onto which it is mapped may be highly complex and intricate, but the relationship does not correspond to the same type of *form-function* relationship that one finds with inflectional morphology and syntax. For example, vocabulary items (including lexical phrases) such as *cushion, evade, intricate, go for a run*, or *keeping up with the Jones'* involve mapping specific meanings onto individual forms, regardless of how complex the forms and how complex and polysemous the meanings may be. Of course the lexical items are subject to morphological rules of the language in question, facilitating use of multiple variants of lexical items within a given word family and allowing for the lexical items to be used in a variety of different morpho-syntactic frames, but the basic relationship in question is one to one: one set of formal properties and one set of semantic properties. This basic relationship holds alongside all of the collocational properties of lexical items that a learner must acquire based on lex-IP over extended periods of time. Lexical items also project syntactic information (e.g., for *give*, allow dative alternation [*John gave Mary the book*]; for *explain*, do not allow dative alternation [**John explained Mary the book*]; for e-mail, allow dative alternation [*John e-mailed Mary the book*]), but this feature does not negate how the basic relationship between form and meaning at the lexical level differs from what it is at the levels of inflectional morphology and syntax.

This distinction between one-to-many versus one-to-one relationships is consistent with (morpho)syntax being a type of procedural (implicit) memory and lexical knowledge being a type of declarative (explicit) memory. With reference to the examples provided above, the English structures *-ed* and third-person *-s* as well as the Spanish personal *a* all correspond to procedural memory whereas the lexical items *cushion, evade, intricate, go for a run*, or *keeping up with the Jones'* correspond to declarative memory. This distinction is critical in understanding the potential effects of explicit instruction directed at (morpho)syntax as opposed to explicit instruction directed at lexis. Whereas the former provides learners with some type of pedagogical rule with the intention of helping them with a one-to-many relationship, the latter does not. In contrast to the case with explicit grammar instruction, explicit vocabulary instruction can promote the development of various aspects (formal, mapping, etc.) of any given one-to-one relationship or set of one-to-one relationships associated with vocabulary learning.

The construct of "intake" in lex-IP

The meanings of the terms *intake* and *developing system* change when one refers to lexical input processing (lex-IP) and lexical acquisition as opposed to sentence-level input processing (i.morph-IP and syn-IP) and the acquisition of (morpho) syntax. With i.morph-IP and syn-IP and the acquisition of morpho-syntax, "developing system" refers to mental representations that develop over time based on examples of "rules" or syntactic procedures (such as for verb movement or question formation) reflected by data provided in the input, and "intake" refers to the subset of information (data) provided in the input about the nature of these mental representations. With lex-IP and vocabulary acquisition, on the other hand, the term *developing lexical system* refers to developing a lexicosemantic system in the target language in which degree of knowledge of individual word forms and the semantic networks associated with each of those word forms gradually develops and is refined over time. In turn, the term *lexical intake* refers to the multiple bits and pieces of word form and the multiple bits and pieces of semantic information associated with word forms that are attended to in the input and made available to the developing lexicosemantic system. Although the developing lexicosemantic system may be much less procedural than a developing (morpho)syntactic system, the system does involve patterns related to different types of morphemes and their meanings (morphological patterns) that build up and can be used for top-down processing with regard to new words presented in the input, such as for adding previously learned prefixes and suffixes to recently learned word stems.

To provide one example of how the concept of *intake* can be conceived when it comes to lexical acquisition, imagine a learner of L2 Spanish is exposed to the word *manzana* 'apple' for the first time and is provided concurrently with a sufficient amount of context to infer that this word refers to the particular fruit that it is. At this point in time, word-level input processing begins to work on the lexicosemantic information (data about the word form and its meaning) provided by this string of word-level input. Lexical intake, in this case, is the subset of the lexicosemantic information provided that the learner is able to pick up, with regard to the form and meaning of the word *manzana*. For example, the learner may only be able to attend to and encode a part of the target word form, such as only the beginning of the word (*man…*) or another strand that may have been more salient to the learner (e.g., *…zana*). Lexical intake refers to the information that the learner is able to pick up about the word form, what the learner is able to activate (based on previous experience or inference) about the meaning of this word form, and the extent to which the learner is able to map the semantic and formal components onto each other based on co-occurring elements in the input. All of this intake (form, meaning, mapping) becomes available to the learner's developing lexicosemantic system, providing the learner with (a) an opportunity to expand that system by including information about the new word *manzana*; (b) a greater potential of being able to comprehend or produce the target word at a later time; (c) a greater opportunity to use the lexicosemantic information encoded about *manzana* in a top-down manner at a later time, such as by relating formal properties of *manzana* 'apple' with those of *manzano* 'apple tree' when exposed to the word *manzano* at some other point in time.

The central role of lex-IP in linguistic development

Given that lexis is central to language and linguistic competence, lex-IP is also central to research and theoretical developments related to input processing and SLA. Regardless of the theoretical approach one adopts regarding the nature of our knowledge of (morpho)syntax, lexis and lex-IP remain critical. From a generative perspective, i.morph-IP and syn-IP and (morpho)syntactic development is constrained by Universal Grammar (UG), but without words and lexical phrases, little meaning can be conveyed, regardless of how many L1- or L2-specific parameters purportedly have or have not been set. More recent instantiations of generativism call for an increasingly central role for lexis in the development of linguistic competence; the process is still constrained, but lexis plays a much more dominant role in the process. Within other theoretical approaches, such as emergentism, constructionism, and cognitive linguistics (Lakoff, 1987), the process of acquiring lexical items provides mechanistic principles by which (morpho)syntax can also be acquired. Following these approaches, learning happens in a more piecemeal (idiosyncratic) fashion, and meaning is represented at different levels of constructions. Following any of these approaches, it is critical to note how the absence of lexical knowledge dramatically impedes one's ability to convey meaning.

Differences in the meaning of "direct teaching" for morphosyntax versus lexis

In Krashen's (1981, 1982, 1985) Monitor Model, direct grammar instruction leads only to learning (explicit learning) and not acquisition (implicit learning) of a target language. The explicit knowledge gained from direct grammar instruction can be used only to monitor one's performance when using the language in question. Krashen (1989) has favored promoting L2 vocabulary development through extensive free reading and, including more recently (see, e.g., Krashen, 2008), argued against direct instruction of vocabulary Even if one agrees with Krashen's position regarding the lack of interface between explicit and implicit knowledge in general terms, when it comes to the nature of the type of linguistic information being encoded and stored with vocabulary learning (as opposed to learning [morpho]syntax), it is important to reconsider what direct instruction and intentional learning really mean and the extent to which claims made by Krashen are applicable. As discussed previously, knowledge of (morpho)syntax is an implicit, procedurally oriented type of knowledge that is encoded and stored differently (and in different areas/networks in the brain) when compared to vocabulary knowledge, which is associated with what is a declarative, more idiosyncratic type of memory. Therefore, direct instruction of vocabulary is not likely to lead to the problem of *no interface* ("learned" or explicit knowledge not becoming "acquired" or implicit knowledge) that Krashen has stressed with regard to L2 instruction.

Incidental and intentional vocabulary learning

Incidental vocabulary learning refers to acquiring new words from context without intending to do so, such as when engaging in a conversation or reading a text for meaning and processing new words as input and inferring their meanings. Intentional *vocabulary learning*, on the other hand, refers to learning new words while consciously attempting to do so, such as when studying a list of new words, trying to learn new words while viewing word-picture pairs, or consciously attempting to learn new words from context while reading a text.

As will be explained in detail in Chapter 4, the intentional-incidental distinction in vocabulary learning makes reference to two endpoints on a continuum with purely intentional vocabulary learning on one end, purely incidental on the other end, and many varying degrees between the two in the middle. For example, if a caregiver of a 3-year old learning an L1 points to many different items in a room and asks *What's that? What's that? What's that? ...*, waiting each time for the caregiver's response, which might be *A picture frame. The vent. The blinds...*, this situation can be considered somewhere in between completely intentional and completely incidental vocabulary learning. The focus in this case remains on meaning and communication, but the child has clearly decided to take some time to learn some new words. The reason that this state of affairs is possible is because vocabulary is the place where form meets meaning at a basic level. When we distinguish between the words *van* (/ban/) 'they go' and *pan* (/pan/) 'bread' in Spanish, we make a lexical distinction that corresponds to two forms and two meanings. The distinction is permitted by a phonetic-phonemic distinction (between /b/ and /p/), but it is realized at the lexical level when we perceive the minimal pair *van-pan* and perceive two different meanings. Because lexical form-meaning relationships of this nature are so different than form-function relationships at the (morpho)-syntactic level, the potential qualitative impacts of direct versus indirect instruction (and their counterparts intentional versus incidental learning) are also different.

For this reason (among others), Barcroft (2012) has advocated promoting both intentional and incidental L2 vocabulary learning as one of ten principles of effective L2 instruction within the overall *input-based incremental* (IBI) approach. Another IBI principle is to use meaning-bearing comprehensible input when presenting target vocabulary in the input. These two principles are compatible with the basic nature of vocabulary learning and how it differs from other types of learning, including the gradual acquisition of (morpho)syntax. The IBI principles are also consistent with the grey areas between the two endpoints on the incidental-intentional continuum (as discussed in more detail in Chapter 4). The continuum itself suggests that even if one attempts to teach all vocabulary indirectly, some intentional L2 vocabulary is going to take place. Similarly, if one attempted to teach all vocabulary directly, some incidental L2 vocabulary learning is going to take place. At the end of the day, we are equipped to learn vocabulary with varying degrees of intentionality, with little or no intention at all in cases of incidentally oriented learning and with highly focused attention in cases of intentionally oriented learning.

Methodological issues in research on lex-IP and vocabulary learning

Finally, when it comes to research methodology, many of the issues related investigating lex-IP differ from those in research on other levels of input processing, such as i.morph-IP and syn-IP. A number of investigations on lex-IP and L2 vocabulary acquisition have focused on lex-IP during intentional vocabulary learning when learners are presented with individual words as isolated items. Studying lexical input processing in this learning context affords a particular set of methodological advantages, such as the possibility of controlling the amount of time learners spend attempting to learn each target word and the amount of time they are allowed to retrieve target items in different types of posttests. If learners are encouraged to produce partial forms of target words on posttests (e.g., producing the partial form *resbalia* for the target L2 Spanish word *resbaladilla* 'slide'), their responses can be used to identify different types of patterns and privileging in partial L2 word form learning. After different types of learning-phase treatments, participants can be asked to produce target words via free recall, cued recall, or both, depending upon the goals of the study in question. Additionally, many of the insights gained from researching lex-IP during intentional vocabulary learning can be extended to contexts of incidental vocabulary learning or, at minimum, can help to generate testable hypotheses for more incidentally oriented learning contexts.

As different subareas of research on lex-IP are presented and discussed in subsequent chapters, note the methodological peculiarities of each area of research, including advantages and opportunities that the various research methodologies provide. The unique position of vocabulary at the place where form meets meaning offers particular advantages when it comes not only to understanding core-level issues in language acquisition but also for advancing our understanding of research on memory in psychology. Many early and persistent misconceptions tied to *levels of processing* (LOP) (Craik & Lockhart, 1972) about the potential of semantically oriented deeper processing to facilitate memory for "items" in general terms could have been remedied by more research on the effects of different semantic and structural tasks on L2 vocabulary learning. Demonstrations of *transfer-appropriate processing*, such as the benefits of a structurally oriented rhyming task at study on the same type of task at test (Morris, Bransford & Franks, 1977), provided a means for questioning unqualified LOP-based predictions early on, but more recent research on the effects of different semantic and structural tasks on L2 vocabulary can help to advance the field more rapidly. Barcroft's (2002a) finding of a double-dissociation between orientation at study (semantic, structural) and language of free recall at test (L1, L2) (semantic facilitating recall in L1 but structural facilitating recall in L2), for example, speaks strongly to what we should and should not expect from different types of processing and their effects on corresponding learning counterparts.

CHAPTER 3

Three key components of learning a word
Form, meaning, mapping

Much of language acquisition is about learning new form and mapping it to the meaning it represents. We acquire language by (a) identifying and remembering linguistic forms, such as the written forms *the, dog, bark, -ed* (the formal component of language acquisition); (b) identifying and remembering different meanings and semantic space, such as identifying and remembering that "the type of sound that dogs produce" or "pastness" are entities that we can consider, think about, and talk about (the semantic component of language acquisition); and (c) making connections between linguistic forms and their meanings, such as learning that the linguistic form *bark* can refer to production of the type of sound that dogs produce and that the linguistic form *-ed* can refer to pastness (the mapping component of language acquisition). These three components allow us to become able to comprehend the meaning of linguistic forms and to use linguistic forms to express meaning. Like language acquisition in general, the story of vocabulary acquisition is a story of form, meaning, and form-meaning mapping. The study of vocabulary acquisition focuses on how we acquire *lexical items*, or individual words, such as *door, kindness, gallop,* and *intriguing,* and multiword lexical phrases, such as *stop sign, MP3 player,* or *a penny for your thoughts.* Therefore, as discussed previously, the study of vocabulary acquisition, or *lexical acquisition,* referring to the acquisition of the words and lexical phrases, is located precisely at the place where linguistic form meets meaning.

This chapter focuses on key elements or basics of what is involved in learning new words. First, we consider what words are and how they relate to other types of linguistic knowledge. Second, we review the various types of knowledge that one must acquire in order to know a word. Among these types of knowledge are the formal, semantic, syntactic, and collocational properties of the word. Third, we identify the basic ingredients and basic mental processes that are needed for successful vocabulary acquisition.

What is a word?

The study of vocabulary acquisition is linked closely to *phonology*, the study of the sound system of languages, and *morphology*, the study of the structural and combinatorial properties of words and word parts. Vocabulary is linked to phonology because, when it comes to the formal aspect of vocabulary learning, we must learn and make use of combinations of sounds that are contrastive (*phonemes*) in spoken languages and visual differences that are contrastive in signed languages. Vocabulary is also closely linked to morphology because, as we learn new lexical forms, we acquire knowledge about the combinatorial properties of *morphemes*, the smallest linguistic units that express meaning. *Morphemes* include both *morphs*, forms that express meaning (e.g., the spoken form [pɛn] or the written word *pen* in English) and *allomorphs*, different phonemic forms for the same morpheme (e.g., in English, *a* and *an* are two separate morphs, but *a* and *an* are also two allomorphs of the same morpheme *a, an*.

In order to understand further what words are, let us consider some different types of morphemes. *Free morphemes* are morphemes that can stand alone as single words. In English, *spoon, cat, smart,* and *peace* are examples of free morphemes. *Bound morphemes* are morphemes that must be combined with other morphemes in order to create a word that can stand alone. Numerous English *prefixes*, such as *pre, re, u-,* and *ex*; *stems*, such as *dem* and *ped* (from *demagogy* and *pedagogy*) and *theo* (as in *theocracy*); and suffixes, such as *er, able, ed,* and *ist*, are bound morphemes. As is the case with words in general, the relationship between morphemes and the meanings they convey is typically arbitrary (e.g., the relationship between the sound of the word *chair* and what it refers to is arbitrary), with some exceptions, such as in cases of *onomatopoeia*, that is, cases in which words refer to the sound that it describes, such as *meow, quack, bang,* or *boom* in English.

Following Hudson (2000, p. 60), a *word* is "one or more morphemes with the freedom of occurrence of a single free morpheme." We also can distinguish between simple words and complex words: "A simple word consists of a single free morpheme, for example, *dog*, and *eat*, and a complex word (also a "free form") consists of two or more morphemes, like *dogs*, with two (*dog-s*), *unhappily*, with three (*un-happi-ly*), or *disagreements*, with four (*dis-agree-ment-s*)" (Hudson, 2000, pp. 60–61). Other definitions further emphasize the single-unit nature and constructive properties of words. As defined by Michnick Golinkoff and Hirsh-Pasek (2000, p. 4), words are "minimal free forms in the languages of the world and therefore, unlike phonemes or syllables, they are units par excellence. As individuated elements capable of recombination, words are the building blocks of language." Definitions such as these further remind us of the central role that words play in language and their uniqueness when it comes to being units that combine form and meaning at such a basic level.

Lemmas are basic or "canonical" forms of words. For example, the lemma *dance* in English co-exists with multiple variants, such as *dances, danced,* and *dancing*. One need not view these variants as completely different words. The group of words that includes a lemma and all of its variants is a *lexeme*. Learning the forms and meanings of bound morphemes, such as *s, ed,* and *ing*, is an important component of learning new words, but once the form and meaning of a bound morpheme is learned, it may be applied to other lemmas. Imagine, for example, that one learns the new (and nonexistent) verb *glack* in English. After learning the form *glack*, one quickly should be able to speak of a *glacker* as someone who or something that *glacks* and have a sense that *glacked* likely will be the past tense of this verb. These abilities are based on one's previous experience with the bound-morpheme suffixes *er*, *s*, and *ed* in English. The process of deducing multiple variants based on previous experience on occasion may be more complicated, however. An L2 learner of English, for example, may come to know the meaning of the English verb *to grow* but make incorrect deductions about the past-participle variant and use **growed* instead of *grown*. In such cases, knowledge of the word variants remains incomplete but can be refined over time.

What does it mean to know a word?

As discussed previously, as with language acquisition in general, knowing a word concerns form, meaning, and form-meaning mapping. Our degree of knowledge of words depends largely on (a) the extent to which we have acquired the form of a new word; (b) the extent to which we have learned and can activate the appropriate meaning(s) of the word, including all of the appropriate referential, conceptual, and semantic associations related to the word; and (c) the extent to which each word form and its meaning(s) are mapped appropriately onto one another. To know the word *miga* 'crumb' in Spanish, for example, one must be able to do the following. (1) Be able to identify, comprehend, and produce the spoken and written forms of this word readily and fluently. (2) Know all of the Spanish-appropriate semantic (including referential and conceptual) space related to the meaning of this word (at least to a given extent given that knowledge and interpretation about word meanings can vary from person to person even among native speakers), such as that *miga* can refer to a tiny piece of bread that has fallen off of a loaf of bread and that *miga* also can be used in the expression *hacer buenas migas* (literally 'to make good crumbs') in some dialects of Spanish to express the idea of *to get along with* or *to hit it off* (see, e.g., Cassagne, 1995, for this and a list of other Spanish idioms). (3) Be able to activate the word *miga* and the Spanish-appropriate semantic space for the word concurrently and in a fluent manner both during comprehension and production of Spanish.

In addition to the basic form, meaning, and mapping components of word knowledge, knowing a word also implies that we know how the word functions in the language with regard to its *morphosyntactic properties*, or the types of forms that the word can take and the roles that it can play in the overall grammar of the language, as well as its *collocational properties*, or the manner in which the word tends to appear or co-occur with other words in the language (*collocations* being sequences of words that tend to co-occur in varying degrees within a given language). Continuing with the example of the word *miga* 'crumb' in Spanish, one would have to learn, however implicitly and unconsciously, that this word is a noun that takes feminine articles and feminine forms of adjectives, that it can be pluralized by adding *-s*, and so forth. In addition to learning these morphosyntactic properties of *miga*, one would have to learn that this word (unlike in English) has unique collocational properties (at least in some varieties of Spanish) that ties it to the words *hacer* 'to make/do' and *buenas* 'good' due to how it is used in the expression *hacer buenas migas con alguien* when expressing the idea of *to get along with someone* or *to hit it off*. Whereas the idea of using the word *good* in combination with *crumbs* may be an odd or unlikely combination when speaking English, the same does not hold for the combination of *buenas* and *migas* when speaking Spanish.

In one sense, our knowledge of the syntactic and collocational properties of words can be viewed, at least to some extent, as aspects of knowing word meaning, the second of the three main components of word knowledge in addition to form and form-meaning mapping. If we know the referential meaning of a word, we usually know a substantial amount about its probable syntactic properties. Knowing the meaning of a word inherently implies that one will know, however implicitly, whether the word is a noun, adjective, or adverb, and other syntactic information related to the word, such as probable syntactic projections of the word. Knowing the meaning of the word *put*, for example, implies knowing that this word refers to an action and is a verb. In addition, one also knows (again, from knowing the meaning of the word *put*) that we must *put something somewhere* and that it is not possible only **to put*, **to put something*, **to put somewhere*. Knowledge of the meaning of the word *put* allows one to anticipate and ultimately to know and make use of word-based syntactic projections of this nature.

The collocational properties of words also may be viewed as being tied to word meaning. We know, again however implicitly, that the two words *football* and *field* are more likely to co-occur in English than *football* and *jellyfish*. In this case, our overall knowledge of the meanings of *football*, *field*, and *jellyfish* help us to do so because *football* and *field* simply have more to do with each other than do *football* and *jellyfish*. Basic knowledge of the referents of the three words in question implies that this is the case. Even in the case of idiomatic expressions with less than "intuitive" collocations, such as the more likely co-occurrence of *rain*, *cats*, and *dogs* as compared to a combination such as *rain*, *elephants*, and *armadillos*, our knowledge about probable collocations can be viewed as one of the many aspects of knowing word meaning. In the minds of English speakers, *rain* is, for better or for worse, forever tied to the semantic space of *cats* and *dogs*. At times we even may visualize cats and dogs falling from the sky, a much more probable event than to visualize elephants and armadillos falling from the sky given the cognitive impact of the idiomatic expression *raining cats and dogs*.

To summarize with some additional nuance, when it comes to what it means to know a word, Ellis (1994, p. 215) asserted the following about what it means to know a word:

> Minimally we must recognise it as a word and enter it into our mental lexicon. But there are several lexicons specialised for different channels of Input/Output (I/O). To understand speech the auditory input lexicon must categorize a novel sound pattern…; to read the word the visual input lexicon must learn to recognise a new orthographic pattern…; to say the word the speech output lexicon must tune a motor programme for its pronunciation; to write it the spelling output lexicon must have a specification for its orthographic sequence…. We must learn its syntactic properties…its place in lexical structure…. its semantic properties, its referential properties, and its roles in determining entailments…the conceptual underpinnings that determine its place in our entire conceptual system. Finally we must learn the mapping of these I/O specifications to the semantic and conceptual meanings: the relation between word form and word meaning is generally arbitrary….

This description makes multiple references to the three key components of word knowledge (form, meaning, and form-meaning mapping) and other aspects of word knowledge while pointing out how these fit into the larger information-processing scheme in different channels, including both spoken and written. In signed languages, the visual modality becomes critical in different ways given the critical roles of hand shape, location in space, and movement, as does the tactile modality for blind individuals comprehending sign language or Braille tactilely.

What are the limits of the conceptual and semantic space of lexical items?

Another important issue in understanding word knowledge concerns which elements of knowledge are and are not included under the label "conceptual" versus "semantic." A *concept* is the referent or idea that a word represents whereas the *semantic representation* includes not only the concept(s) but also its various connotations, pragmatic qualities, and other aspects of knowledge, all of which reflect not only the language and *dialect* (regional variety) one speaks but also the *idiolect* (individual variety of a language) in question. Should we consider syntactic projections to be part of conceptual/semantic representations in the mind? Should we consider visual processing to be a part of learning the conceptual/semantic properties of a word, such as when a child learns the difference between a dog and a cat or an adult participating in an experiment learns novel words for nonobjects (figures they have never seen as referents before) learns to associate these new figures with the novel words they are learning?

Answers to such questions are debatable, and they shape the manner in which we view all of the dimensions of word meaning. Given that knowing the meaning of a verb such as *bring* implies knowing that it requires a direct object (one must bring *something* to the party and never just **bring to the party*), should knowledge of this required direct object be part of the meaning or conceptual/semantic space of the word *bring*? Now consider the relationship between visual processing and learning novel referents of words. When a child visually processes the difference between "cat" and "dog" for the first time, that visual information becomes part of the developing conceptual/semantic representations of those two word referents. Similarly, the adult who learns novel words for nonword referents must process the referents in question in order to learn them as referents. Therefore, such visual processing and learning can be considered part of the conceptual and semantically oriented learning that takes places in a vocabulary learning situation of this nature. It is useful to consider this type of a broad-based view of conceptual/semantic learning and lexicosemantic representation, one in which all of the aspects of knowledge mentioned above are legitimate and necessary components of word knowledge.

How do we learn new words? Necessary ingredients and basic mechanisms

The most basic and necessary ingredient for successful vocabulary acquisition is the provision of *input* (samples of the target language). We learn all of the words that we know because we are given opportunities to hear (in spoken language) or to view (in signed language) the words or, after we learn to read, to read the words in different texts. If we are not exposed to a word as input, we have no chance of learning it. In other words, vocabulary learning is necessarily *input-first*. Input provides us with the information that we need about the formal, semantic, and mapping components of vocabulary. As we are exposed to input, we process the input in ways that allow us to encode aspects of word form, word meaning, and form-meaning mapping gradually in a bit-by-bit manner over time. L2 learners gradually progress in their knowledge of individual words in this manner. Bogaards (2001, p. 325) described the semantic development component of this process as follows: "They learn a first sense here, something about its use there, and another sense somewhere else" (see Bogaards, 2001, for more on how the notion of *lexical units* can be used to as more differentiated element than the notion of "word" to depict this bit-by-bit process). Similarly, L2 learners may pick up part of the form of word on one occasion, another part on another occasion, and then finally encode and retain the entire word form on another occasion.

One of the basic mechanisms involved in learning new words is lex-IP. Learning the three main components of word knowledge (form, meaning, mapping) always involves processing new words as input. We may encounter a new word on one or more occasions, but our ability to learn the word presupposes that the word is processed as input. One can learn a word incidentally by inferring its meaning from context or learn a word intentionally in a more direct manner, such as by looking up the meaning of a word in a dictionary or obtaining a translation of the word in L1. One of the advantages of learning new words in richly meaningful contexts is that these often provide learners with more information about the semantic, syntactic, and collocational properties of the words in question. In this way the strength of the mapping between each word form and its different meanings and uses can continue to increase over time. What is critical for either type of vocabulary learning (incidental or intentional) to take place is that the learner must be given opportunities to process the new word as input and must do so. How different types of learning conditions and tasks affect learners' ability to do so is critically important.

The incremental nature of vocabulary learning

The forms and meanings of words and other lexical items are commonly learned in an incremental manner, that is, in bits and pieces over time. In L1 acquisition, children face the challenge of lexical-level *bootstrapping*, or segmenting different parts of the speech stream in order to make form-meaning connections. Peters (1985) identified some of the general operating principles (OPs) used in doing so. Some of these concern how the child responds to different types of acoustic saliency for different forms in the speech stream and Internal Cues for Segmentation (SG), such as the following related to location:

> SG:BEGIN. Segment off the first syllable of an Extracted unit and store it separately.
> SG:END. Segment off the last syllable of an Extracted unit and store it separately.

According to these two principles, children segment off first and last syllables and store them as units (e.g., *fas* for *faucet* in the case of a first syllable). Another OP available to children learning their L1 concerns stress versus unstressed syllables in the speech stream:

> SG:STRESS. Segment off a stressed syllable of an Extracted unit and store it separately.

In other words, for a word like *return*, the OP SG: BEGIN should encourage segmentation and storage of *re* as a unit, and the OPs SG: END and SG: stress should encourage segmentation and storage of the latter syllable *turn*. According to Peters, the ability of the child to segment and store units in this manner is inborn.

If accurate, the OPs proposed by Peters represent a very useful tool available to children during L1 acquisition. The principles also point to the piecemeal nature in which L1 acquisition proceeds, both at the lexical level and other levels of linguistic analysis. At the lexical level, children have to segment off portions of the word forms to which they are exposed and gradually build up knowledge of these forms over time. Further complicating the issue is that they also have to map partial knowledge of word referents to the partial word forms that they are gradually learning.

When it comes to learning novel words in L2, segmentation can also pose challenges. When presented with spoken input beyond the word level, L2 learners, like L1 learners, apply strategies to determine *word boundaries* (where different words begin and end). After a word boundary is identified, encoding and retaining a novel word based on a limited number of exposures poses another major challenge. As is the case with L1 learners, L2 learners do not have unlimited processing capacity and therefore simply cannot consistently retain novel words based on one exposure or a limited number of exposures over an extended period of time. It may happen from time to time, but it certainly cannot happen all of the time or even on a regular basis (perhaps exempting language savants, at least to some degree).

In one study, for example, Barcroft (2008) focused on patterns in partial L2 word form learning in the written mode. The study assessed properties of word fragments produced by English-speaking learners of Spanish who had attempted to learn a series of new Spanish words when exposed to word-picture pairs. The results of the study revealed that 69% of the learners' responses on a posttest (see picture, attempt to produce the target Spanish word) were partial versus only 31% complete words, that they produced a particularly high percentage of 1-letter fragments, and that they privileged (produced more) fragments in word-initial position as compared to word-medial and word-final positions. In another study, Barcroft and Rott (2010) assessed partial word form learning in the written mode among L2 learners of German and L2 learners of Spanish following a similar experimental methodology. Results indicated that the learners produced (in both languages) approximately 49% more partial words than whole words, a high percentage of 1-letter fragments, and more fragments in word-initial position, extending previous findings for Spanish learners only. Both of these studies demonstrate that learning novel L2 word forms is an incremental process that involves learning bits and pieces of word forms over time.

L2-specific meanings and conceptual/semantic space for words are also learned incrementally over time. Unlike L1 vocabulary acquisition, adult L2 learners typically learn target words for which they already know referents based on their experience in L1. For example, when a Spanish-speaking learner of L2 English learns the word *party* for the first time (see Bogaards, 2001, on how the multiple senses of this English word constitute different lexical units), the learner can transfer knowledge of the Spanish word *fiesta* in the sense of party as a social event in which a group, such as a group of friends, gets together to celebrate something or just to enjoy themselves. This translation works in Spanish. As such, the learner in no way starts from scratch when learning the meaning of *party* in English. However, the use of *party* in the sense of a political party would translate to *partido* in Spanish, and the use of *party* in the sense of a group, such as at a restaurant (e.g, *Johnson, party of six!*) would translate as *grupo* in Spanish. Therefore, the learner must acquire these alternative L2-specific uses of the word *party* over time. Relatedly, L2 learners oftentimes need to reshape the semantic space of L2 words by eliminating certain L1-based options for meanings when functioning in the L2. An English-speaking learner of Spanish, for example, needs to learn that the Spanish word *fiesta* cannot be used in the senses of *political party* (*fiesta política) or *party of six* (*fiesta de seis).

If the L2-appropriate meanings and uses of target words are not taught directly, it may take a considerable amount of time for the L2 learner to acquire all of the meanings and uses in question, even in an immersion context, because the chance that all of the meanings and uses will be provided in the input is slim, as is the chance that when an L2-specific meaning or use does occur that it will be within a context that is sufficiently clear for the learner to be able to infer the target word meaning or use in question. Therefore, the process of shaping the L2-appropriate semantic space and usage of L2 words can be extensive. A learner might go years after learning one meaning of a word before learning additional L2-appropriate meanings and uses or before learning that a particular L1-based meaning of the word is inappropriate in the L2.

CHAPTER 4

Contexts of lexical input processing
L1/L2 and incidental/intentional

Both the provision of input at the lexical level and the phenomenon of lex-IP take place within multiple contexts, each of which impacts upon how lex-IP ensues. Two key variables that affect lex-IP are (a) whether lex-IP takes place in the context of *L1* or *L2* vocabulary learning and (b) whether lex-IP takes place in a primarily *incidental* or primarily *intentional* learning context. This chapter addresses each of these two sets of contexts in turn, clarifying how L2 vocabulary learning does not "start from scratch" but may involve, at least on occasion, the acquisition of completely novel concepts and meanings, and how a substantial amount of both L1 and L2 vocabulary learning can fall on a continuum between the end extremes of purely incidental and purely intentional vocabulary learning.

Lex-IP in L1 and L2 vocabulary learning

To what extent is learning new words in L1 similar to or different from learning new words in L2? As with L1 and L2 acquisition in general, much of what is involved in learning new words in L2 is very similar to what is involved in learning new words in L1. In both cases, one must isolate target word forms, isolate the meanings of these forms, and make bidirectional mental mappings between the forms and their meanings. A large amount of these processes can take place incidentally, without intending or making a special effort to do so. There are, however, fundamental differences between L1 and L2 vocabulary learning. In this section, we first draw attention to key similarities and key differences between learning new words in L1 and learning new words in L2 and then explore in further detail what these similarities and differences imply when it comes to lex-IP.

Similarities between L1 and L2 vocabulary learning

There are a number of important ways in which L1 and L2 vocabulary learning are similar. First, for both types of vocabulary learning, the learner must develop a formal representation of the word based on having processed the word as input. Second, the learner must develop appropriate mappings between the word form and various aspects of its meaning and learn the word's syntactic and collocational properties. Third, for both L1 and L2 vocabulary acquisition, learners can develop new word knowledge based on a range of different types of input sources, including spoken discourse or isolated words, and different contexts of vocabulary learning, including purely intentional vocabulary learning and purely incidental vocabulary learning. Even though children may not seek to learn many new L1 words intentionally, they may do so later on life, such as during study sessions for courses in elementary school, high school, or college or when making attempts to improve L1 vocabulary knowledge as an older adult. Finally, word-based determinants of learnability, such as word length, can affect the relative ease or difficulty that one is likely to experience with regard to learning a given target word in both L1 and L2. Very short words, for example, are easier to learn than very long words in either L1 or L2 (e.g., Ellis & Beaton, 1995).

Differences between L1 and L2 vocabulary learning

There are also a number of key differences between L1 and L2 vocabulary learning. One basic difference is that learners often do not have to learn new concepts when learning L2 words. With L2 vocabulary acquisition, learners commonly make assumptions about the meaning and uses of new L2 words based on their previous experience with L1 words. For example, when an English speaker learns that the Spanish word *mañana* can mean 'tomorrow,' the learner does not need to relearn all of the previously acquired semantic properties associated with the word 'tomorrow,' such as that it refers to the day after today. Similarly, an English speaker learns that the Spanish word *burro* refers to 'donkey,' the learner can make a series of assumptions about the meaning of *burro* in Spanish based on previous experience, such as that it refers to an animal, is related to horses, may carry things on its back, and so forth. Semantic properties such as these do not have to be relearned from scratch. Instead, they arrive at the task of L2 vocabulary learning with some pre-existing conceptual/semantic information about target words based on their experience in L1.

Nevertheless, L2 learners also must be able to refine and redefine L2-appropriate semantic space for L2 words over time. Assumptions about the L2-specific properties of words such as L2-specific meanings and syntactic and collocational usage need to become increasingly crystallized over time. Following the examples of *mañana* and *burro*, an English-speaking learner of Spanish will need to come to realize at some point that the word *mañana* can be used in Spanish to refer not only to 'tomorrow' but also to 'morning' and that the word *burro* can be used in the Spanish expression *el burro hablando de orejas* 'the donkey talking about ears,' which can be used to express the idea of *the pot calling the kettle black*. Initially, the learner may hypothesize that *mañana* and *burro* occupy the same semantic space as 'tomorrow' and 'donkey' in English and then, at some later point in time, may come to realize that *mañana* can also mean 'morning' (*a las nueve de la mañana* 'at nine in the morning') and that *burro* may be associated with the concept of 'talking about its ears' in the sense of *the pot calling the kettle black*. In this manner, the L2 learners must gradually refine their knowledge of the L2-specific properties of words over time.

In addition to semantic overlap, with L2 vocabulary learning, learners stand to benefit from varying degrees of overlap in the form of words in L1 and L2. *Cognates*, words that are similar in two languages, such as the Spanish-English pairs *historia – history, biología – biology, arquitecto – architect*, and *teléfono – telephone*, can facilitate L2 vocabulary learning. False cognates, however, such as *embarazada* (which means 'pregnant') – **embarrassed* and *realizar* (which means 'to bring about' or 'actualize') – *to realize*, can complicate L2 vocabulary learning and cause difficulties.

Finally, one additional key difference between L1 and L2 vocabulary acquisition should be considered. Except in rare cases, the bulk of L1 vocabulary used for everyday communicative purposes is always learned by children. L2 vocabulary, however, is learned by both children and adults. The common case of adults learning an L2, including the vocabulary of the L2 in question, poses a series of important questions that differ from those related to children learning vocabulary. For example: Do children have advantages over adults when learning L2 vocabulary? If so, what are those advantages? Do adults have any advantages over children when learning L2 vocabulary? If so, what are those advantages?

L1, L2, and the "learning burden" in vocabulary learning

Another consideration is how formal and semantic similarities and differences between L1 and L2 versions of a word affect how difficult it is to learn a new L2 word. According to Nation (2001, p. 23) the *learning burden* of a word refers to "the amount of effort required to learn it" whereby "the more the word represents patterns and knowledge that learners are already familiar with, the lighter its learning burden. These patterns and this knowledge can be from the first language, from knowledge of other languages, and from previous knowledge of the second language." From this perspective, one can posit that the greater the formal and semantic overlap between L1 and L2 versions of a given word, the less the learning burden for the L2 word in question, and similarly, the less the formal and semantic overlap between L1 and L2 versions of a given word, the greater the learning burden of the L2 word in question.

The case of learning new words and new meanings for the first time in L2

In some cases, learners can encounter L2 words for which they have not yet learned an L1 counterpart. Most advanced L2 learners should be able to think of circumstances in which they have experienced this type of vocabulary learning. Oftentimes, words of this nature belong to particular semantic fields, such as plants, foods, or specialized areas of expertise (e.g., medicine, linguistics, literature) that the advanced L2 learner has studied in the L2. For example, an English speaker taking a course on linguistics for the first time in L2 Spanish may learn that the meaning of the Spanish word *oclusiva* is 'stop' before learning that the English word *stop* can be used to express the same meaning. As another example, oftentimes when L2 learners travel to a country where the target language is spoken, they may come into contact with fruits, vegetables, and other types of foods that they have not come into contact with previously in their country of origin. In these cases, the L2 learners will be learning both novel word forms and novel word meanings at the same time, unlike the more typical case of having a substantial degree of knowledge about the meaning of a new L2 word based on one's experience learning meanings in L1.

Lex-IP in both intentional and incidental learning contexts

Recall that *incidental vocabulary learning* refers to picking up new words from context without intending to do so, such as when engaging in a conversation or reading a text for meaning and processing new words as input and inferring their meanings. In contrast, intentional *vocabulary learning* refers to learning new words while consciously attempting to do so, such as when studying a list of new words, trying to learn new words while viewing word-picture pairs, or consciously attempting to learn new words from context while reading a text. For a learner to acquire a new L2 word, lex-IP must successfully take place regardless of whether the new word in question is acquired incidentally or intentionally. Consequently, investigations on lex-IP and L2 vocabulary learning have focused on lex-IP during (a) intentional vocabulary learning when learners are presented with individual words as isolated items and (b) incidental learning when learners are not instructed to learn to learn target words and are not told that they will be tested on them (Hulstijn, 1992).

The rest of this chapter considers, from a general perspective, what research in each of these two areas can offer when it comes to the relationship between lex-IP and L2 vocabulary learning. In particular, we focus on the extent to which effects observed in intentional learning contexts do or do not generalize to incidental contexts and the extent to which effects observed in incidental contexts do or do not extend to intentional learning contexts. The goal at present is to provide a general discussion of these issues. More details about the implications of the incidental (or at least incidentally oriented) studies (e.g., Kida, 2010a, 2010b), and combined (both intentional and incidental or at least incidentally oriented) lex-IP studies (e.g., Barcroft, 2009; Burfoot, 2010) appear in subsequent chapters.

What are the parameters of a lex-IP study?

Before delving further into issues about lex-IP during intentional versus incidental vocabulary learning, it is useful to begin by identifying some of the main parameters that distinguish studies on lex-IP from studies on other issues in vocabulary learning. Research on lex-IP – whether directed toward intentional vocabulary, incidental vocabulary learning, or both – focuses on how learners allocate their limited cognitive processing resources while attending to new words or lexical phrases as input. In other words, a central feature of research on lex-IP is that it takes a processing perspective as a means of understanding various phenomena related to vocabulary learning. Certainly, some studies may address issues related to lex-IP even though they were not conceived from a processing perspective or designed to address issues related to lex-IP, but research of this nature may need to be reinterpreted from a processing perspective in order to advance our current understanding of different issues pertinent to lex-IP. In this way the borders between research focused specifically on lex-IP and research on other areas of vocabulary learning sometimes become blurred.

Distinguishing between research on lex-IP and research on lexical processing

It is also important to distinguish between research interested in *lexical processing*, which refers to processing of words and other lexical items during tasks such as spoken or written word identification, and lex-IP. Whereas research on lex-IP by definition focuses on how learners process words and other types of lexical items as input, research on lexical processing commonly does not fall within this particular purview. Research on lexical processing may sometimes involve issues related to how learners process lexical items as input, but its primary focus is not on input processing as it relates to acquisition. Consider, for example, the 2009 book edited volume by Fitzpatrick and Barfield on lexical processing in L2 learners. It includes work on the use of dictionaries with regard to L2 vocabulary learning, different foci on L2 lexical networks, issues related to word association, the types of lexical environments provided in L2 classrooms, and the relationship between the development of lexical and syntactic knowledge, among others. Clearly, the construct of lexical processing is conceived in a broad sense here. Other research on bilingual lexical processing has focused specifically on processing of previously learned lexical items in more the one language. Miozzo et al. (2010), for example, examined the availability of lexical information to bilinguals who were aphasic with regard to whether the items in question were nouns or verbs and whether they corresponded to other morphological characteristics. These areas of research differ from that of lex-IP in that they do not focus specifically on how lexical items are processed as input in light of overall limits on learners' capacity for processing input.

"Incidental" versus "incidentally oriented" vocabulary learning: A clarification

Before discussing issues related to research on lex-IP in intentional, incidental, and combined learning contexts, a clarification on terminology is in order. Hulstijn (1992) provided an operational definition of incidental vocabulary as being situations in which learners are not explicitly told to attempt to learn a set of target words and are not forewarned that they will be tested on the words. This manner of operationalizing incidental vocabulary learning may be helpful from a research methodology standpoint, but it must be pointed out that the two criteria in question (no direct instructions to attempt to learn target vocabulary and no forewarning of pending testing on the vocabulary) do not ensure that one or more learners may decide to learn target vocabulary intentionally. One or more learners may, for example, decide to pay less attention to the meaning of a reading passage and focus on trying to learn new vocabulary or may decide to do so after comprehending the main idea of a reading.

Because the criteria outlined by Hulstijn (1992) for operationalizing incidental vocabulary learning do not fully ensure that learners will not engage in intentional vocabulary learning, a more appropriate term to use in studies that adopt these criteria would be *incidentally oriented vocabulary learning*. By using this term we acknowledge that even though the basic conditions for incidental vocabulary learning may have been met in a particular study, these conditions do not guarantee that some learners will not decide to engage in intentional vocabulary learning on their own. This clarification being made, in this book we use the terms "incidental" and "incidentally oriented" interchangeably for the most part, but there are times to consider the extent to which learners may have decided to engage in intentional vocabulary learning on their own in vocabulary learning contexts that might otherwise be deemed incidental in nature.

The incidental-intentional continuum in vocabulary learning

The clarification made above regarding incidental versus incidentally oriented vocabulary learning is consistent with the fairly easily observed occurrence of vocabulary learning being neither purely incidental nor intentional. The incidental-intentional distinction is more accurately observed as a continuum, ranging from learning that is highly incidental in nature to learning that is highly intentional in nature. Conceptualizing different contexts of L2 vocabulary learning in this manner makes sense along this dimension given that attention is not a dichotomous entity (Gass, 1999; Haynes, 1998, as cited in Wesche & Paribakht, 1999). Relatedly, vocabulary instruction can be viewed as a continuum ranging between activities that are highly indirect and activities that are highly direct (Haynes, 1998, as cited in Wesche & Paribakht, 1999). Therefore, research on lex-IP and vocabulary learning also needs to take into account the continuous nature of the incidental-intentional distinction when studying and making assertions about how learners attend to different aspects of vocabulary learning (e.g., word form, word meaning, form-meaning mappings) in contexts directed toward intentional vocabulary learning versus contexts more directed toward incidental vocabulary learning.

Six areas of research on L2 vocabulary across the incidental-intentional continuum

One reflection of the incidental-intentional continuum in vocabulary learning is how different areas of research on L2 vocabulary learning can be organized with reference to research focused on incidental learning on the one side and intentional learning on the other (cf. Barcroft, 2004b, 2005; Coady, 1997). The following brief review of six areas of research demonstrates how different areas of L2 vocabulary research can be classified, at least roughly, using *incidental* as an endpoint on one side of a continuum and *intentional* as an endpoint on the other side of the continuum.

Incidental vocabulary learning. On the most incidental side of the continuum we find research on how learners are able to acquire new words from context without being instructed to do so. "Read and test" studies have demonstrated the intuitive finding that learners *can* learn new words while reading texts without being instructed to do so (Nagy, Herman & Anderson, 1985). Based on a review of a number of these types of studies, Krashen (1989) argued in favour of free reading as a means for promoting L2 vocabulary learning by emphasizing how learners in the studies reviewed were indeed able to acquire words during free reading. One limitation of this line of research is that many of the studies did not compare the effectiveness of incidental vocabulary learning during reading with other methods available for vocabulary instruction, such as more direct methods of vocabulary instruction. Without comparing the effects of free reading on vocabulary learning to Option B, Option C, or some other option, one cannot make claims about the relative effectiveness of free reading as a method for improving learners' knowledge of L2 vocabulary.

One important development in this line of research is connected to a study by Nagy, Anderson, and Herman (1987), who calculated that the probability of learning a new word from context is between 5–20%. The 5% figure was used to calculate that upon reading a million words in one year children can learn 1000 words per year (Nagy, Anderson & Herman, 1987; see also Nation & Waring, 1997; Nagy, 1997). This figure does not indicate, however, the number of words that could have been learned in the same amount of time using alternative methods of vocabulary instruction. Other research on incidental L2 vocabulary learning has examined the use of inferencing strategies (Paribakht & Wesche, 1999) and demonstrated the positive effects of variables such as topic familiarity, L2 reading proficiency (Pulido, 2003), and increased frequency of exposure to target words (e.g., Rott, 1999, 2007) on L2 incidental vocabulary learning.

Lexical requirements based on word frequency. A second strand of research related to incidental vocabulary learning has focused on *lexical requirements for comprehension*, or the number of words needed to know to reach different levels of reading comprehension. Much of this research has focused on the English language and learners of English as a second language. Nation and Waring (1997) have calculated that with a vocabulary of the 2000 most frequently used words in English one can reach an English text comprehension level of about 80%, which corresponds to about 1 out of 5 words not being known. According to a study by Liu and Nation (1985), this proportion would not be sufficient to allow for extensive success in guessing the meaning of new words from context. In consideration of multiple studies in this area, Nation and Waring (1997, p. 11) advocated teaching learners approximately 3000 words of high frequency in a language, noting that these words are "an immediate high priority" in language instruction.

Input enhancement and text-based factors. Moving a bit further toward the intentional side of the incidental-intentional continuum as a classification system, a third area of research related to L2 vocabulary concerns the impact of input enhancement and text-based factors on vocabulary learning. *Input enhancement* refers to techniques that cause targeted items (e.g., words) in the input to stand out so that learners may pay more attention to them. One can underline, bold, or increase the font size of certain words in a text, for example. Note that research on input enhancement for L2 grammar acquisition has demonstrated a somewhat constrained set positive effects for techniques of this nature when it comes to attention to and acquisition of (morpho)syntactic structures (for a review of these studies, see Wong, 2005).

A limited number of studies have assessed the effects of input enhancement on L2 vocabulary learning. In a study on intentional translation-based L2 vocabulary learning, Barcroft (2003a) found that enhancement via increasing the font size and bolding of target words could increase learning rates for those words provided that the type of enhancement used was sufficiently distinctive (i.e., only 3 out of 24 words enhanced as opposed to 9 out of 24 words enhanced). In another study that included more extensive manipulations of text-based factors, Hulstijn, Hollander and Greidanus (1996) demonstrated positive effects for the following conditions on vocabulary learning during reading: (a) increasing the number of times that a word appears in a text; (b) allowing students to use a bilingual dictionary (as compared to a control group); and (c) including definitions of words in marginal glosses (as compared to the dictionary use group). These studies suggest that input enhancement may promote, at least in some contexts, learning target words.

Vocabulary learning strategies. A fourth area of L2 vocabulary research has focused on the relationship between the use of different learning strategies and vocabulary learning. Studies in this area have focused on strategy use and levels of vocabulary learning success (see Schmitt, 1997, for a review). Schmitt (1997) developed a taxonomy of vocabulary learning strategies by integrating different existing classification systems into a system that sorts fifty different strategies according to those used to infer meaning of new words and those used to consolidate words. Ahmed (1989) found that more successful vocabulary learners tended to utilize a larger and more varied repertoire of vocabulary learning strategies, were aware of their learning, and were more aware of the semantic relationships between new and previously learned words. In a study on learner-selected strategies and intentional vocabulary learning, Barcroft (2002b) found that (a) mnemonic techniques, concurrent visualization of L2 words and their pictures, and repeating words "silently" yielded the three highest levels of performance and that (b) a significant positive correlation emerged between the number of strategies that learners used and their vocabulary learning performance. Finally, one fairly well-known mnemonic strategy that can be used to learn L2 vocabulary is the Keyword Method. When using the *Keyword Method*, learners recode new L2 word forms (the Spanish word *flor* 'flower') into known L1 words ("floor") and create visual images (image of a flower on the floor). In their seminal study in this area, Atkinson and Raugh (1975) demonstrated that L1 English speakers using Keyword were able to learn more L2 Russian words when compared to an unconstrained control group. More recent research has, however, revealed critical costs associated with Keyword, including costs related to the quality of lexicosemantic representations that Keyword promotes (Barcroft, Sommers & Sunderman, 2011; Kole, 2007; van Hell & Mahn, 1997), as is discussed further in Chapter 6.

Combining indirect and direct vocabulary instruction. Another area of research has focused on combining indirect, incidentally oriented vocabulary instruction with direct methods of vocabulary instruction. Paribakht and Wesche (1997) found that combining these two different types of instruction was more effective than using indirect, incidentally oriented instruction alone. In their study, in a Reading Plus (RP) treatment, students of English as a second language (ESL) read a total of four texts (on two themes), after which time they answered comprehension questions and completed a series of vocabulary activities focused on target words from the text. The types of direct techniques of instruction used ranged from less to more mental processing on a hierarchy of exercise types proposed by Paribakht and Wesche: selective attention, recognition, manipulation, interpretation, and production. In a Reading Only (RO) treatment, on the other hand, students from the same population also read four texts (on two themes) and responded to comprehension questions, but instead of completing vocabulary activities, they read a supplementary text in which the target words from the main texts appeared again, the purpose being to provide the students with further exposure to the target words in the context of reading. The findings of the study indicated that although both the RP and RO groups learned new vocabulary (albeit based on a scale that involved self-evaluation of vocabulary knowledge), the RP group scored higher than the RO group.

Intentional vocabulary learning and direct instruction. Finally, a sixth area of vocabulary-related research that can be viewed as the last point on the incidental-to-intentional learning continuum is that of intentional vocabulary learning and direct vocabulary instruction. Although researchers have identified and categorized a variety of different types of activities that can be performed while attempting to learn words intentionally (e.g., see Paribakht & Wesch, 1997), more research has been conducted on the relative effectiveness of the many different types of instructional activities that could be empirically tested. In one study, Prince (1996) compared translation-based L2 vocabulary learning versus presenting L2 vocabulary in the context of sentences. The results of the study indicated that translation-based learning was more effective. In other studies, Barcroft (1998a, 2000a, 2002a, 2004a, 2006) examined the effects of sentence writing, answering questions about word meaning, making pleasantness ratings about or counting the number of letters in words, and copying target words during intentional vocabulary learning.

Folse (2006) also compared the effectiveness of three types of L2 vocabulary learning exercises (one fill-in-the blank, three fill-in-the-blanks, and original sentence writing). The methodology and findings of these studies are discussed in subsequent chapters.

Four other areas of research related to L2 vocabulary

In addition to the six areas of research that we have classified by using the incidental-intentional learning continuum, we also find four other important areas of research related to L2 vocabulary that we can consider separately as the goals of research in these areas is less tied to incidental versus intentional learning issues. These four areas in question concern research on (a) word-based determinants of learnability, (b) the bilingual mental lexicon, (c) receptive versus productive vocabulary knowledge, and (d) lex-IP.

Word-based determinants of learnability. Studies on word-based determinants of learnabiltiy have investigated properties of L2 words that affect the relative difficulty and ease with which they can be learned. Ellis and Beaton (1995), for example, found the learnability of L2 words to be affected by word-based factors such as word length and degree of phonological similarity between L1 and L2 words: longer words and L2 words less similar to L1 words were more difficult to learn. In another study, Laufer (1997) found that "deceptive transparency" can make it more difficult to learn L2 words. *Deceptive transparency* refers to when a learner incorrectly thinks s/he knows the meaning of an expression because s/he knows words with in it. One example of deceptive transparency would be if a learner of English as a second language were to understand the expression "break the ice" in its literal sense instead of in its idiomatic sense.

The bilingual mental lexicon. Another area of research related to L2 vocabulary focuses on the bilingual lexicon. Studies in this area focus on how concepts and word forms are represented in the bilingual mind. In a classic study in this area, Potter, So, Von Eckardt and Feldman (1984) compared two different models of how L1 words, L2 words, and concepts may be represented in bilinguals: the *concept mediation* model, which posits direct connections between L2 words and concepts; and the *word association* model, which posits that L2 words are indirectly connected to concepts through L1 words. Although Potter et al. found evidence consistent with the concept mediation model, the subsequent studies have found that L1 lexical information is activated during L2 comprehension and production, suggesting that activation of L1 and L2 is "nonselective" during language use (see review in Kroll & Sunderman, 2003). Kroll, Michael, Tokowicz and Dufour (2002) also provided evidence suggesting that the ability to perform certain types of tasks in L1 is affected by L2 proficiency level. In their study, Kroll et al. found that more advanced bilinguals named words faster in their L1 than did beginning L2 learners who had the same L1.

Receptive versus productive knowledge. Another body of research has focused on receptive versus productive knowledge of L2 vocabulary. Issues of interest in this area include how receptive versus productive vocabulary knowledge can be measured and why receptive vocabulary knowledge may be larger than productive vocabulary knowledge. As a starting point for a review of research in this area, Melka (1997, p. 84) refers to "the generally accepted assumption that in one's lexicon receptive vocabulary is much larger than productive vocabulary and that reception precedes production." Estimates have been made that receptive vocabulary knowledge is twice as large as productive vocabulary knowledge (see Marton, 1977). One possible explanation of the relationship between productive and receptive vocabulary knowledge concerns the relationship between different ways of testing vocabulary knowledge and degree of knowledge of the formal properties of a word that one may possess. According to this explanation, on a vocabulary test, the more one provides the form of a word, the less one is testing productive knowledge, and similarly, the less one provides the form of a word, the more one is testing productive knowledge. From this perspective, one can view the productive versus receptive distinction as existing primarily at the level of testing, with degree of knowledge of word form remaining the same. This explanation is consistent with the following assessment by Melka (1997, pp. 101–102): "It is certainly not clear whether [reception] and [production] ought be considered as two separate systems dependent on each other, or rather as one unique system (one lexical store) used in two different ways, receptively or productively." This issue is discussed further in Chapter 9.

Lex-IP. A fourth area of L2 vocabulary research that is not located at any one particular point along the incidental-intentional continuum is lex-IP. Regardless of whether a word is learned incidentally or intentionally, it must be processed as input (cf. McCarthy, 1990, on input, storage, and retrieval with regard to vocabulary), but certain minimum conditions need to be in place for lex-IP to take place. Learners must have, for example, access to the form and at least some component of the meaning of the target word in question. This type of access may depend on conditions that are predicated by other levels of IP, such as prag-IP (c.f. Paribakht & Wesche, 1999), during incidental vocabulary learning, although isolated words (and other types of lexical items) are not a trivial portion of the input to which learners are exposed. Additionally, the learner's ability to access and attend to word form and word meaning is incremental in nature (see Hatch & Brown, 1995), regardless of whether the context of learning is intentional or incidental.

These points being made with regard to (a) the nature of the incidental-intentional learning continuum, (b) six areas of research that can be placed (at least roughly) along this continuum, and (c) four areas of research that are difficult to place along the continuum because they are pertinent to both incidental and intentional contexts, the remainder of this chapter focuses on key issues related to lex-IP research in intentional versus incidental contexts and the extent to which research in intentional contexts can and cannot be extended to incidental contexts, and vice versa. We begin with lex-IP research in intentional contexts.

Research on lex-IP and *intentional* L2 vocabulary learning

As mentioned previously, researching lex-IP in intentional learning contexts affords a number of advantages when it comes to research methodology, such as the possibility of controlling the amount of time learners spend attempting to learn each target word. Additionally, many of the insights gained from studying patterns in lexical input processing during intentional vocabulary learning can be extended, at least to some degree, to contexts of incidental vocabulary learning. At minimum, lex-IP research on intentional vocabulary learning can help to generate testable hypotheses about lex-IP in incidental learning contexts. As in incidental contexts, intentional contexts of vocabulary learning require one to attend to novel word forms, to identify and isolate the meanings (referential and otherwise) that the forms represent, and to map the meanings onto the forms.

Focused attention. One important defining characteristic of intentional vocabulary learning is the high degree to which a learner is focused on vocabulary learning instead of other possible tasks or other possible stimuli in the learner's immediate environment. If a learner is asked to attempt to learn a set of target words, is informed about a pending test on the words, or both, the learner typically is highly focused on the target words, regardless of how they are being presented as input within this larger context. *Focused attention* of this nature leads to more vocabulary learning than does the more limited attention learners tend to allocate in more incidentally oriented contexts of vocabulary learning (e.g., Hulstijn, 1992).

Controlled presentation patterns. Another defining characteristic of intentional vocabulary learning is that the number of times that target words appear in the input and the amount of time that they appear tends to be more controlled and predictable as compared to what happens in incidental vocabulary learning contexts. In intentional contexts, a learner may be viewing word-picture pairs, translated pairs, a series of words with definitions, or otherwise, but in any of these cases, the number of times each target word appears and how long it appears tends to be fairly controlled. Even when the learner initially does not know the specific presentation pattern that will follow (with regard to when words and their corresponding referents are presented and reappear), the learner typically gets a sense of the presentation pattern in question, assuming that the pattern is not completely random, after viewing it over a sufficient amount of time.

The two defining characteristics above make it possible for the lex-IP researcher to assess the specific effects of having learners perform different types of tasks concurrent to the vocabulary learning task the learner is by definition already engaged. When the concurrent tasks engage different types of processing, they allow the researcher to assess how each type of processing affects vocabulary learning (*task-based effects*). Additionally, when different components of vocabulary learning (word form, word meaning, form-meaning mapping) are isolated in assessment tasks, the researcher can draw conclusions about how different types of processing affect different components of vocabulary learning. In addition to assessing the effects of different types of concurrent tasks (and the different types of processing they engage), the controlled and attention-focused nature of intentional vocabulary learning allows the researcher to assess the effects of specific modifications in how target vocabulary is presented as input (*input-based effects*). Barcroft and Sommers (2005), for example, found that vocabulary learning improved incrementally when target words were spoken by three talkers and six talkers as compared to when spoken by one talker only, all other properties of the input (number of repetitions, amount of exposure to each word, etc.) being held constant. This finding allowed the researchers to make assertions about the role that increased talker variability plays on the development of new lexical representations, as discussed in Chapter 13.

Research on lex-IP and *incidental* L2 vocabulary learning

With incidental L2 vocabulary learning, on the other hand, the degree to which one's attention is focused on novel vocabulary is more difficult to ascertain and control. In fact, amount of focused attention on new words may be one of the most important, if not the most important, determinants of vocabulary learning success in incidental learning contexts, but focused attention on target words often may be very low if there is any focused attention at all. Therefore, in contrast to what is the case with intentional vocabulary learning, if a given task or input-related factor draws a learner's attention to target words in an incidentally oriented context, the task or input-related factor in question may positively affect word pick-up rates simply by drawing the learner's attention to (potential) target words. Therefore, we need to reconsider the potential impacts of different tasks and the corresponding types of processing they invoke in incidental, as compared to intentional, vocabulary learning contexts. The pattern in which (potential) target words appear in the input is another important way in which incidental learning contexts different from intentional ones. With incidentally oriented contexts the learner typically cannot predict how many times and how often novel words are going to appear as input. Therefore, both lack of focused attention and lack of controlled presentation pattern are commonly critical differences that appear with incidental as compared to intentional vocabulary learning.

The challenge of inferring word meanings. Another important difference with incidentally oriented learning is that the meanings of target words are inferred from context with varying degrees of difficulty. Whereas with intentional vocabulary learning word meanings tend to be very transparent from the immediate context (based on pictures of referents, definitions, translations, and so forth), with incidental vocabulary learning they frequently are not transparent at all. Of course researchers can introduce methodological previsions that help to control for this issue, such as by providing translations of novel words parenthetically, marginal glosses of target words, or text in which target word meanings are particularly clear from context (e.g., *I saw an X, hopping around and eating carrots in my backyard*). When provisions such as these are not provided, however, new word pick-up is determined largely, and oftentimes primarily or even solely, by the extent to which novel word meanings can be inferred from context.

To summarize, we have discussed three key factors that distinguish between L2 vocabulary learning in intentional versus incidental learning contexts: (a) +/– focused attention on vocabulary learning; (b) +/– controlled presentation of vocabulary; and (c) +/– inferable meanings of novel vocabulary from context. Each of these factors strongly affects the extent to which lex-IP as related to intentional vocabulary learning can be extended to lex-IP as related to incidental vocabulary learning and vice versa. As should become clear in the remaining three units and eleven chapters of this book, consideration of these factors is critical when interpreting the generalizability of research findings related to how learners process and learn novel L2 vocabulary. The type of processing – resource allocation (TOPRA) model (Barcroft, 2002a), which is the focus of the next two chapters, makes predictions that have been tested and confirmed in numerous studies on intentional L2 vocabulary learning. However, the predictions of TOPRA are more difficult to test in contexts of incidentally oriented L2 vocabulary learning where the potential impact of different types of processing becomes more difficult to predict than in contexts of intentional L2 vocabulary learning.

UNIT 2

Task-based effects

CHAPTER 5

Specificity in type of processing and learning
The TOPRA model

Unit 1 situated the study of lex-IP within other arenas of research and sorted out some of the key issues involved in lex-IP research, such as the roles of form, meaning, and mapping and comparisons between intentional and incidental contexts of vocabulary learning. The next two units systematically review different areas of research on lex-IP in order to map out key theoretical advances and pedagogical implications of research in each of these areas. Unit 2 focuses on the effects of different tasks that learners may perform while learning new vocabulary whereas Unit 3 focuses on the effects of different ways in which target vocabulary can be presented in the input.

Unit 2 begins with the present chapter (Chapter 5), which reviews research on human memory from different processing perspectives and introduces the type of processing – resource allocation (TOPRA) model (Barcroft, 2002a) and some compelling initial evidence in support of the model. The following chapter (Chapter 6) then systematically reviews a much larger body of research that has put the predictions of the TOPRA model to test from different angles, including studies on the effects of sentence writing, addressing questions about word meaning, and synonym generation. Chapters 7 and 8 then move on to research on the effects of tasks that involve output *without* access to meaning, such as word copying (Chapter 7), and the effects of tasks that involve output *with* access to meaning, such as attempting to retrieve target words after they have been processed as input to at least some extent (Chapter 8).

Most early research on the TOPRA model has focused on how requiring learners to perform different types of semantic tasks (e.g., sentence writing, questions about word meaning) affects intentional L2 vocabulary learning. According to TOPRA, the increased semantic processing invoked by tasks of this nature has the potential (a) to deplete processing resources that might otherwise be allocated toward novel L2 word forms, thereby decreasing word form learning. This prediction does not imply that the same types of increased semantic processing also have the potential (b) to draw learners' attention to target words that may otherwise be ignored in contexts of incidental vocabulary learning and in this way improving L2 vocabulary learning, as predicted by the *attention-drawing* hypothesis (Barcroft, 2009). Another possible effect of increased semantic elaboration in incidental contexts of L2 vocabulary learning is a combination of (a) and (b).

Research on TOPRA predictions in incidentally oriented contexts of L2 vocabulary learning have advanced our understanding of these issues, as has other research on the predictions of TOPRA with regard to the effects of different types of structural tasks (focused on word form) and the effects of increased semantic and structural processing on the mapping component of L2 vocabulary learning.

Whereas the findings and implications of this entire line of research on the TOPRA model are reviewed in the next chapter, the rest of this chapter provides background on the construct of processing resource allocation, the critical role of specificity when defining different types of processing, the history of research on the memorial effects of semantic and structural tasks on human memory, including the research frameworks of levels of processing (Craik & Lockhart, 1972) and transfer appropriate processing (Morris, Bransford & Franks, 1977); and the general and specific versions of the TOPRA model (Barcroft, 2002a). After each of these topics are discussed in turn, the chapter then reviews one particularly pivotal study in the history of research on the TOPRA model (Barcroft, 2002a), which tested the effects of both a semantic task (making pleasantness ratings about word meaning) and a structural task (counting the number of letters in target words) on intentional L2 vocabulary learning and which provided early convincing evidence in favor of TOPRA predictions.

Processing resource allocation

Whereas studies on i.morph-IP and syn-IP input have focused on how learners attend to and parse different items in sentences, studies on lex-IP and L2 vocabulary learning have focused on how learners attend to and parse different components of lexical items when they are presented as input. As with other research on input processing, studies on lex-IP often concern a cognitive construct known as *processing resource allocation*, which refers to how learners distribute their limited cognitive processing capacities toward encoding and retaining different types of data provided in the input. Learners must allocate processing resources in this way because they simply cannot do everything all at once (see Wickens, 1984, 1989) or learn everything all at once. When it comes to lex-IP and vocabulary learning in particular, *processing resource allocation* refers to how learners distribute their limited cognitive processing capacities toward encoding and retaining different aspects of word knowledge, such as word form, word meaning, and form-meaning mapping. Learners must allocate our limited processing resources toward different aspects of learning each new word progressively over time.

A substantial amount of research has been conducted on lex-IP with respect to how limited processing resources are allocated when learners are presented with a new L2 word and are given at least some type of access to aspects of its meaning, such as when viewing a picture of the word, seeing a translation of the word, or attempting to infer the meaning of the word from context. In such cases, limited processing resources can be directed in varying degrees toward perceiving, encoding and retaining the new word form; connecting new word form to its meaning reference; and other types of tasks, such as tasks that require increased semantic processing or output-oriented tasks that may require learners to direct limited resources away from what is pertinent to learning new words.

Specificity in type of processing

One central theoretical and pedagogical contribution of lex-IP research to date concerns the importance of specifying *type* of processing when predicting the learning outcomes of different tasks in which learners can engage during vocabulary learning. As the following sections of this chapter will clarify, the critical finding that one *type* of task, such as a semantic task, may facilitate memory for "items," as proposed by unqualified versions of the levels-of-processing (LOP) framework for research on human memory (Craik & Lockhart, 1972; see below for more details on this framework) and subsequently adopted without sufficient qualification by many L2 researchers and instructors, it may not do so at all for all "items." In fact, the same semantic task may have very different effects on memory for *other* "items," such novel word forms. In such cases, the effect of the semantic task on memory may be negative. Therefore, a new theoretical paradigm is needed to account for when one particular type of task produces very different effects on different types of memory or learning goals.

The type of processing – resource allocation (TOPRA) model was developed for this purpose. It was developed independently of transfer appropriate processing (TAP) (Morris, Bransford & Franks, 1977) based on Barcroft's (2000a) early observations of strong negative effects of sentence writing on L2 vocabulary learning and in consideration of how these findings were inconsistent with unqualified applications of LOP in the realm of vocabulary learning. It was quickly recognized, however, that TAP and the TOPRA model are largely consistent with one another. TAP offers a novel way of viewing LOP and inverse-LOP effects in a manner that Craik and Lockhart (1972) had not previously done in early work on LOP. Specifically, according to TAP, the effect of a variable on memory depends on the nature of the task performed at study and at test: semantic orientation should improve memory for subsequent semantically oriented tasks whereas structural orientation should facilitate memory for subsequent structurally oriented tasks. Nevertheless, the TOPRA model clearly goes beyond the basic assertions of TAP by asserting a series of testable predictions about the "give-and-take" relationship between different types of processing, such as different aspects of vocabulary learning. In particular, the TOPRA model posits that the formal, semantic, and mapping components of vocabulary learning are (at least largely) dissociable and that tasks invoking one of these three types of processing can increase learning for that particular aspect of vocabulary knowledge but at the same time decrease the amount of processing resources available for processing and learning other aspects of vocabulary learning.

Semantic elaboration, LOP, and vocabulary learning

There is a fairly persistent line of thinking within L2 vocabulary research and instruction that maintains that focusing extensively on the meaning of a target word should lead to the better learning and retention of the word in question. This belief has origins in unqualified applications of LOP. According to LOP, memory for an "item" depends on the level or relative depth at which the item is processed. Tasks that involve more elaborate manipulation of information, or *deeper processing*, result in better memory than their counterparts, which involve *shallower processing*. Within this framework, *semantic elaboration*, or when one focuses extensively on word meaning, is associated with deeper processing. On the other hand, *structural elaboration*, or when one focuses extensively on word form, is associated with shallower processing.

To provide one example of semantic elaboration, consider the extent to the word *squid* represents an example of an animal, of a fish, of a food, or of another category. As an example of structural elaboration, count how many letters or syllables there are in the word *squid* or try to think of other words that rhyme with it. Tresselt and Mayzner (1960), for example, compared the effects of semantic elaboration by requiring participants to judge whether words represented an instance of a particular concept (e.g., "economic"), a semantically oriented task, versus requiring learners either to cross out vowels in words or to copy words, both structurally oriented tasks. Hyde and Jenkins (1969) compared having participants judge whether words had pleasant or unpleasant connotations, a semantically oriented task, versus having participants count the number instances of the letter "E" or estimate the total number of letters in words, more structurally oriented tasks. As another example, Schulman (1971) compared having participants scan a list of words to assess whether each word denoted living things, geographic locations, or both (semantically oriented tasks) versus having scanning the list to determine whether the letter "A" was present in each word or whether all the letters in each word were different (a structurally oriented task).

Numerous studies have demonstrated that semantic elaboration can facilitate many different types of memory/learning, including the three studies on semantic elaboration cited in the previous paragraph, when recall of known (previously learned) L1 words was the memory-related dependent measure. Other studies have demonstrated benefits for semantic elaboration on L1 sentence recall (Stevenson, 1981) and L1 text recall (McDaniel, 1984). Indeed the evidence in favor of LOP predictions is substantial, at least for the limited nature of the "items" that were being examined during the early years of research in this area. And again, according to LOP, the positive effects of semantic elaboration in these studies is due to the "deeper processing" produced by increased semantic processing as compared to the "shallower processing" produced by structurally oriented processing.

Impacts of LOP on ideas about semantic processing and vocabulary learning

Craik and Lockhart's (1972) explanation of the benefits of semantically oriented processing gave rise, at least in large part, to the idea that having learners engage semantic processing should improve memory for new words during vocabulary acquisition. Beyond the potential benefits of semantic processing when engaged as part of the Keyword Method (Atkinson & Raugh, 1975), many language researchers and language instructors came to believe that having learners process new words while focusing on their semantic properties should positively affect vocabulary instruction (e.g., Stahl & Fairbanks, 1986; Brown & Perry, 1991). Johnson and Pearson (1978, 1984), for example, developed two instructional techniques focused on different properties of the referents of new words. These techniques are semantic features analysis and semantic mapping. With *semantic feature analysis*, new words and concepts or features associated with those words appear on a grid. When the instructor presents a new word, students fill in the grid by determining whether the concepts or features listed are positively or negatively associated with the new word. With *semantic mapping*, students attempt to connect new words in semantic networks by identifying explicitly how the words may or may not be grouped together. L2 instructors also have engaged their students in other semantically elaborative types of vocabulary learning activities, such as talking about the meaning of new words and relating the meanings to personal experiences; focusing on varying contexts in which the words can be used; asking and answering questions about the meanings of new words and the contexts in which they appear; comparing and contrasting the meanings of new words; and writing new words in sentences. However, what does research actually indicate about the relative effectiveness of these types of semantically elaborative activities as compared to other tasks and no-task controls?

Transfer appropriate processing

In answering this question, let us first consider Morris, Bransford, and Franks' (1977) proposal of *transfer appropriate processing (TAP)* as an alternative framework for research on human memory as compared to that of LOP. As mentioned previously, according to TAP, the effect of a variable on memory depends on the nature of the task performed at study and test. Semantic orientation facilitates performance on subsequent semantically oriented tasks, and structural orientation facilitates performance on subsequent structurally oriented tasks. Morris, Bransford, and Franks provided evidence for TAP by demonstrating that recall of L1 words after learning with a structurally oriented rhyming task was improved when the task performed at test involved rhyming as well. Following this alternative theoretical framework (in contrast to LOP) and the research findings that support it, one may begin to question whether increases in semantic processing (invoked by different types of semantic tasks) do or do not really facilitate learning novel word forms. If a structural (rhyming) task is more effective than a semantic (pleasantness ratings) task when the to-be-remembered "item" is structural in nature, then perhaps certain structural tasks are more effective than semantic tasks when it comes to encoding and retaining novel word forms. TAP did not go as far as to make predictions of this nature, but it provided a new way of viewing previous findings that had been interpreted from the LOP perspective alone. TAP debunked the notion that (deeper) semantically oriented processing (as compared to [shallower] structurally oriented processing) should lead to better memory across the board.

The type of processing – resource allocation (TOPRA) model

Consistent with the general proposals of TAP, the *type of processing – resource allocation (TOPRA) model* (Barcroft, 2000a, 2002a) visually represents how different types of processing can produce different types of learning outcomes. Three versions of the model appear in Figure 5.1. In each version, the thicker outer lines do not move because they represent the restricted amount of processing resources available to a learner at a given point in time. The overall distance between the two thicker outer lines necessarily vary based on the learner in question as they would reflect differences in the overall processing capacities of different learners. Once the outer lines are established for any given individual in any given learning situation, however, those lines should not move. In such cases, the overall available processing resources are established for the learner and learning situation in question. The inside lines do move, however, reflecting how different types of processing and their corresponding types of learning increase or decrease. The basic idea of

Chapter 5. Specificity in type of processing and learning

A. General version: Types of processing and learning

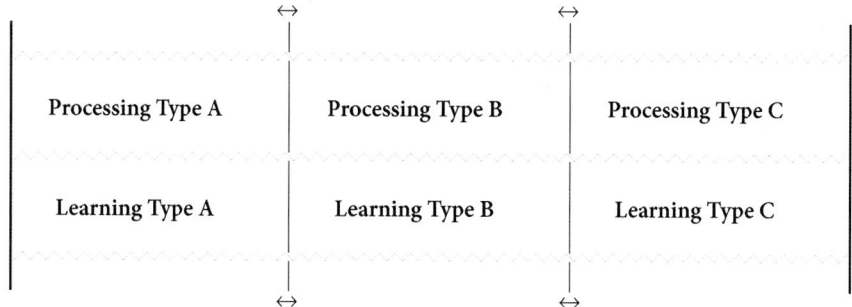

B. Components of vocabulary learning: Semantic, formal, and mapping

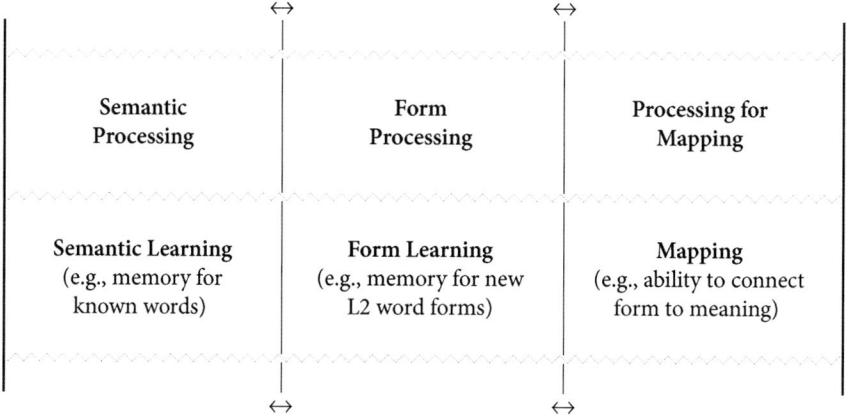

C. Semantic and formal components of vocabulary learning

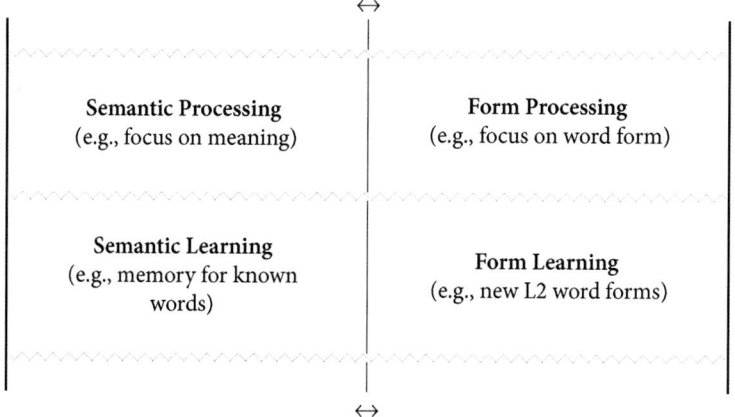

Figure 5.1 Type of processing – resource allocation (TOPRA) model.

the model is that each specific type of processing necessarily exhausts processing resources that now become unavailable for other types of processing. As one type of processing increases due to a specific type of task being performed, other types must decrease in order to accommodate. The amount and type of learning that ultimately take place reflect the end result of the trade-off between the different types processing and learning counterparts in question.

The TOPRA model can focus on how different types of processing affect learning rates for different aspects or components of word knowledge, such as word form, word meaning, and form-meaning mapping. Version A (see Figure 5.1) is the general version of the model. Version B focuses on processing for word meaning, word form, and form-meaning mapping. Version C focuses specifically on the semantic and formal components of word learning for contexts in which these two types of processing come into play. It demonstrates most clearly the prediction that, when processing demands are sufficiently high, increased semantic processing can increase learning for the semantic properties of words while decreasing learning for their formal properties. The formal component of word learning (the written form of the target word, the spoken form of the target word, or otherwise) decreases under these conditions because fewer processing resources remain available to process for word form.

The TOPRA model makes predictions about how different types of tasks are likely to affect processing resource allocation during L2 vocabulary learning, predictions that ultimately could be quantified. According to TOPRA, more semantically oriented tasks facilitate learning the semantic or meaning-related properties of target L2 words (unless these are already known) while decreasing learning of the formal and mapping-related aspects of learning the words in question. Although studies on lex-IP do not focus solely on questions related to the TOPRA model, a number of studies, many of which are reviewed in Chapter 6, have tested the predictions of the model in contrast to unqualified extensions of LOP that predict improved L2 vocabulary learning for semantic tasks (as compared to structural tasks or no-task controls).

A pivotal study on TOPRA and intentional L2 vocabulary learning

Barcroft (2002a) reported one particularly telling study on the TOPRA model. The study tested TOPRA predictions by examining the effects of both increased semantic processing and increased structural processing on memory for previously known (L1) word forms and memory for novel (L2) word forms. Increased semantic processing was operationalized by having learners perform a semantic task during a time-controlled period of intentional L2 vocabulary learning. Increased structural processing was operationalized by having learners perform a structural task during the same period of intentional L2 vocabulary learning. A no-task control condition was also included.

Participants in the study were English-speaking students of L2 Spanish. All of the participants were asked to do their best to learn 24 new Spanish words while viewing word-picture pairs on a screen at the front of their classroom. For one group of 8 words, the participants were asked to make pleasantness ratings about the meaning of target L2 words based on their prior experience while attempting to learn the words. This semantic task was designed to increase semantic processing. For another group of 8 words, the participants were asked to count the number of letters in the words while attempting to learn the words. This structural task was designed to increase structural processing. Finally, for another group of 8 words, the participants were asked only to do their best to learn the target words and were not required to perform any additional task. After the learning phase, the participants performed three posttest tasks. First, they completed a free recall of the target words in Spanish. In a *free recall* task, participants simply try to remember words to which they have been exposed, in this case by writing them and numbering them on a blank sheet of paper. Second, they completed a free recall task of the words in English. Third, they completed a picture-to-Spanish cued recall task. *Cued recall* refers to when one is asked to recall something based on the presentation of another item as a stimulus, in this case a picture of the referent of each target Spanish words.

Before considering the findings of the study, let us review what predictions the TOPRA model would make for each of the three learning conditions. To begin, the model would predict that the structural task would increase processing and learning for the formal aspects of the overall task but decrease processing and learning for aspects that are dependent on semantically oriented learning or memory. Therefore, given that the Spanish free recall and the picture-to-Spanish cued recall were largely dependent on how well the participants had learned the new word forms, the TOPRA model would predict higher Spanish free recall for the structural (letter counting) as compared to the same type of free recall for the semantic (pleasantness ratings) task. In addition, given that the English free recall was not dependent on learning new word form (because the participants already were English speakers) and more dependent on semantically oriented memory (being able to activate the meaning of the words in one's mind in order to recall it), the TOPRA model would predict higher English free recall for the semantic task as compared to the structural task. This second prediction regarding the effects of the semantic task is also predicted by the LOP view of memory.

The results of the study were consistent with the predictions of the TOPRA model on all fronts. Spanish free recall scores were higher for letter-counting (+structural) task than for the pleasantness-ratings (+semantic) task, but English free recall was higher for the pleasantness-ratings (+semantic) task than for the letter-counting (+structural) task. These findings, which are depicted in Figure 5.2, suggest, as predicted by the TOPRA model, that the increased semantic processing invoked by the +semantic task decreased processing resources that otherwise could have been allocated toward processing and encoding the new L2 word forms. Furthermore, the results of the indicated that Spanish cued recall, which is also dependent on learning new L2 word forms, was not higher for the +semantic task as compared to the +structural task. Based on one scoring method sensitive to partial knowledge of target word forms (LPSP-written), Spanish cued recall means were 1.58 for the +semantic task versus 1.96 for the +structural task, but this difference did not reach a level of statistical significance ($p = .089$). Clearly, any so-called "deeper processing" associated with the semantic task was of no benefit to learning the new L2 word forms. Finally, the findings of the study indicated that overall free recall scores and Spanish cued recall scores were higher in the no-elaboration control condition as compared to both the +semantic and +structural tasks. This finding suggests that both tasks essentially "got in the learners' way" of being able to encode the target words as input in the most effective manner.

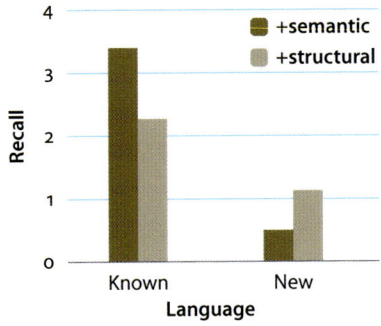

Figure 5.2 Effects of making pleasantness ratings (+semantic) versus letter counting (+structural) on free recall in a known language (English) and a new language (L2 Spanish).

Figure 5.2 demonstrates a *double dissociation* that is wholly consistent with the predictions of the TOPRA model for the semantic and formal components of vocabulary learning. The structural task improved recall of the new word forms, or the new L2 Spanish words, whereas the semantic task improved recall that depended on semantic memory, or memory for the English words, which were not new forms to the learners. The effect that we observe on the right side of Figure 5.2 for Spanish free recall is an *inverse levels-of-processing effect* whereas the effect that we see for the English free recall on the left side of the figure is a standard levels-of-processing effect.

The increased semantically oriented processing invoked by the semantic task in the study functioned like a double-edged sword. It helped learners to remember previously acquired forms but hindered them in their ability to remember the truly novel word forms. With direct reference to the TOPRA model for the formal and semantic components of word learning (Figure 5.1C), the effects observed for the pleasantness-ratings semantic task can be accounted for by moving the center bar in the model to the right, which increases semantic processing and learning while decreasing structural processing and learning. The effects observed for letter-counting structural task can be accounted for by moving the center bar in the model to the left, increasing structural processing and learning while decreasing semantic processing and learning. This overall pattern is precisely what is predicted by the TOPRA model.

Specificity in type of processing and type of human memory and learning

The main theoretical implications of this study concern the relationship between semantic processing, structural processing, and form learning. Whereas numerous studies have demonstrated that increased semantic processing facilitates various types of semantically oriented memory and learning (e.g., Craik & Tulving, 1975; Hyde & Jenkins, 1969; Johnson-Laird, Gibbs, & de Mowbray, 1978; Stevenson, 1981; Tresselt & Mayzner, 1960), the findings of Barcroft (2002a) and numerous other studies (reviewed in the next chapter) suggest that increased semantic processing can inhibit memory for and learning of novel forms, and in this case in particular, novel word forms. This general finding highlights the need to reevaluate the relationship between increased semantic processing, structural processing, and the various types of learning in which human beings can engage. In other words, research in this area suggests that when we examine the relationship between input processing and memory/learning, it is important that we distinguish between learning that is semantic in nature (semantic learning) and learning that is directed at the formal properties of the target stimuli in question (form learning).

Different types of processing as a double- or multiple-edged swords. As is consistent with the study reviewed here and the predictions of the TOPRA model, when processing resources are being utilized at maximum levels, increased semantic processing may facilitate different types of semantically oriented learning while at the same detract from form-oriented learning or vice versa. In this sense, in contrast to unqualified extensions of the LOP paradigm to the realm of novel word learning, increased semantic processing can function like a double- or multiple-edged sword, increasing semantically oriented learning while decreasing form-oriented learning, other types of learning, or both. When task demands exceed what available processing resources can meet, one particular type of processing (semantic, structural, mapping-oriented, or otherwise) facilitates one type of learning while decreasing another type because resources are distributed in an unequal (unbalanced) manner.

Pedagogical implications of specificity in type of processing. The predictions of the TOPRA model, as supported by the findings of Barcroft (2002a) and other research on the effects of different types of semantic and structural tasks (as reviewed in the next chapter) also has important implications for language instruction. The predictions of TOPRA speak to the need to identify the specific type(s) of processing a given task is likely to promote when predicting its probable effect on different types of learning. With regard to L2 vocabulary in particular, developers of L2 instructional materials, language program directors, and language instructors should expect tasks that invoke semantically oriented processing to facilitate semantically oriented types of learning, such as learning novel word meanings. They should not, however, expect the same semantically oriented tasks to facilitate form-oriented learning, such as learning novel word forms. Similarly, they should expect tasks that invoke structurally oriented processing to facilitate structurally oriented types of learning, such as learning novel word forms, but in no way should they expect the same structurally oriented tasks to facilitate semantically oriented learning, such as learning novel word meanings. Finally, it is important to be cautious when making predictions related to the potential effects of different semantic and structurally oriented tasks on the mapping component of L2 vocabulary learning. According to the TOPRA model, what is most appropriate to strengthen form-meaning mappings at the word level is, precisely, mapping-oriented processing, whereas increases in semantic processing, structural processing, or both have the potential to detract from mapping-oriented learning by exhausting limited processing resources in other directions.

CHAPTER 6

Effects of tasks involving semantic and structural elaboration

The study described in the previous chapter (Barcroft, 2002), which provided strong support for the TOPRA model by comparing the effects of both semantic and structurally oriented tasks on recall of known L1 words and novel L2 words, is only one of many studies to test the predictions of the TOPRA model in different contexts of L2 vocabulary learning. This chapter reviews the larger body of studies that have tested the predictions of the TOPRA model. They include (a) studies on the effects of various semantic and structurally oriented tasks on different aspects of intentional L2 vocabulary learning but also (b) one study focused on the form-meaning mapping component of L2 vocabulary learning based on learning novel L2 homonyms (e.g., "*foot* with five toes" versus "*foot* the bill") and (c) various studies on the effects of semantic and structural tasks on incidental L2 vocabulary learning. As should become evident as the chapter progresses, these studies provide convincing evidence in support of the predictions of TOPRA model, particularly with regard to intentional L2 vocabulary learning, but also to a large extent with regard to the potential of the TOPRA perspective when it comes to improving our understanding of the role of specificity in task type in incidental L2 vocabulary learning.

It also should become clear, on the other hand, that not all semantically oriented tasks are created alike when it comes to how they affect different components of vocabulary learning. Some semantic tasks tend to produce stronger negative effects on word form learning than others, for example. The same holds true for structurally oriented tasks. Research to date also suggests that it is more challenging to test the predictions of the TOPRA model in incidental (as compared to intentional) contexts of vocabulary learning. This state of affairs appears to be due in large part to methodological difficulties related to how semantic processing is utilized in more incidentally oriented contexts. Do increases in semantic processing draw learners' attention toward words in incidental contexts, increasing the likelihood that the words will be learned, as predicted by the *attention-drawing hypothesis* (Barcroft, 2009)? Alternatively, do increases in semantic processing exhaust processing resources that otherwise could be utilized to encode and learn novel word forms in incidental contexts, as predicted by the *resource-depletion hypothesis* (Barcroft, 2009)? As a third option, do increases in semantic processing result in both of these effects, rendering the net effect of increased semantic processing less visible? These questions are critical when attempting to understand the relationship between the task type, type of processing, and incidental L2 vocabulary learning outcomes.

The rest of this chapter is divided into three main sections. The first two review research on different types of semantic, structural, and mapping-focused tasks in different contexts of vocabulary learning. The first section focuses on research on intentional vocabulary learning, including studies that examined the effects of writing target words in sentences and answering questions about target word meanings as well as a study on the effects of referent token variability, which concerns effects related to how input is presented but which yielded telling results when it comes to the effects of contexts of increased semantically oriented processing. This section also includes one study that tested the predictions of the TOPRA model from a different angle by examining the effects of increased semantic and structural processing on the mapping component of intentional L2 vocabulary learning. Finally, additional consideration is given within this section to research on the Keyword Method (Atkinson & Raugh, 1975) and how this method relates to the predictions of the TOPRA model and lex-IP in general.

The second section focuses on the effects on different types of semantic and structural tasks, such as synonym generation (semantic) and letter counting (structural), on incidental L2 vocabulary learning during reading. A subset of these studies included both structural and semantic tasks. This section provides analyses regarding the extent to which research supports the predictions of the TOPRA model in incidental vocabulary learning contexts of this nature. It also includes consideration of the proposals of Hulstijn and Laufer's (2001) involvement load hypothesis, existing research on the involvement load hypothesis, and the degree to which the existing research does or does not support the proposals of the hypothesis. The third and final section of the chapter then provides summary and analyses of research in this area as it relates to basic assertions that can be made about the relationship between different types of tasks, the processing that they invoke during lex-IP, and the effects that these tasks and their corresponding types of processing have on vocabulary learning.

Studies on intentional vocabulary learning

To begin, we consider studies that have tested the predictions of the TOPRA model in different ways. Most of these studies focused on the effects of different semantic and structural tasks on intentional L2 vocabulary learning. However, the final two studies in this section assessed (respectively) (a) the effects of increased semantic processing by means of increased referent token variability in the input on intentional L2 word learning (Sommers & Barcroft, 2013) and (b) the effects of a semantic and a structural task on the mapping component of intentional L2 vocabulary by means of learning secondary meanings of homographs (Kida & Barcroft, 2014). The questions addressed by studies in this section are the following:

1. What is the effect of writing target words in sentences?
2. What is the effect of questions about word meaning?
3. What is the effect of different types of instructions regarding focus on word meaning and word form?
4. What is the effect of referent token variability?
5. What is the effect of pleasantness ratings and letter counting on the mapping component of L2 vocabulary learning?

The first two questions concern the effects of increased semantic processing, which the TOPRA model predicts will not facilitate and may detract from novel word form learning. The third question parallels questions addressed by Barcroft (2002a) on the effects of both semantic and structural tasks but regarding tasks that are more open in nature – tasks that learners can complete "in their mind" without needing to circle numbers. The fourth question concerns predictions of TOPRA regarding the possible negative effects of increased referent token variability (e.g., presenting six different pictures of a bear instead of only one picture six times for the L2 Spanish target word *oso* 'bear'). Finally, the fifth question concerns the viability of TOPRA predictions with regard to its predictions of potential negative effects of either increased semantic processing or increased structural processing on the mapping component of L2 vocabulary learning.

What is the effect of sentence writing?

To begin, Barcroft (1998a, 2000a, 2004a) reported a series of studies on the effects of requiring learners to write target L2 words in sentences as compared to not having them do so. This task is a semantically elaborative in nature because one must activate various aspects of the semantic properties (meaning) of the target word and related words in order to be able to write the word in a sentence. Traditionally, there has been widespread belief among instructors and researchers that writing target words in sentence should be an effective technique for intentional vocabulary learning, but how does this type of semantic task actually pan out when put to the test and compared to conditions without sentence writing?

To answer this question, we will focus here on a study reported by Barcroft (2004a), who asked English-speaking learners of L2 Spanish to attempt to learn 24 new Spanish words while writing 12 of them in original sentences and by simply viewing the other 12 words as input only. The results indicated that productive vocabulary learning was much better on both immediate and delayed measures when learners were not required to write the target words in sentences. Figures 6.1 and 6.2 depict the negative effects of sentence writing in two experiments (both reported in Barcroft, 2004a) on immediate (Time 1) and delayed (Time 2 = 2 days later; Time 3 = 1 week later) measures of productive vocabulary learning over time. The results depicted in Figure 6.1 (Barcroft, 2004a, Experiment 1) are based on learning conditions of one 48-second trial for sentence writing versus four 6-second trials for no sentence writing. The results depicted in Figure 6.2 are based on learning conditions of one 24-second trial for both the sentence-writing and no-writing conditions.

Contrary to intuitions that one might have about sentence writing positively affecting vocabulary learning, these findings suggest that writing new words in sentences can draw processing resources away from what is needed to encode and retain new word forms, mappings between the word form and its meaning, or both. As predicted by the TOPRA model, increased semantic processing associated with the sentence writing condition exhausts processing resources that otherwise could be used to encode new word form, and in terms of L2 instruction, this finding suggests that having students write new L2 words in sentences is an ineffective vocabulary learning activity, at least when compared to not having them do so and simply focus on target words as input during the early stages of L2 word learning.

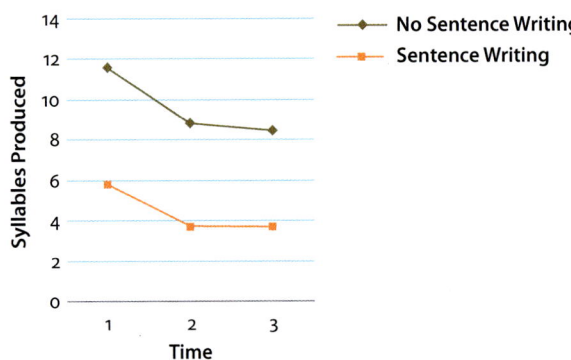

Figure 6.1 Negative effects of sentence writing on L2 vocabulary learning (Experiment 1).

These findings are consistent with those of Barcroft (1998a, 2000a) regarding the negative effects of sentence writing on L2 Spanish vocabulary learning. In another study, Wong and Pyun (2012) assessed the effects of sentence writing among English-speaking learners of L2 French and L2 Korean. In that study, the researchers followed the same basic design and methods used by Barcroft (2004a) but

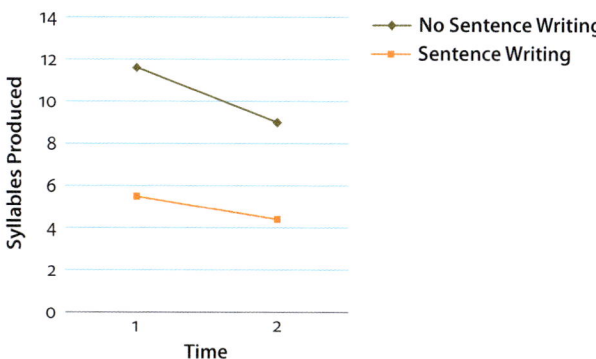

Figure 6.2 Negative effects of sentence writing on L2 vocabulary learning (Experiment 2).

examined L2 (French, Korean) as an additional factor. The results of their study indicated strong negative effects for sentence writing, helping to confirm Barcroft's previous findings, but they also indicated that the vocabulary learning scores in the sentence-writing condition of the L2 Korean learners were much lower than those of the L2 French learners. In their interpretation of these findings, they argue that the potential negative effects of sentence writing may be more pronounced when an L2 script is more distant from one's L1, which provides support for the role of L1–L2 orthographic distance in the learning and retention of L2 words. Note that this pattern of results is precisely what the TOPRA model would predict: the more successful learning of a target depends on processing and retaining novel form, the more semantic tasks and the increased semantic processing they invoke can detract from processing and learning the target item in question.

It is important to clarify that the studies reviewed thus far in this section compared conditions of sentence writing versus no sentence writing. In this way the studies assessed how the increased semantic processing associated with sentence writing affected the allocation of processing resources toward learning the new L2 words. The nature of these studies made it unnecessary to make predictions or assumptions about how much any other task might or might not increase semantically oriented processing. This methodological advantage is an important one because when it comes to making predictions about the degree to which a given task invokes semantically oriented "deeper" processing, researchers certainly can make errors in what they deem to be the most semantically oriented "deeper" one when comparing two or more possible tasks. To illustrate this point further, let us consider two studies that included sentence writing as one of three tasks being assessed: one study by Coomber, Ramstad, and Sheets (1986) and another study by San Mateo Valdehíta (2013).

Coomber, Ramstad, and Sheets (1986) compared the effects of three rehearsal methods on learning pseudowords. The three rehearsal methods were (a) definition, or matching the words to one of five definitions; (b) examples, or matching the words to one of five usage examples, and (c) sentence composing, or writing and underlining the words in sentences. The examples and the sentence composing methods were intended to operationalize increased semantic elaboration and were expected to result in greater learning than the definition condition, which was based on the following idea: "How much of a stimulus one retains depends primarily upon how deeply one elaborates on the material during coding, or practice. The deeper the analysis, or the greater the elaboration, the greater is the amount of verbal material retained" (p. 281). In other words, the researchers expected definitions condition to require the least amount of processing, the examples condition to require somewhat more processing than that, and sentence writing condition to require the most processing.

In their study, 134 college students were divided into the three treatment groups: definitions ($n = 43$), examples ($n = 46$), and sentence composing ($n = 45$). The ten "synthetic" pseudowords words constructed were verbs composed of two highly frequent trigrams: *bulfor* 'to solve a problem,' *camill* 'to inhabit,' *fodive* 'to progress,' *herzon* 'to destroy,' and so on. For each treatment, the researchers used two reinforcement booklets. On the top of each page of the reinforcement booklets appeared a target word that was followed by exercises that corresponded to the treatment in question. In the definitions condition, there was a list of 50 possible definitions of the target word, some correct and some incorrect. In the examples condition, there was a list of fifteen possible examples of the target word, some valid and some invalid. In the sentence-writing condition, there were instructions to answer a stimulus question ("Answer the following question in one sentence, using the underlined target word in your sentence. Underline the target word in your sentence. To be counted correct, your sentence must demonstrate that you know the meaning of the target word.") and the stimulus question itself (e.g., "What is one campus organization to which you belong, and where does it *morwil*?" Sample Response: "I belong to the debate team, and we *morwit* in Academy Hall.") (p. 286). All three treatment groups completed the same posttest. The posttest contained three parts that corresponded to the three learning conditions (definitions, examples, sentence writing), but with stimulus items. Sentences in the posttest were rated as "acceptable" or "unacceptable" and, accordingly, scored as correct or incorrect. Four minutes were allowed for definitions, 4 minutes for examples, and 8 minutes for sentence writing.

The results indicated a significant main effect for condition and for posttest. The actual means for each of the conditions (for definitions, examples, and sentence writing posttests respectively) were as follows: definitions = 6.4, 5.2, 4.4;

examples = 6.6, 5.4, 5.2; and sentence writing = 7.5, 5.8, 6.2. The difference between the definitions and sentence writing groups was found to be significant. The researchers argue that the results obtained support their hypothesis about more deeply processed words being retained better. They conclude that their study "supports composing as an effective means of learning specified lexical items" (p. 290).

There are several other possible reasons for the nature of the findings on sentence writing in Coomber, Ramstad, and Sheets' study. The first concerns the operationalization of variables in their study. The three treatments examined were deemed to require different amounts of semantic elaboration (processing levels). Sentence writing was deemed to require the most and definitions the least. However, the actual amount of semantic elaboration (and processing depth) associated with each of the three learning conditions may not have corresponded to what they were purported to be in terms of semantic elaboration. For example, in the definitions condition, the participants had to process the new words based upon their semantic properties by comparing the meaning of each word to five different possible definitions. Therefore, the participants had to make a variety of different types of semantically oriented evaluations. In the sentence writing condition, on the other hand, the participants only had to write one sentence for each word. Therefore, the participants may have evaluated the meanings of the new words in more ways in the definitions conditions than they did in the sentence writing condition. If this is the case, then the hypothesis that semantic elaboration can inhibit (word) form processing and learning, as predicted by the TOPRA model, would explain the lower performance in the definitions condition and the superior performance in the sentence writing condition.

In addition, on the posttests in Coomber, Ramstad, and Sheets' study, the participants were provided with each of the target words and asked (a) to match it to a definition, (b) to match it to a usage example, or (c) to write it in a sentence. Word form production was not tested. It is evident that the provision of target word forms in posttests is a characteristic of many studies (with some exceptions) on semantic elaboration and lexical learning. Requiring learners to produce new word forms may result in very different results, however. When learners are required to produce novel L2 word forms themselves, their performance reflects their degree of knowledge of the word forms in question to a greater degree than when learners are provided with the target forms and tested in a more "receptive" manner.

In another more recent study, San Mateo Valdehíta (2013) compared the effectiveness of three activities (tasks): choose the right definition of each target word; choose the example that includes a semantic equivalent of each target word; and write each target word in an original sentence (sentence writing). Without expanding upon methodological details of the study to the extent provided for the Coomber, Ramstad, and Sheets' study, it should be immediately clear that

San Mateo Valdehíta's study did not compare sentence writing with no sentence writing, and therefore any claims about the relative effectiveness of sentence writing need to be interpreted in this light. As was the case with Coomber, Ramstad, and Sheets, San Mateo Valdehíta necessarily makes predictions or assumptions about which of the three tasks in the study involved more semantically elaborative "deeper processing," and these predictions or assumptions may not be correct. San Mateo Valdehíta's results indicated higher vocabulary learning scores for the sentence task as compared to the other two tasks, but we are left with the same issues described above regarding Coomber, Ramstad, and Sheets' study and which tasks are "deemed" to be more or less semantically elaborative.

Had one or both of these two studies included a no-sentence-writing "do your best to learn the words" condition, they may have revealed much more about the impact of sentence writing on learning novel L2 vocabulary learning in intentional contexts. San Mateo Valdehíta also interprets the 2013 findings as providing support for predictions of the involvement load hypothesis, which extends the potential problems with deeming certain tasks to be more semantically elaborative than others and including tasks for which it is difficult to determine their relative degree of semantic elaboration. From this perspective San Mateo Valdehíta's interpretation of the findings of the 2013 study as providing support for the predictions of the involvement load hypothesis is drawn into question. Other issues related to the involvement load hypothesis, such as the extent to which it is a hypothesis about effort prior to lex-IP, are discussed later in this section of the chapter.

As a final example of the importance of the exact nature of tasks, Kondo (2007) conducted a study that compared the effects of sentence writing with sentence translation (from L1 to L2) on L2 vocabulary among Japanese learners of English. The results of the study indicated lower vocabulary learning for the participants who completed the sentence-translation task. Again, this study demonstrates that sentence writing (as one variety of a semantically oriented task) is by no means the only task that can detract learners from attending to and processing new L2 words as input. There are a variety of ways in which learners can be detracted from attending to novel L2 word forms, and sentence translation is one among them, but the fact that other tasks can detract from L2 word learning more than sentence writing does not imply good evidence for the benefit of semantically oriented tasks on L2 vocabulary learning. For example, requiring learners to perform some other type of non-form-oriented tasks, including many types of visual, motor, or cognitive tasks that are not pertinent to target word learning and that detract attention from word learning may lead to lower amounts of word learning than does sentence writing, but such a comparison is one of varying degrees of increased non-form-oriented processing. For tasks of this nature, the TOPRA model predicts that the more non-form-oriented processing increases, the more form-oriented processing and its learning counterpart should decrease. A sentence-translation task such as the one examined by Kondo may not be very form-oriented at all when it comes to the target words because the learner's attention and resources are necessarily directed toward all of the other words in each to-be-translated sentence and all of the other subtasks involved in sentence translation.

What is the effect of questions about word meaning?

In another study, Barcroft (2003b) investigated the effects of asking L2 learners to address questions about word meaning while attempting to learn the words. The learners, who were English-speaking learners of L2 Spanish, were presented with 24 novel Spanish words. For 12 of the words, they were instructed to answer (in their minds) questions related to the meaning of the target words, such as *In what ways can this object be used?* For the other 12 words, they were instructed only to do their best to learn the target words in question. Among the posttest measures were immediate and delayed cued (picture-to-L2) recall. The delayed posttest was administered only 10 minutes after the first cued recall posttest, and in the interim the participants completed a distractor task. As can be seen in Figure 6.3, the results of the study indicated higher L2 vocabulary learning scores (based on picture-to-L2 cued recall scores) in the no-questions condition and, interestingly, a small increase in scores from Time 1 to Time 2, most likely due to a reminiscence effect in this particular learning context.

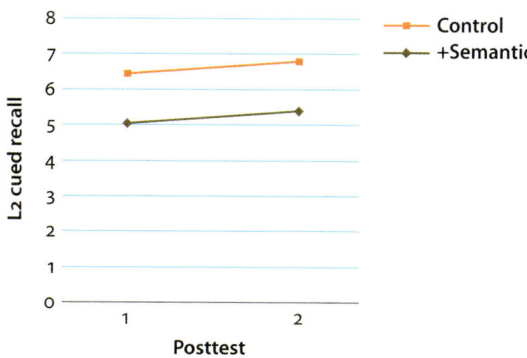

Figure 6.3 Effects of questions about word meaning on intentional L2 word learning.

The findings of the study are clearly consistent with the predictions of the TOPRA model. The condition with questions about word meaning increased semantically oriented processing to a sufficient extent so that it also necessarily reduced the amount of form- and mapping-oriented processing in which the learners could engage. The negative effects of the semantic task in this study were not as pronounced as those in the sentence-writing (versus no-sentence-writing) studies, potentially due to how sentence writing involves so many other subtasks that could detract further from processing and encoding target L2 words. The relative impact of the two different types of semantic tasks may be different, but the most important point is that the effects of both are *negative*, which stands in stark contrast to any position in favor of a direct application of LOP proposals regarding purported benefits of the "deeper processing" invoked by semantically oriented tasks in the realm of L2 vocabulary learning.

What is the effect of different types of instructions regarding focus on word meaning and word form?

Further exploring the theme that not all semantic and structurally oriented tasks are alike, Barcroft (2004c) reported two experiments on different possible methods of inviting (if not requiring) learners to engage in increased semantic and structural processing while attempting to learn a set of target L2 words. In the first experiment, the instructions in the semantic condition were: "For the next 12 words, focus as much as you can on the MEANING of each word. For example, you may focus on (a) whether or not you own this item; (b) how much it might cost to purchase the item; (c) contexts in which the item may or may not be used; (d) the last time that you used the item; and so on. Please do your best to learn these words. Good luck!" The instructions in the structural condition, on the other hand, were the following: "For the next 12 words, focus as much as you can on the FORM of each word. For example, you may focus on (a) what the word looks like; (b) how long the word is; (c) how many syllables there are in the word; (d) the first and last letter of the word; and so on. Please do your best to learn these words. Good luck!" Using these instructions, no differences were observed in L2 vocabulary scores between the two conditions, and reports regarding task performance were fairly low, with only 67.6% of the participants reporting being able to perform the semantic task and 54.4% reporting being able to perform the structural task.

In Experiment 2, the instructions for the semantic task were to consider the extent to which each target word represented an instance of the concept "economic" on one occasion and instance of the concept "recreation" on another occasion. Instructions for the structural task were to consider what each word looked like on one occasion and what each individual letter in each word looked like on another occasion. A "do your best" control group was also included in this experiment. The results of Experiment 2 indicated no significant differences between the semantic, structural, and control groups. Regarding task performance, of the

46 participants, 3 reported 0% task performance; 2 reported 1–10%; 6 reported 10–20%; 1 reported 20–30%; 5 reported 30–40%; 4 reported 40–50%; 3 reported 50–60%; 7 reported 60–70%; 8 reported 70–80%; 6 reported 80–90%; 0 reported 90–100%; and 1 gave no answer.

These two experiments demonstrate no benefit for semantic tasks over structural tasks or a no-task control, as an unqualified extension of LOP to L2 vocabulary learning would predict. What is more is that they provide a great deal of information about how difficult it is for participants to engage in externally imposed tasks when they are attempting to learn a set of target words. The reports of task performance on the part of the participants to a large extent speak for themselves, which is something that both researchers and instructors need to keep in mind when asking learners to perform different types of tasks concurrent to attempting to learn a set of target words intentionally. Even though learners may want to follow instructions for the task in question, they may find it difficult to do and inconsistent with their efforts to encode and retain the novel words in question. The lack of difference between conditions and groups in these two experiments needs to be interpreted in light of the fairly low degree of task performance reported.

What is the effect of referent token variability?

In another study, Sommers and Barcroft (2013) tested the effects of referent token variability on intentional L2 vocabulary learning. Referent token variability refers to varying the referent tokens of a given target word. If an English speaker is learning a new L2 Spanish word such as *oso* 'bear' by viewing 6 repetitions of pictures while hearing the target word each time, the same picture of a bear can be used each time (no referent token variability) or three different pictures of a bear can be used for 2 times each, totaling 6 presentations (moderate referent token variability), or six different pictures of a bear can be used once each, totaling 6 presentations (high referent token variability). This manipulation, which was carried out within-groups in the study, does not constitute a "semantic task" per se in the traditional sense, but the researchers argued that increased token variability would increase the amount of semantic processing (including visual processing to whatever degree that is appropriate) required on the part of the participants and that, according to the predictions of the TOPRA model, the increased semantic processing associated with referent token variability would decrease learners ability to process and encode the target word forms.

The results of the story bore out this prediction. L2 vocabulary scores were less accurate and slower in the high referent token variability condition than in the moderate and no variability conditions and less accurate and slower in the moderate referent token variability condition than in the no variability condition. These findings provide strong support in favor of the TOPRA model and are unique from those of other studies in that they demonstrate the graded negative effect of incremental increases in semantically oriented processing on intentional L2 vocabulary learning.

What is the effect of pleasantness ratings and letter counting on mapping?

Whereas the studies reviewed above focused on the effects of different semantic and structural tasks on intentional L2 vocabulary learning with regard to TOPRA model predictions, at least one study to date has attempted to test TOPRA predictions from a different angle by isolating the mapping component of L2 vocabulary learning and examining the effects of a semantic and structural task on that particular component. In the study in question, which was conducted by Kida and Barcroft (2014), Japanese-speaking learners of L2 English learners were presented with 24 English words whose primary meanings they already knew. The participants were instructed to attempt to map alternative (secondary) meanings (that they already knew in Japanese) onto these 24 L2 words. The words in question were homographs such as *foot* for which the participants already knew their primary meanings (足, as in "hand and foot") but had not yet learned to map secondary meanings (支払う, as in "foot the bill") onto the words in question. Given this state of affairs, the learning task at hand was mapping only (no new word forms or new word meanings were to be learned). All of the participants studied the secondary meanings in each of three conditions: (a) make pleasantness ratings about each word's meaning (semantic task); (b) count the number of letters in each English word (structural task); and (c) do your best only (no-task control). After the study phase, two free recall tests – in L1 and L2 – and two cued recall tests – L2 to L1 and L1 to L2 – were administered.

The results of the study indicated significantly higher L1 free recall for +semantic than +structural and significantly lower cued recall for +semantic and +structural when compared to the no-task control. These results provide strong evidence in support of the TOPRA model, which predicts that increases in semantic processing or structural processing (or both) can decrease processing and learning of the mapping component of novel word learning. The study also debuts a useful new methodological technique for isolating the mapping component of L2 vocabulary learning.

The Keyword Method, mnemonics, and the TOPRA model

Whereas the combined findings of the studies above provide convincing support for the TOPRA model, it is worth clarifying how semantic tasks and increased semantic processing in the context of those studies differs from increased semantic processing in mnemonic techniques designed to help learners recode novel forms into known forms and connect them through visualization and other methods of improving memory retention. The most well-known of such mnemonic techniques for L2 vocabulary is the Keyword Method (Atkinson & Raugh, 1975), which involves two stages. First, a learner recodes an L2 word into some familiar code based on L1 orthographic or acoustic properties in the word. Second, the learner produces a compound image which connects the recently created familiar code and the object being learned. Below are three examples taken from a study by Barcroft, Sommers, and Sunderman (2011) for English speakers learning L2 Spanish:

1. *Chiste* (joke) – Imagine a piece of swiss *cheese* telling a joke.
2. *Cabra* (goat) – Imagine a goat taking a ride in a taxi *cab*.
3. *Sapo* (toad) – Imagine a poisonous toad on a leaf covered in *sap*.

In each case, the learner creates a mental image that connects an L1 word (which could also be a group of words) with the referents of the L2 words being learned. To provide an example with another L2, in a study by Ellis and Beaton (1995, Table 1 on p. 124), to remember the German word Ecke 'corner,' participants were instructed to "imagine an echo in a corner."

Studies on the Keyword Method have demonstrated that groups learning with Keyword often obtain higher vocabulary learning scores as compared to alternative unconstrained or self-selected strategy groups (e.g., Atkinson & Raugh, 1975; Ellis & Beaton, 1993; Sagarra & Alba, 2006). Brown and Perry (1991) also concluded that learners using Keyword who also were presented with definitions and examples of words in sentences (Keyword-Semantic) learned significantly more vocabulary than learners using Keyword alone. Other research has demonstrated, however, that L2 words learned via Keyword can be more prone to long-term forgetting as compared to a nonmnemonic technique such as rote rehearsal (Wang & Thomas, 1995) or result in worse performance than rote rehearsal in some contexts (e.g., Van Hell & Mahn, 1997). In addition, from the perspective of the quality of the semantic representation of each developing L2 word, it turns out that the Keyword Method can be problematic. Barcroft, Sommers, and Sunderman (2011) found that the introduction of Keyword primes during a translation task, which were similar in form to the target L2 words, *speeded* recall for a group who had studied vocabulary via rote rehearsal but *slowed* recall for a group who had studied the same vocabulary using the Keyword Method (see also Kole, 2007; van Hell & Mahn, 1997).

Regardless of the relative utility and consequences of using the Keyword Method, what needs to be clarified is that a study on the relative effectiveness of the Keyword Method is not the same as a study on the effects of generalized increases in semantic or structurally oriented processing. The Keyword Method is a mnemonic device for which the act of recoding novel (L2 or in some cases L1) word forms into more familiar (L1) word forms, not a method that involves increasing semantic processing as related to the meaning of the target words in question. Therefore, studies that test the relative effectiveness of the Keyword Method are not tests of the predictions of the TOPRA model.

Studies on incidental vocabulary learning

We now move on to consider studies that have assessed the extent to which predictions of the TOPRA model may be applicable in contexts of incidental L2 vocabulary learning, potentially adding to other findings about L2 vocabulary learning in this context, such as the role of inferencing strategies (Paribakht & Wesche, 1999) and the positive effects of variables such as topic familiarity and L2 reading proficiency (Pulido, 2003). Clearly, the issues that come into play in incidental learning differ substantially from those in intentional learning contexts, such as the extent to which the TOPRA model's predictions about the dissociability of the form, meaning, and mapping components of vocabulary and the interplay among these three components. A key issue here is whether these different components, the processing for which is proposed to be dissociable, can be isolated and measured to a sufficient degree in order to test TOPRA predictions in a fair and useful manner. Despite such challenges, some studies (e.g., Barcroft, 2009; Burfoot, 2010; Barcroft, 2005; Kida, 2010a, 2010b) have attempted to test the viability of the TOPRA model in incidental contexts of L2 vocabulary learning during reading. These studies have addressed the following questions:

1. What is the effect of synonym generation?
2. What is the effect of pleasantness ratings and letter counting?
3. What is the effect of type (semantic, structural) and amount of processing?

The rest of this section reviews this research and analyzes the extent to which the predictions of the TOPRA model may be useful in incidental vocabulary learning contexts.

What is the effect of synonym generation?

Barcroft (2009) examined the effects of synonym generation on L2 vocabulary learning during reading in both incidental and intentional vocabulary learning contexts. Participants in the study were Spanish-speaking adult learners of L2 English. They read an English passage that contained 10 target words that were translated in the text. Each participant was randomly assigned to one of four groups: (1) "Read for meaning only" (incidental). (2) "Read for meaning and try to learn the translated words" (intentional). (3) "Read for meaning and generate Spanish synonyms for the translated words" (incidental + semantic). (4) "Read for meaning, try to learn the 10 translated words, and generate Spanish synonyms for the translated words" (intentional + semantic). After the reading session, the participants were asked to complete tests of English-to-Spanish and Spanish-to-English recall of ten target words.

This experimental design was used to assess two competing hypothesis about the potential effects of synonym generation (a semantic task): (1) the *attention-drawing hypothesis*, which predicted null or positive effects for the semantic task because it would draw learners' attention to the novel words, which otherwise they may simply overlook or to which they might not pay sufficient attention; and (2) the *resource-depletion hypothesis*, which predicted negative effects for the semantic task because the learners may focus specifically on the meaning of the target words primarily, which could exhaust processing resources that might have been used to encode the novel form and form-meaning mapping component of the target words.

As can be seen in Figure 6.4, vocabulary learning was greater when explicit instructions to learn new words were provided and greater when synonym generation was not required. In other words, the synonym-generation tasks produced negative effects on L2 vocabulary learning in both the incidental and intentional learning conditions, providing support for the resource-depletion hypothesis and in favor of the potential applicability of TOPRA to incidental contexts of L2 vocabulary. What the findings suggest, importantly, is that regardless of whether a learner is engaged in intentional or more incidentally oriented learning, specificity in *type* of processing and what to expect in terms of learning outcomes remains an important issue. If a learner is to learn more novel L2 word forms, increased semantic processing toward the meanings of the target word should not be expected, in and of itself, to produce better word form learning. In fact, it may exhaust processing resources in the wrong direction away from processing and encoding the novel word forms in question, as the negative effects observed in this study clearly suggest.

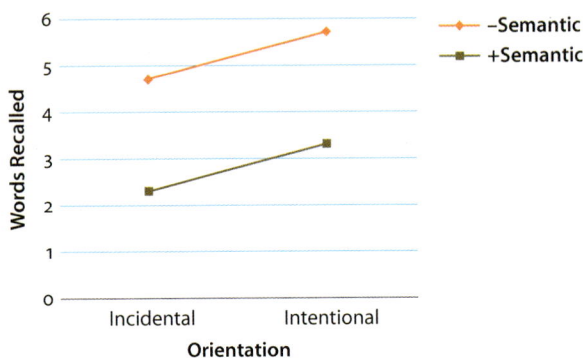

Figure 6.4 Effects of L1 synonym generation on intentional and incidental L2 word learning during reading.

Burfoot (2010) reported a partial replication of Barcroft's (2009) study in which Chinese learners of L2 English read the same reading passage as that of Barcroft (2009) and in which the other materials were the largely the same (except with regard to providing instructions in Spanish and so forth) as those used by Barcroft (2009). The procedures for data collection were also the same, except that in Burfoot's study separate sheets of paper instead of overall packets were used (in neither study were participants allowed to return to previous pages they had completed, including when using packets in the earlier study). The times allowed, the test battery, and scoring also paralleled those of the earlier study, but the two different levels of proficiency were not examined in the study by Burfoot. The results of Burfoot's study, although pointing in the same direction as the earlier study with regard to the overall pattern of which means were higher than other means, indicated (a) little difference and no significant difference between scores in the incidental condition between −semantic (5.92) and +semantic (5.8) conditions and (b) only slightly higher scores in the intentional condition between scores in the −semantic (7.2) condition than in the +semantic condition, a difference that was not indicated to be significant. It is also important to note that even though overall scores for intentional orientation (6.91) were significantly higher than those for incidental orientation (5.86), the numerical difference between the two means is quite small (only slightly over 1 point), which is notably different from the results of Barcroft (2009) and other previous studies that compare incidental versus incidental orientations during reading (see, e.g., Hulstijn, 1992).

What might account for the difference in results between these two studies? In addition to the importance of accounting for why incidental and intentional orientations resulted in such numerically close overall means in the Burfoot's study, which clearly has an impact on the −semantic/+semantic variable as well, one may also consider the nature of how target L2 English words were provided in the text. Whereas in the earlier study the translations were in Spanish, using the same Roman script, in Burfoot's study, the translations were written in *hanzi*, simplified Chinese characters. Even though necessary and appropriate for the participants in the later study, the distinction between the two writing scripts may have drawn attention to target words to a greater degree than when the same script was used in the earlier study, in this way increasing the attention-drawing potential of the +semantic task and working toward cancelling out any potentially visible negative effect of the +semantic task. This possibility is just one of or among many (others potentially being tied to the lack of strong difference between intentional and incidental orientations in the study), but it is certainly worth noting. Furthermore, it is important to note the +semantic task in Burfoot's study in no way facilitated learning the target words in the study as the actual means for the +semantic condition always remained lower (although not largely or significantly so) when compared to the -semantic condition.

What is the effect of pleasantness ratings and letter counting?

Barcroft (2005) also tested the predictions of TOPRA in contexts of both incidental and intentional L2 vocabulary during reading while using pleasantness ratings and letter counting as tasks. Spanish-speaking learners of English read the same passage with the same translated target words. Participants were assigned to one of six conditions: (1) Incidental = "Read for meaning." (2) Incidental + Semantic = "Read for meaning and make pleasantness ratings about the meaning of each translated word." (3) Incidental + Structural = "Read for meaning and count the letters in each translated word." (4) Intentional = "Read for meaning and try to learn the translated words." (5) Incidental + Semantic = "Read for meaning, try to learn the translated words, and make pleasantness ratings about the meaning of each translated word." (6) Incidental + Structural = "Read for meaning, try to learn the translated words, and count the letters in each translated word." After reading, the participants completed two free recalls (English, Spanish) and two vocabulary posttests (Spanish-to-English, English-to-Spanish). Passage comprehension also was assessed. Orientation (incidental, intentional), task (+semantic, +structural, read-only), proficiency level (low-intermediate, high-intermediate), and recall type (Spanish-to-English, English-to-Spanish) were independent variables. Free recall and vocabulary scores were higher in the intentional condition. No significant differences emerged based on task.

These findings, in combination with those of Barcroft (2009), provide support for TOPRA within contexts of both intentional and incidental vocabulary learning during reading and demonstrate the critical role of task type when predicting learning outcomes related to vocabulary during reading. Not all semantically oriented tasks yield negative effects, but clearly the findings do not support the idea that semantic elaboration will improve new word form learning, as would be the prediction of an alternative view, one that maintains that semantically oriented "deeper processing" should result in improved word form learning.

What are the effects of type (semantic, structural) and amount of processing?

In another study on incidental vocabulary learning only alone (without intentional orientation in the study), Kida (2010b) asked one group of Japanese speakers learning L2 English to complete a semantically oriented condition pleasantness ratings task. This task resulted in significantly lower vocabulary learning scores, using both stringent and lenient types of scoring, when compared to scores of participants who performed a structurally oriented (phonological) task involving writing the pronunciation of the English words of interest in the text in Japanese script. Furthermore, performance was not statistically different for the group that performed the semantically oriented task as compared to the performance of a no-task control group. The actual means were lower for the semantically oriented task as compared to the no-task control, but the difference did not reach statistical significance. The semantically oriented pleasantness-ratings task was clearly not effective at promoting learning of the novel word forms, but the form-oriented structural task was more effective at doing so. Based on the more lenient scoring protocol, the phonologically oriented task resulted in significantly higher means than was the case for the no-task control group. Finally, the study in question also assessed the effects of quantity of processing and potential interaction between quality and quantity of processing by including conditions of both one versus three exposures to the target words in question (the text was modified in order to achieve these two different amounts of processing. With regard to this manipulation, the results of the study indicated no interaction between quality and quantity of processing, which Kida interpreted as being consistent with multiple-trace theory (e.g., Hintzman & Block, 1971), and the study confirmed that increasing the number of presentations of each target word from 1 to 3 appearances produced a significant positive effect on incidental vocabulary learning of this nature.

This study provides at least partial support for the TOPRA model in that the semantic task examined resulted in lower actual means than the no-task control even though the difference did not reach a level of statistical significance. Moreover, the benefits of the structural task examined is wholly consistent with TOPRA predictions regarding the potential positive effects of increased structural processing on learning form-oriented items, in this case, the novel L2 word forms.

From both a theoretical and pedagogical, the success of the structurally oriented "change-script" task with regard to incidental L2 vocabulary learning in this study should pique interest as it is rare to find a demonstration of a form-oriented task producing significant benefits of this nature in an otherwise incidental context of L2 vocabulary learning.

In another study, Kida (2010a) compared incidental L2 vocabulary learning among three different groups, one of which performed the semantic task of pleasantness ratings, one of which performed the structural task of writing down the pronunciation of the target L2 English words in Japanese Katakana, and one of which did not perform any additional task during reading. The findings of this study provided additional support for the viability of the TOPRA model within incidental contexts by demonstrating, when using a stringent scoring protocol, positive effects of the structural task whereas the effects for the semantic task approached being significantly lower than those in the no-task control group. Again, the findings of this study suggest that at least some types of structural tasks can facilitate incidental L2 word learning during reading. Writing out target words in Kanakana appears to be a particularly strong type of structural task in this regard, perhaps because of the involvement of L1, as in the case of the Keyword Method. The Kanakana strings written by the participants in the structural group may not have been "as familiar" as L1 words used to recode L2 words via the Keyword Method, but the strings somehow seem to be quite useful for remembering the novel L2 word forms in question.

The involvement load hypothesis, the TOPRA model, and lex-IP

Whereas most of the studies reviewed above focused specifically on testing predictions of the TOPRA model, a number of studies have assessed the effects of different semantically oriented tasks in other research domains, as illustrated, for example, by the study by Coomber, Ramstad, and Sheets (1986) reviewed above. Since the introduction of Laufer and Hulstijn's (2001) *involvement load hypothesis*, other studies have investigated the impact of semantically oriented tasks within that particular research domain. According to the involvement load hypothesis, word retention in incidental L2 vocabulary learning is positively affected by three factors: need, search, and evaluation. *Evaluation*, for example, includes semantic evaluation and concerns "a comparison of a given word with its other meanings, or combining the word with other words in order to assess whether a word (i.e. a form-meaning pair) does or does not fit its context" (p. 14). According to Laufer and Hulstijn, tasks that involve semantic evaluation of this nature should result in better word retention during incidental vocabulary learning. If this is the case, then the negative effects of semantically oriented tasks discussed in the previous section may be limited to the realm of intentional L2 vocabulary learning only and do not extend to the realm of incidental L2 vocabulary learning.

Hulstijn and Laufer (2001) tested the predictions of the involvement load hypothesis by assessing how three learning tasks affected retention of the meaning of 10 English words among L2 English learners in Israel and the Netherlands. An involvement index was used to classify the three tasks with regard to the factors need, search, and evaluation. (1) Reading comprehension with marginal glosses was assigned an involvement index of 1 because it was deemed to induce moderate need but no search or evaluation. (2) Reading comprehension plus a fill-in-the-gap task was assigned an involvement index of 2 because it was deemed to induce moderate need, no search, and moderate evaluation. (3) Writing a composition and incorporating target words was assigned an involvement index of 3 because it was deemed to induce moderate need, no search, and strong evaluation. Immediate and delayed retention posttests on word meaning were administered. Results of the study indicated higher retention for the composition task than for the other two tasks, and Israeli students (but not Dutch students) demonstrated higher retention scores for the fill-in-the gap task than for reading with marginal glosses, but time on task was not held constant for each of the three conditions: 40–45 minutes was allowed for reading-with-glosses (the task associated with the lowest retention); 50–55 minutes was allowed for fill-in-the-gap (the task associated with the second highest retention); and 70–80 minutes was allowed for composition (the task associated with the highest retention).

Regardless of methodological issues such as time on task with this and subsequent studies on the involvement load hypothesis, for present purposes what is important to note is that the involvement load hypothesis, in contrast to the TOPRA model, makes claims about what may lead to more successful incidental vocabulary learning and not about specific aspects of words are processed in either intentional or incidental contexts of vocabulary learning. The notion of "search," for example, is typically not applicable in the context of intentional vocabulary learning when one is already focusing on a specific set of target vocabulary. In fact, the involvement load hypothesis may be viewed as largely a theory of the relationship between the overall effort that a learner allots and amount of incidental vocabulary learning, as would be consistent with Laufer and Hulstijn's (2001) substantial consideration of previous research on motivation when discussing and putting forth the hypothesis. If a learner needs and searches for given words to a greater degree, it is likely that the learner increases overall effort with regard to the words in question. Furthermore, even in the areas where the hypothesis goes beyond issues of overall effort – as may be the case with the "evaluation," for example – it does not focus on specifying (and dissociating) different types of processing for different components of vocabulary learning (in particular, the form, meaning, and mapping) in either intentional or incidental learning contexts. In contrast, the TOPRA model is designed to make predictions of this nature and at this level of lex-IP. It focuses on processing resource allocation among different types of processing that are dissociable or at least largely dissociable, such as semantic processing and processing directed toward encoding novel word form, and the consequences of this type of allocation when it comes to learning.

Summary and analysis

The combined findings of the studies reviewed in this chapter provide strong support for the predictions of the TOPRA model. These studies demonstrate that, during lex-IP, increases in semantically oriented processing can decrease available resources for structurally oriented processing, mapping-oriented processing, or both. Some of the studies also demonstrate that increases in structurally oriented processing can decrease available processing resources for semantically oriented processing, mapping-oriented processing, or both. The ability to dissociate these three different types of processing and to observe the interplay between them with regard to allocation of processing resources and resultant learning outcomes has been, at least to date, more pronounced in research on intentional L2 vocabulary learning. Kida and Barcroft's (2014) study on the effects of structural and semantic tasks on the mapping component of intentional vocabulary learning is a telling most recent example of this ability. Using learning of secondary meaning of homographs as a means of isolating the mapping component of L2 vocabulary learning, the findings of their study exhibited the significant negative effects of increasing semantic processing (by means of pleasantness-ratings task) and increasing structural processing (by means of letter-counting task) on the mapping component of intentional L2 vocabulary learning.

Studies on the potential viability of TOPRA in incidental contexts of L2 vocabulary also suggest that the model can be useful in making predictions related to different processing types and expected learning outcomes. Barcroft's (2009) study provides particularly strong evidence on this front, demonstrating the resource-depleting potential of a semantic task (based on lower vocabulary learning scores) in conditions of both intentional and incidental orientation during reading. The fact that these findings were not obtained in a partial replication study by Burfoot (2010) may speak at least some extent to the attention-drawing potential of a semantic task, in this case possibly in combination with the attention-drawing potential of the point at which two different writing scripts come into contact in order to translate a target word. In fact, given the range of different possible types of semantic tasks that can be included during incidental contexts of L2 vocabulary, it makes sense to consider both the *resource-depleting* and *attention-drawing* potential of semantic tasks when considering the potential effects of these tasks on vocabulary learning within this context. In addition, Kida's demonstration of improved incidental L2 vocabulary learning scores for requiring learners to rewrite words in a different script speaks to the potential of at least some types of structurally oriented tasks to focus processing on and increase learning of L2 vocabulary learning contexts.

From a theoretical perspective, research findings in this area suggest three key assertions that can be made with regard to lex-IP:

1. Semantic and structural processing are (at least largely) dissociable.
2. Semantic and mapping-oriented processing are (at least largely) dissociable.
3. Structural and mapping-oriented processing are (at least largely) dissociable.
4. Increases in one of these three types of processing (semantic, structural, mapping-oriented) increases processing and learning for the type of processing in question, which is reflected in increased learning for the component of vocabulary learning in question.
   On the other hand ...
5. Increases in one of these three types of processing (semantic, structural, mapping-oriented) can decrease available processing resources for the other types of processing, which is reflected in the relative amount of learning associated with the different types of processing and learning counterparts in question.

From a larger perspective, these five assertions speak to the importance of specificity in type of processing when making predictions about the potential effects of different types of tasks and the types of processing that they invoke on L2 vocabulary learning and, for that matter, on any to-be-remembered item when it comes to human memory. All five assertions are inherent in the basic structure of the TOPRA model (lines separating different types of processing indicating how these types of processing are dissociable) and in the predictions that the TOPRA model makes, such as with regard to the potential of increases in semantic processing decreasing available processing resources for structural and mapping-oriented processing and their learning counterparts.

Instructional implications

From a pedagogical standpoint, the theoretical precepts of lex-IP outlined above, and the growing body of research supporting them, have called for and continue to call for radical changes when it comes to L2 vocabulary instruction. Traditional notions about supposed positive effects of semantically oriented tasks being effective during the early stages of L2 vocabulary learning need to be reassessed and, to a large extent, discarded. They simply do not match up to what research findings on the TOPRA model and lex-IP continue to indicate. The idea that tasks such as writing target words in sentences or addressing questions about the meaning of the words should be effective means of facilitating the acquisition of a recently introduced set of target words run directly in the opposite direction of what the data suggest. Furthermore, the potential negative effects of imposing a particular semantic task during the initial stages of L2 word learning can be quite large. Barcroft's (2006) findings, for example, indicated approximately *half* as much vocabulary learning scores when participants were required to write target words in sentences as when they were not required to do so. Wong and Pyun (2012) demonstrated how the negative effects of sentence writing can be even more pronounced when one is attempting to learn word forms that are more novel when compared to what one is familiar with based on their previous experience in L1, such as when the L2 in question has a novel script as compared to the L1.

The *input-based incremental (IBI)* approach to L2 vocabulary instruction (Barcroft, 2012) includes a principle (Principle 7) incorporated specifically to address issues related to the predictions of the TOPRA model as they relate to semantically elaborative tasks, the increased semantic processing that they invoke, and the potential negative impact of both on processing for and learning novel word forms: *Limit forced semantic elaboration during the initial stages* (all ten of the IBI principles appear in Appendix A). This principle in no way implies that vocabulary-focused lessons should not focus on meaning or should not be task-oriented, content-oriented, or both. It simply means that learners should be allowed to attend to and process the formal component of novel words without being forced to *elaborate* extensively on the meaning of those words, particularly when the aspects of meaning are redundant with what learners already know based on their experience with word meanings in L1. When learning L2-specific meanings of a word that do not exist in the L1 in question (and refining knowledge of the L2-specific semantic space for the word), semantically elaborative tasks may be a better use of time, however. The issue is more one of specificity in terms of what to expect from different types of tasks – semantic, structural, mapping-oriented, or otherwise – in terms of learning outcomes. As is consistent with the TOPRA model, semantic tasks should be expected to increase semantic processing and semantically oriented learning but should not be expected to increase structural and mapping-oriented processing and learning, at least to a large extent. Similarly, structural tasks should be expected to increase structurally oriented processing and learning but semantic and mapping-oriented processing and learning. The key issue here is specificity in the processing type invoked by different tasks and specific learning outcomes that should be expected with regard to different components of vocabulary learning.

CHAPTER 7

Effects of output with and without access to meaning

In addition to the misconception that elaborating on word meaning (increased semantic processing) should be an effective means of learning new L2 words, which the research reviewed in Chapter 6 should dispel, another widely held belief related to L2 vocabulary learning and instruction is that copying target words or repeating them while trying to learn them should always be an effective approach. The research reported in this chapter should help to draw this belief into question and, at least to some degree, dispel it. We will review a series of experiments on the effects of copying target words (Barcroft, 2006) and a study on copying both target words and word segments (Barcroft, 2007b) as well as a study on the effects of choral repetition (Wong & Barcroft, 2012). The combined findings of these studies are inconsistent with the idea that written or spoken repetition of target words is an effective means of teaching and learning vocabulary. In fact, many of the research findings in this area point to the potential detrimental effects of these types of output-oriented activities when it comes to L2 word learning.

A larger goal of the chapter, however, is to distinguish between two distinct types of output as they relate to vocabulary learning and to demonstrate each of these two types of output produces a distinct pattern of effects on L2 vocabulary. One of the pattern of effects is largely not favorable; the other is quite favorable. The two types of output in question are output *without* access to meaning and output *with* access to meaning. *Output with access to meaning* refers to output that involves "activating the lexical items and grammatical forms necessary to express particular meanings" (VanPatten, 2003) whereas *output without access to meaning* refers to output more of a repeat-after-me parroting nature, which does not require the same type of activation and use of mental networks involved in expressing meaning as output with access to meaning does (see Lee & VanPatten, 2003 and VanPatten, 2003 for more on this distinction). As should become clear from the research reviewed in this chapter and the next, the distinction is critical when predicting and understanding the effects of different types of output on lexIP and L2 vocabulary learning.

The rest of the chapter is divided into three main parts. The first focuses on research on different types of output without access to meaning and their effects on intentional L2 vocabulary learning. These include copying target words, copying target words and word segments, and choral repetition of target words. The second part of the chapter presents a representative study on the effects of output *with* access to meaning on intentional L2 vocabulary learning. Only one study on output of this nature is presented in this chapter because the next chapter is devoted entirely to the beneficial effects of output *with* access to meaning and opportunities for target word retrieval on vocabulary learning. Finally, the third part of the chapter analyzes what the combined findings of research on output both with and without access to meaning suggest when it comes to general principles of lex-IP.

Research on output *without* access to meaning and L2 vocabulary learning

We begin by focusing on research on the effects of different types of output *without* access to meaning on intentional L2 vocabulary learning. Studies in this area suggest that several types of output without access to meaning, such as copying target words (Barcroft, 2006), copying target words and word segments (Barcroft, 2007b), and choral repetition of target words (Barcroft, 1998a; Wong & Barcroft, 2012), do not, on the whole, positively affect intentional L2 vocabulary learning and in many cases produce negative effects when compared to no-output conditions of "do your best to learn the words" only.

What are the effects of copying target words?

Barcroft (2006) conducted two experiments that addressed the "Can writing a new word detract from learning it?" In both experiments, English speakers attempted to learn 24 novel L2 Spanish words. While doing so, they copied 12 of the target words and wrote nothing for the other 12 target words. Word groups and presentation orders were counterbalanced across an equal number of participants. Results of both experiments indicated that productive vocabulary learning (picture-to-L2 recall) on immediate and delayed (2 days later) measures was higher in word-copying condition than in the no-task control condition. These findings suggest that this type of forced output *without* access to meaning can detract from early word learning. From a theoretical perspective, Barcroft argued that it does so by exhausting processing resources that otherwise could have been utilized to process and encode novel lexical forms. In other words, this type of output (without access to meaning) is not as effective as allowing learners to attend to target words as input at the most initial stages of L2 vocabulary learning. As such, the findings of both experiments are consistent with the resource depletion for output (RDO) hypothesis (Barcroft, 2006, p. 488), which posits that output without access to meaning "may decrease new word learning by exhausting cognitive processing resources that could be used to encode new word forms and establish new form-meaning mappings."

An earlier study by Thomas and Dieter (1987), on the other hand, had indicated that word writing positively affected word learning performance among L2 learners of French when the scoring in question was based on complete words produced and completed words produced in addition to words produced with one letter wrong but not when scoring included word fragments. The researchers interpreted these findings as evidence for the potential of word writing to facilitate learning of the complete orthographic representations of the target words in question. Barcroft (2006, p. 495) offered the following differences related to task difficulty, presentation format, and scoring as a possible explanation of the combined results of the two studies:

> First, more target words were used in Thomas and Dieter's study, but the inclusion of an additional repetition for each word and an additional 4 seconds for every repetition may have resulted in a less demanding vocabulary task than that of the [2006] study. If so, the negative effect of word writing via resource depletion may have been less detectable. Second, Thomas and Dieter presented target words both visually and orally. As such, word writing may have enabled participants to attend to sound-to-spelling correspondences in a manner that was more beneficial to encoding the new forms. Third, Thomas and Dieter's scoring method most sensitive to partial word form knowledge (most inclusion of partial word fragments) did not yield positive effects. In the [2006] study, negative effects were obtained using LPSP-written scoring, which is very sensitive to partial word knowledge. Therefore, the potentially negative effects of word writing may be more detectable with measures that are more sensitive to partial word form knowledge.

This explanation, which focuses largely on the extent to which posttest measures are or are not a precise reflection of the formal component of L2 vocabulary learning, also begs future research that may help to continue to reconcile the at least apparent differences in the pattern of results of these two studies.

What are the effects of copying target words and word fragments?

In another study, Barcroft (2007b) partially replicated and expanded upon the 2006 study on word writing in order to assess (a) whether negative effects of word copying would emerge using both productive and receptively oriented measures of vocabulary learning and (b) whether word fragment writing, writing only specific fragments of each target word, would affect L2 vocabulary learning similarly or differently when compared to word writing. Fragment writing was a task for which participants wrote a selected underlined syllable in each target word. It was noted: "[b]ecause writing a single syllable of a word involves less writing than writing the entire word, one might argue that the fragment-writing condition in this study could reduce, at least ostensibly, the cognitive load of the task (as compared to word writing). Alternatively, one might argue that identifying and isolating a syllable within a word could increase cognitive demands due to various subtasks involved in fragment writing, such as noting where the fragment in the word is underlined with regard to other letters in the word and ensuring that one writes only the underlined letters within each word" (p. 716).

The results of the study indicated that vocabulary learning scores for the no-writing condition were significantly higher than in both the word-writing and fragment-writing conditions. In addition, scores in the fragment-writing condition were even lower than those in the word writing condition, which is consistent with the proposition of increased resource depletion for fragment writing in light of the all of the different subtasks involved in fragment writing. These findings were interpreted as additional support for the RDO hypothesis, rounding out a total of three demonstrations of negative effects of word writing (copying) and an additional demonstration of the negative effects of fragment writing. Given that both of these tasks are instances of output without access to meaning, they speak strongly against any potential value of output without access to meaning when it comes to novel L2 word learning.

What are the effects of choral repetition?

To date, only a limited number of studies (Barcroft, 1998a; Seibert, 1927; Wong & Barcroft, 2012) have assessed the effects of choral repetition on L2 word learning, which is surprising given the extent to which this technique tends to be used in L2 classrooms when presenting a set of new L2 words. There is also research on whether or not overt repetition is necessary for L1 vocabulary learning, and that it indicates that overt repetition is not necessary (e.g., Abbs, Gupta & Khetarpal, 2008). Existing research on choral repetition and intentional L2 vocabulary learning indicates that choral repetition is not beneficial to L2 word learning (Wong & Barcroft, 2012; compare also, however, with Seibert, 1927, who, after comparing self-study conditions of "learning silently," "learning aloud," and "aloud, with an "immediate written recall," reported modest gains over the silent condition) and borders on suggesting that, at least in certain circumstances, that choral repetition may be detrimental (Barcroft, 1998a).

In a pilot study on the potential effects of choral repetition on L2 vocabulary learning, Barcroft (1998a) examined the effects on having English-speaking learners of L2 Spanish repeat target words out loud in a classroom setting on the acquisition of a set of target Spanish words. For half of the words, participants repeated target words out loud after hearing the words produced for them, and for the other half of the words, they studied the target words only (in both cases, as the words appeared on a screen at the front of the class). Immediate and delayed posttests were administered. Actual means were higher in the condition of no choral repetition, but no significant differences were observed except for the difference on one delayed posttest, in which case means for no choral repetition were significantly higher than for choral repetition.

In a more recent study, Wong and Barcroft (2012) assessed the effects of different types of choral repetition on the initial stages of L2 vocabulary learning among English-speaking learners of L2 French. Two experiments were conducted. Experiment 1 compared the effects of choral repetition versus no choral repetition without presenting the target words as spoken input in the no-choral repetition condition. Experiment 2 compared the effects of choral repetition versus no choral repetition with target words in the no-choral repetition condition being spoken out loud. The results of Experiment 1 revealed no significant differences in scores for choral repetition as compared to no choral repetition. The results of Experiment 2 also revealed no significant differences between choral repetition versus no choral repetition. The researchers concluded that potentially negative effects of choral repetition (in consideration of the pilot study by Barcroft, 1998a, which had no spoken input in the condition of no choral repetition) may be offset when modality-appropriate input (spoken input in this case) is provided.

What are the effects of spoken output on learning novel L2 phonemic contrasts?

Interestingly, some more recent research also has revealed what might be considered counter-intuitive findings regarding the effects of production on learning L2 phonemic contrasts. In one study, Baese-Berk and Samuel (in press) were motivated by a previous finding by Leach and Samuel (2007) demonstrating negative effects of producing target words on "perceptual recalibration" (learning to adjust to idiosyncratic variability in the speech signal, such as what is tied to variants of a word forms produced by different talkers) of those words among English speakers learning nonwords whose forms corresponded with what could possibly be English word forms. Baese-Berk and Samuel (in press) expanded upon this finding at the lexical level in an L1-approximated context (which in itself is also consistent with the idea that choral repetition may not benefit and might detract from novel L2 word form learning as well) by conducting three experiments in which participants were trained on a L2 phonemic distinction that did not exist in their L1. The L2 phonemic distinction in question exists in Basque but not in Spanish, and the training was at the level of syllables, not in the context of lexical learning.

In Experiment 1 of Baese-Berk and Samuel's study, Spanish-speaking participants with minimal experience in Basque were trained on the Basque phonemic distinction with Perception Only training or a Perception + Production training. In both training regimens the participants made perceptual judgements related to the stimuli, but with Perception + Production training they also repeated the final token in each set. The results indicated that the participants' development of perceptual discrimination for the contrast in question was negatively affected if they produced tokens during training. Experiment 2 included participants with some prior exposure to Basque to see if some initial familiarity with the Basque distinction might have an impact. The results of Experiment 2 provided some evidence that previous experience with an L2 (in this case Basque) may reduce the negative (disruptive) effect of production on perceptual discrimination for an L2 phonemic contrast. Finally, Experiment 3 compared the effects of producing target versus other items during training and provided evidence that producing target items themselves can disrupt the development of L2 phonemic distinctions to a greater degree than producing other items does. These findings provide evidence at the phonemic level of how choral repetition during lexical learning in a classroom context may not benefit and might inhibit word form learning, although clearly much more research is needed in this area, including research that systematically investigates the effects of different types of spoken output on different aspects of word learning in a laboratory setting.

Research on output *with* access to meaning and L2 vocabulary learning

The combined findings of research on output without access to meaning in both the written and spoken mode speak strongly against any potential beneficial effect of this type of input. The findings to date are much more convincing with regard to the spoken mode than with regard to the written mode, but no evidence of any clear benefit of either written- or spoken-mode output without access to meaning (with regard to L2 vocabulary learning) has been produced to date, at least to our knowledge. In contrast to the lack of any demonstration of benefits in this area, research on producing target words in cases of output *with* access to meaning has yielded a very different pattern of effects. When it comes to L2 vocabulary, output with access to meaning refers to attempts to retrieve (and possibly produce) target words after the target words have been processed, at least to some degree, as input. Attempting to retrieve target words in this manner has yielded a very different pattern of *positive* effects, as exemplified the 1973 seminal study by Royer presented in the rest of this chapter and all of the additional convincing evidence presented in the next chapter on the positive effects of providing learners with opportunities for target word retrieval, a form of output with access to meaning at perhaps the most basic level.

Output with access to meaning and L2 vocabulary: A study by Royer (1973)

Expanding on previous work of memory researchers such as Izawa in the 1960s, Royer (1973) opted to assess the effects of providing learners with opportunities to retrieve words during the study of L1-L2 translated word pairs. The pairs consisted of Turkish-English vocabulary, such as the pairs *Ridvan-Satisfaction*, *Komsu-Neighbor*, and *Cenk-War*. Vocabulary learning performance was examined for three groups. The first group (T) utilized a self-test that provided retrieval opportunities for the participants. Participants in this group "were given a deck of 3-in. X 5-in. index cards with the Turkish word and its English equivalent typed on one side of the card and the Turkish word alone typed on the other side. On the initial trial Ss were instructed to study the words from the Turkish-English side of the card. On subsequent trials Ss [subjects] were instructed to use the Turkish word alone side of the card and only to turn the card over when they were not certain of the English equivalent. After each run through the deck of cards Ss were presented with a new randomized deck for the study of the next trial" (p. 196). The second group (S) attempted to learn the same pairs but under a condition that made it difficult to use the self-test procedure. The third group (SM) also studied the same words but simply studied the words until they felt they had mastered them. Participants in all groups continued to study the pairs until they felt that they had mastered them. After the study phase, all participants were tested by having them attempt to produce each English word when presented with the Turkish translation of the English word in question.

The results of the study indicated means of 19.3 for Group T, 16.9 for Group S, and 17.95 for Group SM. Given that there were ceiling effects in the study, Royer conducted a nonparametric statistical analysis, which indicated significantly higher scores in Group T when compared to scores in Group S (but not when compared to SM). Royer interpreted these results as "rather strong support for the notion that S's self-testing leads to more efficient acquisition of a foreign language vocabulary list" (p. 197). In spite of a series of key methodological drawbacks related to Royer's study, such as allowing learners to train to a level at which scores were likely to be at ceiling, the results of the study are a critical first demonstration of the positive effects of providing learners with opportunities for retrieval during L2 vocabulary learning when compared to at least one other type of studying.

In the case of Royer's study, retrieval meant attempting to retrieve L1 translations of target L2 words, which is quite different than providing learners with opportunities to retrieve target L2 words on their own (after having processed them to at least some extent beforehand in the input). The former (Royer's) type of retrieval focuses more on the mapping component of L2 learning whereas the latter (retrieval of target L2 word forms) focuses more on the formal component. In this sense, Royer's study may not be an example of output with access to meaning per se because target (L2) words were not being retrieved (they were used instead as cues), but the study is a first example of the value of retrieval in enhancing memory in the realm of L2 vocabulary learning. In this case, the focus of memory concerned the mapping component of L2 vocabulary learning.

The present purpose for reviewing Royer's (1973) study is to provide an initial demonstration of how providing learners opportunities for retrieval while studying L2 vocabulary can produce very different patterns of effects than different types of output without access to meaning, such as copying target words, copying word fragments, and engaging in choral repetition of target words while attempting to learn them. Whether the task used in Royer's Group T can truly be considered a form of output with access to meaning is debatable because the participants were attempting to retrieve L1 words instead of the novel L2 word forms. As discussed more extensively in the next chapter, subsequent studies (e.g., Barcroft, 2007a) have provided learners with opportunities to retrieve target L2 words themselves, which is definitely a type of output with access to meaning, and these studies have indicated even more pronounced benefits than those observed by Royer. In fact, given the nature of the retrieval in Group T and the aspect of asking participants to study up to ceiling levels, it is somewhat surprising that the benefits of retrieval opportunities emerged in Royer's study at all. Nevertheless, it did, and as such, it provided a first set of data pointing toward the potential positive effects of providing learners with retrieval opportunities during L2 vocabulary learning.

Summary and analysis

The research reviewed in the next chapter (e.g., Barcroft, 2007a; Harrington & Jiang, 2013; McNamara & Healy, 1995) expands greatly upon Royer's initial study, confirming the strong potential of retrieval opportunities as a technique for improving L2 vocabulary learning and assessing what the data indicate with regard to the potential mechanisms underlying the positive effects of retrieval. This larger body of research further confirms the importance of distinguishing between output *without* versus output *with* access to meaning when it comes to L2 vocabulary learning. Whereas different types of output without access to meaning, such as word copying and choral repetition, do not positively affect and can negatively affect L2 word learning, different types of output with access to meaning positively affect L2 word learning. Output of this nature (with access to meaning) implies that learners have processed target L2 words to at least some extent prior to attempting retrieval because without at least some prior exposure and attempted lex-IP, a learner has no level of knowledge at all of the target L2 word in question.

From a theoretical perspective, when comparing the distinct pattern of effects of output with versus without access to meaning on lex-IP and vocabulary, we see how two tasks that may appear similar at first blush are actually very different at a foundational level. Different types of output without access to meaning, such as copying target words, can deplete processing resources that otherwise could be utilized toward successful lex-IP of a given target word (Barcroft, 2006). Output with access to meaning, on the other hand, enhances lex-IP and increases L2 vocabulary learning by strengthening developing lexical representations in the mind, as discussed more extensively, including with reference to the larger body of research on the benefits of retrieval and testing in research on human memory, in the next chapter. At present, three key assertions can be with regard to output without access to meaning, output with access to meaning, and lex-IP:

1. Output without versus with access to meaning result in two distinct types of processing during lex-IP.
2. Output without access to meaning does not facilitate and can detract from efficient and successful lex-IP by depleting processing resources that otherwise could be directed toward lex-IP.
3. Output with access to meaning can facilitate efficient and successful lex-IP.

The mechanisms underlying the beneficial effects of output with access to meaning are discussed further in Chapter 8.

As is the case with tasks that involve semantic versus structurally oriented processing, from a pedagogical perspective, understanding the distinction between output without versus with access to meaning is critical when it comes to predicting probable learning outcomes for L2 vocabulary learning. Tasks that involve output without access to meaning may look similar to tasks that involve output with access to meaning at first blush, but they are completely different at a fundamental level, and the more that L2 instructors, language program directors, and developers of course materials are aware of this distinction and the probable impacts of each, the better. IBI vocabulary instruction, for example, includes a principle (Principle 6) with a warning with regard to different sources of output without access to meaning: *Limit forced output without access to meaning during the initial stages.* It also advocates the use of different types of output with access to meaning, however, including the incorporation of different types of practice quizzes that require learners to retrieve target L2 words at different points in time after they have had opportunities to process the target L2 words as input to a sufficient degree prior to attempting to retrieve and to produce the target words (output *with* access to meaning) on their own.

CHAPTER 8

Effects of opportunities for target word retrieval

Sometimes the particular effect of a given task on one aspect of human memory is not maintained when it comes to other aspects of human memory. For example, the positive effects of semantically elaborative tasks on memory for having been presented with a previously acquired L1 does not hold for memory for novel word forms, such as novel L2 words. For this reason ideas about the beneficial effects of LOP-based "deeper" semantically oriented processing on memory for "items" across the board is definitely a misnomer that should be corrected (in introductory Psychology textbooks, for example) and, instead, should be constrained only to the areas in which they are applied and not be extended in an unqualified manner to novel L2 word learning. On other occasions, however, we find remarkable consistency for the effect of a particular task on specific aspects of human memory. Such is the case with having learners attempt to retrieve target stimuli while memorizing them. Providing learners with opportunities to retrieve target stimuli in this manner has positive effects that are ubiquitous, extending across different types of human memory.

In this chapter, we first briefly review some of the history of research on the beneficial effects providing learners with retrieval opportunities, including different types of testing events, while they are attempting to memorize different types of target stimuli. This review includes consideration of the testing effect (Gates, 1917) and the generation effect (Slamecka & Graf, 1978) and some of the research these related phenomena have inspired within the history of research on human memory. Second, we present the research that has been conducted to date on the effects of retrieval opportunities on L2 word learning, including studies by McNamara and Healy (1995), Barcroft (2007a), and Harrington and Jiang (2013), all of which expand upon the first study on retrieval and L2 vocabulary, the study by Royer (1973) that was summarized in the previous chapter and provided an initial point of departure to distinguish between the different pattern of effects that we find for different types of output *without* access to meaning (e.g., word copying, choral repetition) versus different types of output with access to meaning, the latter including attempting to retrieve L2 words in different ways after the words in question have been presented as input to a degree that allows one to be able to make an attempted retrieval. Here we begin with research on intentional L2 vocabulary learning and then proceed to the limited research that has been conducted to date on the effects of retrieval opportunities in incidental contexts of L2 vocabulary learning. Finally, we conclude the chapter by summarizing a series of key theoretical implications of research on retrieval opportunities and L2 vocabulary learning with regard to lex-IP as well as pedagogical implications, which speak to the effectiveness of providing learners with different types of opportunities to retrieve L2 words on their own (after they have processed the words as input to a sufficient degree) over time.

Retrieval opportunities and research on human memory

The term *retrieval* refers to the cognitive process of "accessing stored information" (Roediger & Guynn, 1996, p. 197). The stored information in question necessarily must have been processed as input, encoded, and retained to a sufficient degree to be able to make a retrieval attempt in the first place, all of which is based on the previous experience (previous input processing, etc.) on the part of the individual attempting to retrieve an item. As should be clear from the previous chapter, for L2 vocabulary learning, retrieval is no way the same thing as simply copying a target word or repeating it out loud as different types of output without access to meaning of this nature have not been found to positively affect L2 vocabulary learning and can, at least under some circumstances, detract from this type of learning.

Research on the benefits of retrieval opportunities has a long history in the field of psychology. In 1914, for example, Myers reported a study in which written recall of words in a list had a positive effect on the ability to reproduce the words in question, which was a first demonstration of the *testing effect*, which refers to how having participants take a test enhances memory (see, e.g., Glover, 1989; Wheeler & Roediger, 1992). Interestingly, it has subsequently been exhibited that test taking can improve learning even more than additional exposure to target items (e.g., Hogan & Kintsch, 1971; Tulving, 1967). In 1939, Spitzer demonstrated that having an individual recall facts learned during reading facilitated later recall of the facts in question. In 1978, Slamecka and Graf made reference to the *generation effect*, which refers to how human beings are able to remember items better when they are required to generate the items on their own. Importantly, self-generation of a target item inherently involves at least a certain degree of retrieval of that item. Finally, the pivotal beneficial role of retrieval for memory continues to permeate research on and our understanding of human memory, as reflected, for example, by comments made by Roediger (2009): "what is important for long-term retention … is not the number of study episodes, it's the number of test episodes."

In order to provide at least one more detailed review of research demonstrating the positive effects of retrieval opportunities, let us consider the seminal study reported by Slamecka and Graf (1978) on the generation effect. Slamecka and Graf (1978) compared the effects of "read" versus "generate" conditions while using different types of generation rules, including "associate," *lamp-light*; "category," *ruby-diamond*; "opposite," *long-short*; "synonym," *sea-ocean*; and "rhyme," *save-cave*). In the "read" condition, participants were presented with word-word pairs (e.g., *rapid-fast*) and instructed to read each of the words aloud. In the generate conditions, they were presented with the various generation rules (e.g., "synonym") along with word-cue pairs (e.g., *rapid-f*) and asked to attempt to generate items on the basis of the generation rule in question when presented with the cue, which a single letter, such as *f* for the target item *fast* (p. 593). In other words, the generation tasks always involved attempting to recall previously acquired L1 words whereas different possible generation tasks during L2 vocabulary learning will necessarily be tied to the extent to which learners have previously been exposed to the target L2 words in question as input. Slamecka and Graf's findings indicated superior performance in generate conditions as compared to read conditions based on measures of cued and uncued recognition, free and cued recall, and confidence ratings regarding word recognition. The beneficial effect "generate" over "read" also held across a variety of learning contexts, including timed and self-paced learning and learning with and without expecting a pending test.

Subsequent studies have helped to define the extension and limits of the generation effect and other related retrieval-related effects. Some point to the robustness of the generation effect. For example, the effect may be obtained when participants do each of the following activities: (a) switch two letters in order to arrive at a target word (e.g., Greene, 1988; Nairne & Widner, 1988); (b) perform mathematical calculations in order to arrive at target numbers (Gardiner & Rowley, 1984); and (c) listen to ads designed in a manner that makes the listener tend to generate fictitious product names (Thompson & Barnett, 1981). Furthermore, in a study on the effects of a particularly challenging generation task based on relatively unfamiliar opposites (e.g., *trivial-v* as a cue for *trivial-vital*), Slamecka and Fevreiski (1983) demonstrated that when participants attempted but failed to generate words, their memory for those words was still better than for words that they read only. In another study, Smith and Healy (1998) examined the time-course of the generation effect and found that it could be obtained even when participants have only a few hundred milliseconds to process the target stimulus. Lastly, the generation effect has been demonstrated in bilingual translation tasks (O'Neill, Roy, & Tremblay, 1993) and has been found to be more pronounced in compound as compared to coordinate bilinguals (Basi, Thomas, & Wang, 1997).

It also has been demonstrated, however, that the generation effect may not emerge for all types of generation task, target item, learning task, and experimental design. Crutcher and Healy (1989) found no significant difference, for example, when comparing a condition in which participants generated numbers while using a calculator and a condition in which they simply read numbers. When participants were required to do mathematical calculations on their own (without a calculator), on the other hand, they performed better than they did in the read-numbers condition. Importantly, with regard to retrieval opportunities and the nature of the target item, certain studies have failed to demonstrate the generation effect when using nonwords as target stimuli (Greene, 1988; McElroy & Slamecka, 1982; Payne, Neely, & Burns, 1986). Other studies have demonstrated the effect with nonword items, however. Johns and Swanson (1988) revealed generation effects when displaying target words at the end of each "attempt-to-generate" trial whereas Schmidt and Cherry (1989) demonstrated how generation facilitated free recall and recognition memory of target words but decreased free recall of word pairs and cued target word recall. Finally, some research using between-subject studies have yielded generation effects (e.g., McDaniel, Waddill, & Einstein, 1988) whereas other research using between-subjects designs, have not (Begg & Snider, 1987; Slamecka & Katsaiti, 1987), suggesting that within-participant allocation of processing resources may be an important contributor to the overall pattern of effects of retrieval- versus no-retrieval oriented conditions in studies in this area.

Researchers have posited a variety of theoretical accounts of the generation effect, including increased cognitive effort (e.g., Griffith, 1976); increased semantic memory (e.g., McElroy & Slamecka, 1982); increased compatibility between study and test conditions (Slamecka & Graf, 1978); selective displaced rehearsal, or increased rehearsal of generated items at the expense of read items (e.g., Slamecka & Katsaiti, 1987); generalized inhibition, or normal encoding of read items being suppressed by generating items in the same list (Begg & Snider, 1987); a two-factor theory (Hirshman & Bjork, 1988); a three-factor (contextual) theory (McDaniel, Waddill, & Einstein, 1988); and the resource-allocation hypothesis (Schmidt, 1990). Given that generating different types of stimuli involves retrieval of items in question, from a more general perspective, we can assert that the generation effect may be best accounted for in terms of an account that emphasizes the beneficial effects of prior retrieval. Partially or fully retrieving a target item can strengthen the representation of the item in memory because the process of partially or fully retrieving the item changes the learner's retrieval mechanism and modifies their existing knowledge (see, e.g., Bjork, 1975; Roediger & Guynn, 1996). Therefore, some variety of a retrieval-based explanation of the generation effect makes sense.

Consistent with this position is research indicating that the positive effect of retrieval increases as a function of the degree of difficulty of the act of retrieval (e.g., Gardiner, Craik, & Bleasdale, 1973; see also Bjork's [1975] discussion). Bjork (1975, p. 143) has interpreted this finding from the LOP perspective (Craik & Lockhart, 1972), positing that "... deeper, more difficult, more complex retrieval processes have two distinct long-term advantages over shallower, less difficult, and less complex retrieval processes: (a) they reactivate or strengthen encodings of an item that are more durable, less susceptible to interference, and therefore, more supportive of long-term retention, and (b) because they involve taking a slower and more complex route to an item in memory, they multiply or elaborate the routes available for subsequent retrieval."

Retrieval opportunities and intentional L2 vocabulary learning

Only a limited number of studies have assessed the effects of providing learners with retrieval opportunities on intentional L2 vocabulary learning (Barcroft, 2007a; Harrington & Jiang, 2013; McNamara & Healy, 1995a; Royer, 1973). Whereas Royer's (1973) study was reviewed in the previous chapter as a first step toward understanding the potential benefits of retrieval-oriented conditions on L2 vocabulary learning, in this section we consider two more recent studies (Barcroft, 2007a; McNamara & Healy, 1995) in this area. Both point to the positive effects of providing learners with opportunities to retrieve target L2 words while they are in the process of attempting to learn them. As such, both studies speak to the effectiveness of engaging learners in tasks that require output *with* access to meaning in contrast to tasks that require output *without* access to meaning (such as word copying and choral repetition) during intentional L2 vocabulary learning.

To begin, McNamara and Healy (1995a, Experiment 2) assessed the performance of participants who attempted to learn a series of novel nonwords (heretofore referred to as "target words") by associating them with English nouns. Training condition, which was either "read" or "generate," was treated as a between-subjects variable. All of the participants were first presented with the target words and were allowed to study them using any self-selected method. The participants in the read group then were instructed to copy each target word in a blank space. Participants in the generate group, on the other hand, were asked to attempt to write each target word on their own when presented with the English translation of the target word. All of the participants then completed a posttest and a retention test one week later. On both tests, the participants were required to write the target words when presented with English counterparts only. The results indicated higher learning of the target words in the generate group as compared to the read group. The mean retention rate was .756 for the generate group as compared to .658 for the read group, suggesting that that the retrieval opportunities positively affected intentional L2 vocabulary learning.

McNamara and Healy interpreted these findings as support for extending the generation effect to the type of learning or skill that takes place over multiple episodes or trials. The researchers proposed a *procedural account* of the generation effect (see McNamara and Healy, 1995b), according to which the act of generating target words promotes development of the cognitive operations involved in retrieving word forms and, in this manner, facilitates word learning. Applying the procedural account to vocabulary learning in particular, providing learners with opportunities to retrieve novel words based on meaningful cues (cues that activate semantic networks) should facilitate subsequent retrieval of those words when cued in a similar manner. They interpret the results of their study (McNamara & Healy, 1995a) as being consistent with this account.

In another study, Barcroft (2007a) explored how providing learners with opportunities to retrieve target words on their own would affect intentional L2 vocabulary learning in a classroom setting. English-speaking learners of L2 Spanish attempted to learn 24 new Spanish words while viewing word-picture pairs on a screen at the front of their regular classroom. They first viewed all 24 pairs in order to be able to process the target words as input to some degree. They then viewed 12 pairs in a retrieval-oriented condition and 12 words in a no-retrieval oriented condition. For retrieval-oriented, they viewed each picture for 6 seconds before seeing both the picture and the written word below it for another six seconds, allowing them time to attempt to retrieve the target words in their mind. For no-retrieval, each word was always presented with its corresponding picture without the 6-second lag. Therefore, the overall study time was held constant for each target word in each condition. Target word groups and learning orders were counterbalanced across an equal number of participants following a latin-square design. After the study phase, the participants took posttests immediately after study (Time 1), 2 days later (Time 2), and 1 week later (Time 3). As depicted in Figure 8.1, the results revealed that vocabulary learning scores were higher in the

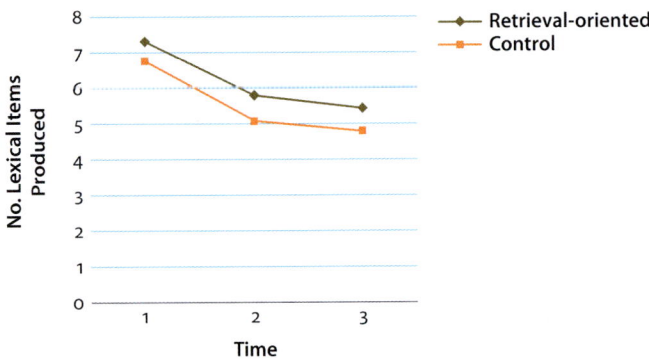

Figure 8.1 Effects of opportunities for target word retrieval on intentional L2 vocabulary learning (Time 1 = immediate; Time 2 = 2 days later; Time 3 = 1 week later).

retrieval-oriented condition as compared to the no-retrieval condition and that this positive effect was maintained over time. These findings, which provide another demonstration of the positive effects of retrieval opportunities, are consistent with the proposal that attempting to retrieve target words (with varying degrees of success) modifies one's existing knowledge when it comes to novel word form, and in this case L2 word forms.

Lastly, in a more recent study, Harrington and Jiang (2013) examined the effect of providing English-speaking third-semester students of Chinese over a more extended period of time. The students engaged in retrieval of target vocabulary (either single or two-character words) by completing a series of form recognition tests that were administered over a period of four weeks. The tests were administered using PowerPoint and involved having the students indicate whether vocabulary items had appeared previously as a part of the materials in the course. As such, the students' responses reflected episodic memory (regarding whether or not the target word forms in question had appeared previously) with no requirement of processing of semantic information for the target words in question. The results of the study indicated higher amounts of vocabulary learning for the vocabulary items in the retrieval tasks when compared to control words appearing in a supplementary list on (midterm and final) vocabulary tests.

These findings are consistent with other findings on the benefits of retrieval opportunities on intentional L2 vocabulary learning but also expand upon the previous findings by demonstrating how a retrieval task focuses specifically on target word form (no cues requiring mapping from meaning to form, for example, were included) can benefit L2 vocabulary over an extended period of time when incorporated as part of the class. With regard to L2 instruction in particular, the researchers state the following (p. 142): "We believe the findings of this study, along with those of Royer (1973), McNamara and Healy (1995) and Barcroft (2007a) indicate that the introduction of retrieval practice can have a positive effect on vocabulary learning in the classroom, without making undue demands on the instructor and learners' time."

Do benefits of retrieval opportunities extend to incidental vocabulary learning?

While the evidence for facilitative effects of retrieval opportunities on intentional L2 vocabulary appear to be mounting, what about the effects of retrieval opportunities in contexts of incidental L2 vocabulary learning? At least two studies (Barcroft, 2013, 2015) have addressed this question to date with regard to incidental L2 vocabulary learning during reading. One of the studies assessed the effects of asking learners to attempt to recall words in a text two times on their own after the word and its translation had already appeared once in the text. The other study expanded upon the first by comparing a series of different possible patterns of presenting target words as input in the text and providing opportunities for target word retrieval.

To begin, Barcroft (2015) assessed how word retrieval opportunities would affect incidental by comparing generate versus no-generate control conditions. Seventy-four Spanish-speaking intermediate learners of L2 English completed an embedded pretest on 6 target words (the embedded pretest format avoided letting the participants know that they were being tested on the six words in question in particular) and were then instructed to read an English text for meaning. None of the participants were told that the study concerned vocabulary learning. Each of 6 target words (e.g., *smidgen*) appeared 3 times in different parts of the text. Participants in the control group ($n = 37$) always viewed Spanish translations of the target words. Participants in the generate (experimental) group ($n = 37$) viewed a Spanish translation for each target word the first time it appeared and attempted to retrieve and produce (write) each of these words on their own for the final two instances in which the words appeared. After the reading task, the participants completed two previously unannounced vocabulary learning posttests, one of which was L1-to-L2 and the other of which was L2-to-L1. The results of the study indicated a highly significant 37% increase in vocabulary learning for the generate group over the control group, which was interpreted as new evidence of how (both partial and complete) target word retrieval can strengthen developing lexical representations within a lexical network and how opportunities for word retrieval can be utilized to improve not only intentional but also incidentally oriented L2 vocabulary learning.

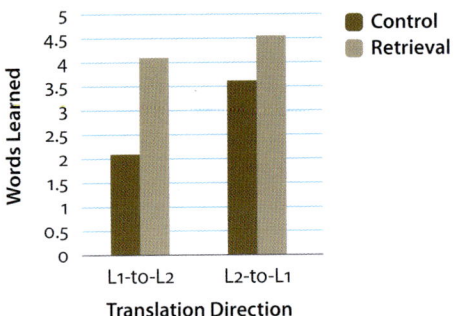

Figure 8.2 Benefits of a retrieval opportunities on incidental L2 vocabulary learning during reading.

In another study, Barcroft (2013) compared four different patterns of input (target words translated) and retrieval (blanks in which to write target L2 words). Seventy-five Spanish-speaking learners of L2 English read an English text for meaning. Each of the 6 target words (e.g., *smidgen*) appeared 3 times in the text. The participants were randomly assigned to one of four groups based on input (I) – retrieval (R) patterns. Group 1 (control) ($n=19$) always viewed Spanish translations of the target words (pattern III). Group 2 ($n=19$) received the pattern of IIR. Group 3 ($n=19$) received the pattern of IRI. Group 4 ($n=19$) received the pattern of IRR. L1-to-L2 and L2-to-L1 posttests were administered. The results of the study indicated greater gains for the IRI and IRR groups than for the III (control) group and greater gains in the IRI group than in the IIR group with no significant differences between the IRI group and the IRR group. As compared to III (control), the vocabulary learning gains were 34.9% in the IRR group and 42.0% in the IRI group. These findings suggest that retrieval strengthens developing lexical representations while interacting with input in an identifiable and telling manner.

Summary and implications

The research reviewed in this chapter provides convincing evidence of the positive effects of retrieval opportunities on both intentional and incidental L2 vocabulary learning. McNamara and Healy (1995) and Barcroft (2007a) demonstrated such positive effects with regard to cued recall of target L2 words, involving the mapping component of L2 vocabulary learning whereas Harrington and Jiang (2013) demonstrated positive effects using a retrieval task that focused purely on target word form and that did not require processing of the semantic or mapping-oriented components of L2 vocabulary learning. All of these studies provide direct evidence of the benefits of tasks that involve different types output *with* access to meaning in contrast to the effects of tasks that involve output *without* access to meaning (such as word copying and choral repetition), as should be clear from the research findings reviewed in the previous chapter.

From a theoretical perspective, these research findings suggest that target word retrieval – be it full, partial, or even less than partial as in cases of only activating retrieval pathways without even successful partial word retrieval – modifies one's existing knowledge when it comes to developing lexical representations. This proposal is consistent with all of the research findings to date on retrieval and intentional L2 vocabulary learning as well as research findings by Barcroft (2013, 2015) indicating positive effects of retrieval opportunities in incidental contexts of L2 vocabulary learning. Overall, research in this area points to the pivotal facilitative role that retrieval opportunities can have during lex-IP when it comes to strengthening and consolidating target words in memory. As such, it is also consistent with the much larger body of the research findings demonstrating benefits of a wide range of different types of retrieval for a wide range of types of target stimuli in the history of research on human memory.

With regard to L2 instruction, research findings in this area strongly favor incorporating retrieval opportunities as a major component of L2 vocabulary instruction. Language instructors, language program directors, and developers of course materials should make use of the facilitative effects of providing learners with opportunities to retrieve target words (after they have been processed to a substantial degree as input) as a means of providing more effective, evidence-based instruction. The current demonstrations of the positive effects of retrieval opportunities should also inspire new research in this area with regard to both intentional and incidental contexts of L2 vocabulary learning. The more types of retrieval-oriented techniques explored, the better our understanding of how each of these might positively affect different components of L2 vocabulary learning.

UNIT 3

Input-based effects

CHAPTER 9

Privileging and patterns in partial word form learning

Whereas the research discussed in Unit 2 provided information related to lex-IP on the basis of the effects of different types of tasks that learners can perform during L2 vocabulary learning, Unit 3 (Chapters 9 to 13) focuses on issues related to lex-IP based on the relationship between different ways that target words can be presented as input and how these affect L2 vocabulary learning. Chapter 9 concentrates on what partial form word learning can tell us about how different features of words are attended to and privileged in varying degrees when the words appear in spoken or written input to a degree that learners do not acquire the ability produce the complete version of the words. Chapter 10 centers on effects of increased exposure, an element that is both facilitative and critical when it comes to word learning, and different possible regimes for spaced exposure. Chapter 11 appraises a series of studies on the effects of learning words in semantic versus thematically based sets. Chapter 12 then considers research on the impact of different sources of input enhancement. Finally, Chapter 13 focuses on one particularly useful type of enhancement for lex-INPUT in the spoken mode: phonetically relevant acoustic variability.

To begin, in the present chapter we focuses on the implications of research on partial word form learning for lex-IP and L2 vocabulary learning in general. Whereas a vast amount of research on L2 vocabulary has addressed issues related to the number (breadth) of words learners know and the semantic and collocational properties of words (depth), insufficient attention has been given to how learners attend to and process the formal component of L2 word learning. As a consequence, more research is needed to address critical questions such as the following: When novel word forms appear as lex-INPUT in, for example, an intentional context of vocabulary learning, how do learners attend to different aspects of the formal features of words as lex-IP ensues? Particularly in contexts of L2 in which learners come to the task of L2 vocabulary already having an existing semantic system (based on L1) that gives them information about basic meanings of target L2 words, lex-IP of novel L2 word *form* is particularly critical to successful word learning. When an L2 learner of Basque attempts to learn the Basque word for "apple," for example, the learner does not "start from scratch" when it comes to knowing what an apple is and how it differs from other items in the world, such as "pear," "strawberry," or "apple tree." What is of utmost priority when attempting to learn the word for "apple" in Basque is to know that the form for the word in question is *sagar*. Similarly, when attempting to learn the Basque word for "wheel," what is of immediate importance is the (quite) novel word form *gurpila* moreso than the fact that bicycles have two wheels, tricycles have three wheels, and so forth.

When word forms actually are broken down into their individual physical components, we find that spoken words are ultimately composed of sound vibrations in the air; signed words are composed of hand shape, location, and movement in space; words in Braille and other tactile systems are composed of edges in physical space (made of paper, metal, or otherwise); and written language is composed of print in one script or another on paper, another surface, or in digital form. Understanding how these different physical properties are attended to and encoded during lex-IP is central to our understanding of lex-IP and L2 vocabulary learning in general. Furthermore, even though L2 vocabulary testing often does not go in the direction of requiring learners to produce target L2 word forms, degree of knowledge of word form may be an excellent predictor not only of the size of so-called "productive" vocabulary knowledge but also of so-called "receptive" vocabulary knowledge. Before moving on to research about patterns and privileging in partial word form learning, let us consider the extent to which the "productive-receptive" distinction in L1 vocabulary knowledge may be a simple artefact of the degree of partial word form knowledge an individual has at any particular point in time for any particular target L2 word.

Is the "receptive-productive" distinction an artefact of partial word form knowledge?

Could it be that the alleged "receptive-productive" distinction is only a reflection of accessing word form in different ways from a single lexical store? As a case in point in favor of this position, imagine that a learner has studied and attempted to learn (intentionally) a set of new words in a Language X (an invented language here) by viewing word-picture pairs. The learner was not able to learn all of the word forms for the target words in question, and for a number of the target words only partial word form knowledge was achieved. Below is an indication of the amount of target word form that the learner managed to encode and retain (symbols represent target word referents; translations are in parenthesis; dashes indicate parts of words that are missing from learner's knowledge of each of the target word forms in question):

> | Amount of target word form learned ("Knowledge Bank") | | |
> |---|---|---|
> | ♀ | ('person') | dl--o--d |
> | ○ | ('circle') | gl-n---- |
> | → | ('arrow') | li-- |
> | □ | ('square') | s--l-pil |
> | ☼ | ('sun') | -bi |

While referring to this "Amount Learned" section only, attempt to complete both of the posttests below. Complete Posttest 1 in its entirety before completing Posttest 2 and without looking at Posttest 2. Notice the type of knowledge that you are relying on when generating each response. You may refer to the information above (your partial word form knowledge) as much as needed in order to complete each of the two posttests (but again, Posttest 1 first and Posttest 2 second while focusing solely on the posttest in question and the "Knowledge Bank."

> *Posttest 1 ("Productive")*. Produce as many of the target words (in whole or in part) that you learned for each of the items that you see. You may look above in the "Knowledge Bank" section as much as you want to complete the productive test because that is how much you would have learned after trying to learn the words.
>
> ♀ _____
> ○ _____
> → _____
> □ _____
> ☼ _____

> *Posttest 2 ("Receptive")*. Draw the item (or write the English word) that each of the following Language X words represents. Again, you may look above in the "Amount Learned" section as much as you want to complete the productive test because that is how much you would have learned after trying to learn the words.
>
> 1. dlinobid   _____
> 2. glinalor   _____
> 3. lili   _____
> 4. sorlapil   _____
> 5. ebi   _____

After completing the two posttests (again, while using "Knowledge Bank" as much as possible in order to get the best score possible on each type of posttest, score each of the two posttests. Give a score of .5 for any response of one half or more of the target word correctly and a score of 1 for any completely correctly produced word on Posttest 1. Give a score of 1 for each correctly produced picture or L1 word on Posttest 2 (it is likely that no partial scores are needed to score Posttest 2.

Below are the correct Target Words in Language X that you had attempted to learn. You may use these words when scoring:

Target Words in Language X
(1) ♀ ('person') = dlinobid   (2) ○ ('circle') = glinalor   (3) → ('arrow') = lili
(4) □ ('square') = sorlapil   (5) ☼ ('sun') = ebi.

Now answer each of the following questions. (1) On which of the two posttests did you perform better? Why? (2) On what type of knowledge were your responses based? Was it the same basic knowledge source ("a single lexical store") for both Posttest 2 and Posttest 1? (3) What does this activity indicate about the nature of purported "receptive" versus "productive" vocabulary knowledge? Relate your experience to one particular proposal first made by Melka (1997), namely, that the receptive-productive distinction may be best viewed as two distinct ways of accessing a single lexical score. (4) What implications does this activity have with regard to testing L2 vocabulary? If target L2 word forms are provided for learners on a test, to what extent does it or does it not ensure that they have learned the target words in question?

This activity should help to illustrate why the supposed "receptive-productive" distinction in L2 vocabulary learning may, at the end of the day, be a construct that is inconsistent with reality when it comes to the nature of L2 word learning. A more appropriate construct, one that could replace "receptive-productive," may be *degree of partial word form learning*, which makes reference to the amount (proportion, percentage, etc.) of an entire word form that one has managed to learn and retain at any given point of time. When one has learned and retained 100% of a target word form, at that point so-called "receptive" and "productive" knowledge are the same (at 100%), but when one has learned and retained less than 100% of a target word form, the less of the word form the individual knows, the greater the individual's so-called "receptive" knowledge becomes as compared to so-called "productive" knowledge with regard to the word in question.

The rest of this chapter will focus on the limited amount of research that exists on observable patterns in L2 partial word form learning, primarily based on studies by Barcroft (2000b, 2008) and Barcroft and Rott (2010). These studies have assessed the extent to which learners tend to learn partial instead of complete L2 word forms when they are challenged by immediate L2 vocabulary learning tasks in which mean scores are not even near 100%. They also have explored issues such as how long segments of partially learned target words tend to be, the location of word segments within the target words, and so forth. Prior to presenting this L2-focused research, however, in the following section we briefly review some previous research on different word-internal locations that tend to be privileged for L1 language users. As it turns out, word-initial and word-final positions tend to be more privileged than word-medial positions in this regard.

Research on the bathtub effect

The *bathtub effect* refers to the phenomenon that people tend to remember and are able to access word parts at the beginnings and ends of words as opposed to in the middle of words. According to Aitchison (1994, p. 134), the bathtub effect is "perhaps the most commonly reported finding in the literature on memory for words." Brown and McNeill (1966) provided evidence for this effect when testing subjects who were in the tip-of the-tongue state with regard to words that came to their mind as they were attempting to retrieve L1 words. Their findings indicated that other words that the subjects reported as being similar in sound to the target word tended to share sounds at the beginnings and ends of the words. In a subsequent study that focused on memory for correct parts of target words in malapropisms, Aitchison and Straf (1982) demonstrated how the bathtub effect was influenced by word length: the beginnings of short words (1–2 syllables) were remembered marginally better than the beginnings of long words (3 or more syllables) whereas the endings of long words were remembered substantially more than the endings of short words. In the next section we consider research on whether the bathtub effect holds true beyond knowledge and use of target words into contexts of L2 vocabulary learning. Meyer and Bock (1992) also reported on patterns of incomplete word form retrieval in tip-of-the-tongue states and argued that incomplete word production in these states was due to insufficient word-form activation.

Research on partial word form learning

Barcroft (2000b, 2008) conducted studies in which English-speaking learners of L2 Spanish attempted to learn 24 new words in Spanish in word-picture repetition paradigm. After attempting to learn the words, the participants were instructed to produce as much of each target word as they could, either in spoken or written form, when presented with pictures only. The primary goal of the study was to analyze all of the partial and complete word forms that the learners had produced. The researcher focused in particular on (a) percentage of partially versus fully produced target words, (b) approximate amount of each word that they produced (if one considers that a completely produced word corresponds to 100%), (c) the mean length of the partial-word segments that the participants tended to produce, and (d) the word-internal location of the segments that the participants tended to produce.

The results of these two studies indicated the following. (1) There was substantially greater production of partial words: in Barcroft's (2008) study, for example 69% were partial words whereas 31% were whole words. (2) There was a high percentage of 1-letter fragments as compared to segments of longer length, as illustrated in more detail in Table 9.1 based on the 2008 study by Barcroft. (3) There was also heavy privileging for word-initial position but not as much for word-final position. This finding is only partially consistent with the above-described demonstrations of the bathtub in contexts of L1 lexical processing given that word-final positions are not as prominently privileged as would be expected for a bathtub effect. When combined, the results of the study indicate that partial word form learning is more prominent than whole word learning when it comes to identifying the norm between these two options in L2 vocabulary learning.

Table 9.1 Means for fragment length in partially produced words (Barcroft, 2008).

Fragment length	Mean	SD
One letter	.57	.11
Two letters	.20	.10
Three letters	.13	.07
Four or more letters	.10	.07

Barcroft and Rott (2010) expanded upon these findings by analyzing partial word form learning in L2 German and Spanish while controlling for the effects of number of syllables in target words. Production data from an L1-to-L2 translation task (administered after a learning phase) from both English to Spanish and English to German were analyzed to determine percentage of partial versus fully produced words; overall amount of target word produced in partial words; fragment length in partial words produced; and word-internal location of target segments. The target words used in this study are provided in Appendix B.

The findings of the study indicated production of approximately 49% more partial words than whole words; a high percentage of 1-letter fragments, as is consistent with the previous findings of Barcroft; and privileging for word-initial position but not other word-internal positions for both languages. More specifically the findings indicated the following: (a) partial words were much more prevalent than complete words (approximately 49% more partial words than whole words); (b) two-syllable words were produced as complete words when compared to three-syllable words; (c) the difference in the amount of partial versus full words was larger for learners of German than it was for learners of Spanish; (d) three-fourths of a word was the amount most often, more so than one-half or one-fourth of a word was produced, (e) privileging for three-fourths of a word was favored for two-syllable words more than for three-syllable words; (f) one-letter fragments were produced much more than two-letter fragments than fragments with more letters (single-letter fragments 40% of the time, two-letter fragments 24%, three-letter fragments 19%, and four-or-more-letter fragments 17%); (g) target letters were produced more in word-initial locations as compared to other locations (49% of the time in word-initial position, 24% in word-medial position, and 27% in word-final position; (h) the word-initial advantage was more pronounced in two-syllable words than in three-syllable words; and (i) patterns of produced segments for medial and final position were different for the two L2s (learners of L2 German produced fewer fragments in word-medial position than in word-final position whereas learners of Spanish had slightly higher means for word-medial than for word-final position). These findings are consistent with the earlier findings but also demonstrate that shorter 2-syllable words were produced completely more often than longer 3-syllable words, which makes sense if one considers overall allocation of limited processing resources during lex-IP.

Bathtub versus recliner effects

With regard to the word-internal location of fragments retrieved, the findings based on both L2 Spanish and L2 German data, along with those of the earlier studies, are more consistent with the idea a *recliner effect* than that of a bathtub effect, as Barcroft and Rott (2010) pointed out and as can be seen in Figure 9.1. In the case of L2 German, the effect looks more like a bathtub effect as compared to the case of L2 Spanish, but the pattern of results in both language indicates greater privileging for word-initial segments as compared to word-final segments, which differs from what would be considered a bathtub effect in the traditional sense that it has been observed in L1 contexts. Looking at scores for the word-final position for both languages, the most appropriate metaphor would seem to be a recliner effect for a recliner that has an adjustable foot area that can be raised up and down.

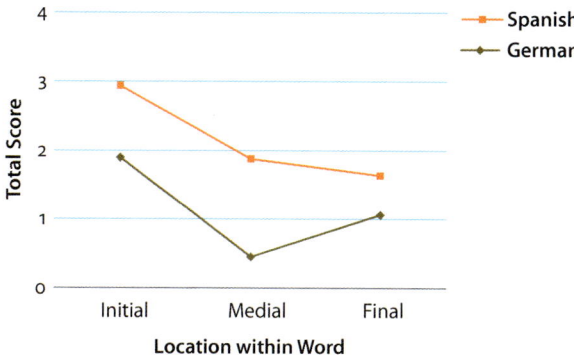

Figure 9.1 A "recliner effect" based on word-internal locations of word fragments recalled (Barcroft & Rott, 2010).

Barcroft and Rott (2010, p. 646) provided four possible explanations with regard to why word-initial positions are favored in this context of vocabulary learning:

> One possible reason that word-initial positions are favored is simply that they are more easily perceived. An alternative, however, concerns efficient parsing. Even if word-initial positions are not perceptually more salient, learners may parse word-initial positions to a greater extent as a strategy that allows for the most efficient word-level parsing overall. A third possibility is that word-initial privileging is due to some combination of both of the above and is in part due to perceptual salience and in part due to parsing mechanisms employed by the learner.

New research in this area should help to discern which of these possible explanations is the most viable.

Importantly, a more recent study by Chen-Chun (2013) has shed new light in this area by demonstrating that for shorter words (6-letter words in this case) the recliner effect emerged such that word-initial positions were most often recalled whereas much more word-final segments were produced for longer words. In the case of the longest words examined (12-letter words in this case), the amount of word-final segments produced was highest, actually going beyond what one might call a bathtub effect in the direction of a recliner effect in the opposite direction. In interpreting these effects, Chen-Chun posited the following (on the bottom of the poster presentation) with regard to the relationship between word length and the prevalence of segments in word-initial versus word-final positions: "The finding suggests] that the participants might manipulate and shift their available lexical processing strategies (i.e. word segmentation skill using affix knowledge [and] word word structure knowledge [and] word decoding skill using phoneme-grapheme mappings and syllable structure knowledge) to promote the learnability of L2 words."

Summary and implications

The research that has been conducted to date on partial L2 word form learning indicates that after attempting to learn a set of target L2 words in a challenging context of intentional vocabulary learning, they produce substantially more partial than complete words. This finding is critical to our understanding of lex-IP and vocabulary learning as a highly incremental process when it comes not only to acquiring the appropriate semantic space for target words but also to learning target word forms themselves. L2 word forms are processed and learned in bits and pieces over time, but there are identifiable patterns, such as the recliner effect, that can be discerned by analyzing the partial words that learners can produce when they are provided an appropriate context in which to do so.

Four key observations related to be lex-IP can be summarized on the basis of the data reviewed in this chapter:

1. L2 word forms are processed and learned in bits and pieces incrementally over time.
2. When challenged by a vocabulary learning task that does not lead to near-ceiling levels of performance and when encouraged to produce as much of each target word form as possible, learners produce substantially more partial word segments than complete words.
3. When learners produce partial L2 word forms, they produce a greater number of smaller segments (e.g., 1-letter segments) as compared to larger segments (e.g., 2-letter, 3-letter, or 4-letter segments).
4. When learners produce partial L2 word forms, the segments that they produce appear more in word-initial position as compared to word-medial or word-final condition. We refer to this phenomenon as the recliner effect. However, there is evidence that with longer words (10-letter and 12-letter words in the case of Chen-Chun's study) that word-final segments are produced to a much greater degree, even exceeding the degree to which word-initial segments are produced.

These observations help to paint a larger picture of what is involved in lex-IP and successful L2 vocabulary learning, and hopefully, future research in this area can provide a new body of data to help expand upon the present assertions and improve our understanding of patterns in partial word form learning and how they relate to lex-IP and L2 vocabulary learning in general.

CHAPTER 10

Effects of increased and spaced exposure

"All other things being equal, our memory for information will depend on the number of times that we have encountered or studied it." Greene (p. 132) noted this fundamental point in 1992, but, well over a century ago, Ebbinghaus (1885/1964, as cited in Greene, 1992) was already demonstrating how memory for stimuli improves as we increase the number of times to which one is exposed to the stimuli in question. Since the early work of Ebbinghaus in this area, numerous studies have explored various aspects of how the effects of repetition function in a *learning curve*, that is, a graph that can depict the positive effects of repetition over time (on the X axis) on learning (on the Y axis). The prototypical learning curve is *monotonic* (the curve goes in one direction, upward, only) and *negatively accelerated* ("the rate of the upward movement is always slowing down") (Greene, 1992, p. 132–133).

Time of exposure and the meaning of effectiveness

Increased repetition alone implies increases in overall time of exposure, however. This point is critical when it comes to learning *effectiveness*, which refers to the amount that one learns within a given amount of time. If a researcher or language instructor is interested in learning effectiveness with regard to L2 vocabulary, the question to be asked is: What is the best way to present target words as input given a limited overall amount of time X for each target word? For example, if a total of 24 seconds is to be allotted to the presentation of each target word within a larger set of target words (with each word appearing below a picture of its referent, for example), what is the best way to distribute the overall time of exposure? How long should each presentation interval be? How many exposures (repetitions) should be included? As the number of exposures increases (from 2 to 4 to 8, for example), the interval length of each exposure must necessarily decrease (from 12 to 6 to 3 seconds, for example) in order not to exceed the maximum overall amount of time of 24 seconds.

Length of exposure interval and number of exposures (repetitions)

Barcroft (1998b) conducted a study that addressed this issue directly by comparing the effects of three presentation patterns on the productive vocabulary learning of English-speaking learners of L2 Spanish. Participants in the study attempted to learn 24 new Spanish words while viewing word-picture pairs. Each word appeared below a corresponding picture of the target word referent. Overall amount of exposure to each target word was held to 24 seconds. Three presentation patterns based on the length of the presentation interval and number of exposures (repetitions) were compared, however. The patterns in question were (a) 8 repetitions at 3 seconds each (high repetition, short interval), (b) 4 repetitions at 6 seconds each (moderate repetition, moderate interval), and (c) 2 repetitions at 6 seconds each (low repetition, high interval). Each participant attempted to learn 8 words in each of these three conditions. Learning conditions and word groups were counterbalanced in a latin-square design.

How did each of these three presentation patterns affect L2 word learning? As can be seen in Figure 10.1, the results of the study indicated that eight 3-second repetitions resulted in the highest vocabulary learning scores, four 6-second repetitions in the second highest, and two 12-second repetitions in the lowest. Although the actual mean differences between the three presentation patterns may not be extremely large, it is important to note that the only variables being manipulated here are interval length and number of repetitions, without any change in the overall amount of time of exposure to each of the target words.

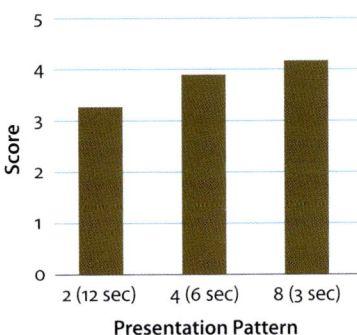

Figure 10.1 Effects of three presentation patterns varying repetitions versus interval length (Barcroft, 1998b).

With regard to allocation of processing resources during lex-IP, one must consider why learners are able to attend to and encode novel word forms and form-meaning mappings more readily when target words are presented using more repetitions as opposed to longer intervals. One possible explanation that with longer intervals, the extent to which learners can encode the new word forms form-meaning mappings decreases within each interval as the learner habituates to each new word as a stimulus. With more repetitions of shorter intervals, on the other hand, learners are exposed to each word form more frequently and with less time for habituation to each new word as a stimulus. Processing resource allocation is therefore more efficient with more repetitions of shorter intervals, at least for the intervals and numbers of repetitions examined. If interval lengths were to continue to be reduced beyond 3 seconds in order to increase repetitions, it may be that at some point the interval lengths would be so short that this feature would begin to negatively affect L2 vocabulary learning.

Clearly, the study reported here varied only one possible presentation pattern regarding interval length and number of repetitions. Many more studies are needed in order to understand better the relationship between a wide range of different possible presentation patterns. For example, would an additional presentation pattern of presenting target words for 1.5 seconds each for 16 repetitions result in more learning than intervals of 3 seconds repeated 8 times? At some point the beneficial effects of increasing repetitions by decreasing interval length may result in a learning curve that asymptotes and begins to fall. In addition, many other overall time frames for each target word need to be explored in addition to the 24-second-per-word time frame used in the study reported here. Additionally, measures of more long-term retention need to be included in studies on interval length and repetition number in this area. The more studies of this nature that are conducted in the future, the better we will understand the relationship between exposure interval and number of repetitions on intentional L2 word learning of this nature.

The spacing effect in L2 vocabulary learning

In addition to manipulations in interval length and repetition, another variable tied to the relative effectiveness of presenting target words while controlling overall time concerns the amount of spacing between each presentation of a target word. The effects of spacing can be investigated with regard to immediate contexts of L2 vocabulary learning – seconds, minutes, hours, days – or more long-term contexts of L2 vocabulary learning – weeks, months, years. Studies in this area have assessed the viability of the *spacing effect* (first noted by Ebbinghaus, 1985), which refers to improved memory for different types of target stimuli when the stimuli in question are presented in a more spaced as opposed to massed manner.

In one study, Bahrick (1979) measured the effects of different amounts of time elapsed between training sessions – 1 day versus 7 days versus 30 days – on recall for Spanish-English word pairs when participants engaged in successive relearning. The findings of the study indicated better learning performance for the shorter amounts of elapsed time on shorter-term measures but better performance for longer amounts of elapsed time on longer-term measures of performance. More specifically, there was a significant decrease in learning for participants who trained on the 1-day lapses when measured after a 30-day delay when compared to learning of the participants who trained with 7- and 30-day lapses. These findings suggest that longer time lapses are more efficient when it comes to long-term retention of target words, which is also consistent with the spacing effect, or at least one particular instantiation thereof. In another much more longitudinal study, Bahrick, Bahrick, Bahrick, and Bahrick (1993) compared intersessions of 14, 28 and 56 days and tested retention rates after 1, 2, 3, and 5 years after the end of training. Although the longer time intervals between training resulted in a disadvantage during the more immediate training period, they resulted in higher retention rates over longer periods of time. Finally, in another study with less of a focus on long-term retention, Bloom and Shuell (1981) compared the effects of a massed versus spaced presentation pattern over the course of three days. The massed practice involved a single 30-minute session whereas the spaced practice involved three 10-minute sessions on the three separate (but consecutive days). The results of the study indicated that studying in the spaced format led to substantially greater vocabulary learning as compared to overall learning in the massed condition. All three of these studies speak to the benefits of spaced over massed retrieval practice when it comes to L2 vocabulary learning over different periods of time, and, as such, they provide fairly robust evidence in favor of the viability of the spacing effect in the realm of L2 vocabulary learning (see also Dempster, 1987, for additional support for distributed spacing in this area).

Hintzman (1974) and Greene (1989) have proposed theoretical accounts of the benefits of spaced over massed study regimens while focusing on issues of deficient processing (in massed presentations) and the role of retrieval. From the perspective of *deficient processing*, Hintzman argued that subsequent presentations of a target stimulus are not attended to as much in conditions of massed presentation whereas they are attended to more so in conditions of spaced presentation. Greene (1989) argued that this proposal holds for memory tasks that depend largely on information about target items and little on issues related to learning context, as is supported in cases when the spacing effect does not emerge in incidental learning contexts. Also taking into account the perspective of *study-phase retrieval theory*, which posits that benefits of spacing are due to more elaboration on subsequent retrieval of the same target stimulus, Greene proposed a *two-factor account* that combined deficient processing and study-phase retrieval. According to this account, the benefits of spacing on free recall are due to study-phase retrieval given how performance on free recall depends on contextual associations and spacing allows for more encoding of the contextual information in question.

With regard to L2 vocabulary learning in particular, the benefits of spacing (over massed presentation) appear to be tied to the benefits of less deficient processing during retrieval opportunities, but further research is needed to isolate precisely how spaced versus massed presentation affects different subcomponents of word learning, such as the formal and mapping components. It may be that massed versus spaced presentation affects one subcomponent more than others, but there is no immediate reason to postulate that this should be the case given the wide range of target stimuli that have been tested to date. What is clear, however, is that the spacing does lead to a lexical representation that is more easily accessed in the long run due to quantitative changes, qualitative changes, or some combination of both that result from the increased space between the time of presentation of the target L2 words in question.

Expanding rehearsal and L2 vocabulary learning

Another issue related to the spacing effect concerns presentation patterns that involve *expanding retrieval*, which refers to the gradual increase in time that elapses between each presentation of a given stimulus over time. Is presenting target L2 words in an expanding manner of this nature more effective than presenting them in a manner in which there is an equal amount of time between each presentation? The answer appears to be *yes*, as evidenced, for example, by findings in favor of learning with increasing ratio review in one study by Siegel and Misselt (1984) on computer-based L2 vocabulary instruction. Additional research in this area is needed, however, in order to examine the multitude of different presentation patterns – expanding, equally spaced, or otherwise – that can be considered when it comes to L2 vocabulary learning over different amounts of time (seconds, minutes, days, weeks, and so forth). Nevertheless, researchers such as Landauer and Bjork (1978) advocated the use of expanding rehearsal early on, and it appears that this technique may result in superior L2 vocabulary learning, at least with regard to certain amounts of overall time, as Siegel and Misselt's findings demonstrated.

Summary and implications

The research reviewed in this chapter illustrates the critical role that repetition and presentation pattern play in the development of L2 lexical knowledge over time. From a theoretical perspective, three key observations can be made in light of the research in question:

1. Increased exposure to target L2 vocabulary in the input leads to stronger and more robust developing lexical representations over time. This assertion has been demonstrated in both intentional and incidental contexts of L2 vocabulary learning (see, e.g., Kida, 2010b for one demonstration in an incidental context).
2. Increasing the number of exposures to a target L2 word in the input leads to better L2 word learning than increasing the interval length of each exposure. This assertion was demonstrated in a study comparing interval length and number of repetitions when each target word was allotted 24 seconds of exposure overall: eight 3-second repetitions resulted in more L2 word learning than did four 6-second or two 12-second repetitions, and four 6-second repetitions resulted in more L2 word learning than did two 12-second repetitions. Decreasing the interval length even further should eventually begin to decrease the benefit in this area because at some point the target words will not even be able to be perceived as input (perhaps at 500 milliseconds or less, for example).
3. Spacing the presentation of target L2 vocabulary in the input leads to more learning than does presentation of a massed nature.

Each of these three observations speaks to the critical role of providing learners with sufficient opportunities for lex-IP by having target words appear as lex-INPUT a sufficient number of times and in a manner that makes use of learners' limited overall processing resources in an efficient manner.

From a pedagogical standpoint, findings of research in this area continue to echo what many researchers on human memory have been asserting with regard to many different types of target stimuli over the years, beginning with Ebbinghaus. Target vocabulary should be presented frequently and repeatedly in the input and in a sufficiently spaced manner. Details about the extent to which words should be spaced and whether expanding rehearsal is the best option are somewhat less clear than the importance of multiple repetitions over time, but there is evidence indicating the value of spaced and expanding presentation patterns, at least for certain learning contexts. As is consistent with the research findings in this area, the proposal to *present new words frequently and repeatedly in the input* appears as Principle 2 in the ten principles of input-based incremental (IBI) vocabulary instruction (Appendix A). Although at first glance it may appear to be an obvious recommendation that L2 instructors must already be incorporating in their instruction, oftentimes it is not the case as instructors can forget about the critical role of increased exposure frequency to target vocabulary when their attention may be focused elsewhere, such as on a particular aspect of a communicative activity or a task that learners in the class are attempting to complete. The IBI approach emphasizes the importance of increasing exposure frequency in both intentional and incidental contexts of vocabulary learning and, importantly, without straying from the frequent use of meaning-bearing comprehensible input when presenting target words. In this way the benefits of increased exposure frequency can be attained in a manner that fits seamlessly with an overall focus on meaning, completion of tasks, and focus on content in the L2 classroom.

CHAPTER 11

Effects of semantic versus thematic sets

As spelled out and demonstrated in Chapters 5 and 6, the formal, semantic, and mapping subcomponents of L2 vocabulary learning are largely (if not completely) dissociable and independent from one another when it comes to the effects of increasing one type of processing on the amount of another type of processing and the corresponding learning counterparts of both. As is consistent with the predictions of the TOPRA model, we find that tasks that increase semantically oriented processing can, as a consequence (assuming overall processing demands are sufficiently high), decrease form-oriented processing/learning, mapping-oriented processing/learning, or both. Semantic activation is undoubtedly a necessary part of L2 vocabulary learning, however. In order for a novel word form (in L2 or otherwise) to be mapped onto its basic meaning and the rest of its appropriate semantic space, the semantic representation (or a substantial part thereof) must be activated, which leads to issues about how the activation of the semantic space of different types of words and different types of word groups may affect lex-IP and resultant amounts of L2 word learning. One issue of this nature concerns the extent to which the semantic space of target words being presented as lex-INPUT overlaps. When target words are presented in *semantic sets* or as *semantic clusters*, they are all related in their meanings, as in the case of (a) *eye, nose, ear, mouth,* and *chin* or (b) *cashier, clerk, manager, receptionist, secretary, supervisor,* and *typist* (examples from Gholami & Khezrlou, 2013/2014). What is the effect of presenting target words in semantic sets of this nature?

Arguments in favor of semantic clustering

In their review of pedagogical practices and research related to semantic and thematic clustering, Gholami and Khezrlou (2013/2014) note how the use of semantic sets or semantic clustering (also called, as noted [p. 152], "lexical fields, semantic mapping, semantic clusters, semantic fields, semantic sets, and lexical sets") has a history of being considered an effective technique. Scholars such as Machalias (1991) and Hatch and Brown (1995), for example, have advocated the use of semantic sets under the assumption that the similarity on the semantic front should facilitate the ease with which target words are learned while allowing learners to perceive distinctions between words more clearly. Gholami and Khezrlou (2013/2014, p. 153) summarize how notions about the supposed benefits of using semantic sets are tied to *semantic field theory*, which (at least purportedly):

> ... provides evidence for the efficiency of presenting semantically related sets and leads to the assumption that semantic sets can bring about:
> 1. Common approaches of establishing complex lexical networks (Amer, 1986; Channel, 1988);
> 2. Efficient and fruitful acquisition of words, in which learning of a new word motivates learning of its neighbors (Seal, 1991; Wajnryb, 1987); and
> 3. A means of illustrating the distribution of meaning of related lexical items (Dunbar, 1992; Machalias, 1991).

Gholami and Kherzrlou then go on to provide specific examples of how semantic sets are used so commonly in instructional materials, noting how the use of semantic sets is "a very popular approach" (p. 154).

Arguments against semantic clustering

West (1988), who used the term "catenizing" (chaining) to refer to the semantically oriented chaining of words in this manner, was among the first to oppose this manner of presentation, arguing that semantically oriented groupings of this nature are not a natural frame from a linguistic standpoint as they are not commonly found in the normal course of language learners' experience in their real lives. A very limited amount of existing research at the time (e.g., Schmidt, 1985) appears to have been consistent with West's pedagogically oriented argument based in reasoning about natural tendencies in language acquisition. In subsequent years, however, research findings demonstrating the potentially negative effects of presenting target words in semantic sets (or semantic clusters, semantic groups, etc.) began to accrue (Erten, & Tekin, 2008; Finkbeiner & Nicol, 2003; Tagashira, Kida & Hoshino, 2010; Tinkham, 1993, 1997; Waring, 1997).

Research on semantic and thematic clustering

In a seminal study in this area, Tinkham (1993) demonstrated higher vocabulary learning rates when target words were presented in semantically unrelated groups as compared to when they were presented in semantically related groups. Tinkham (1997) conducted additional experiments in both written and oral modalities and demonstrated, again, negative effects of presenting target words in semantically related groups, in this case when compared to thematically related clusters in both the written and oral modalities. Waring (1997) provided an additional demonstration of the negative effects using Japanese-artificial word pairings. The findings of all three of these pivotal studies are consistent with interference theory and the distinctiveness hypothesis. *Interference theory* posits that words that are very similar to one another share common underlying semantic properties and are therefore more challenging to learn (because of the underlying overlap in semantic properties). According to the *distinctiveness hypothesis* (see Eysenck, 1979), on the other hand, learners are able to encode and retain stimuli that are different from one another better than items that are similar to one another. Both of these theoretical proposals are consistent with the above described early demonstrations of the negative effects of semantic clustering as compared to thematic clustering.

In more recent research, Finkbeiner and Nicol (2003) assessed the impact of using semantically grouped sets by having participants attempt to learn 32 novel L2 names from four semantic categories while grouping items from the categories based on whether they were related or unrelated. The results of the study revealed a semantic interference effect in measures taken at both the encoding and retrieval stages for the translation task in question. In another study, Erten and Tekin (2008) compared two different methods introducing 80 new words to a group of 60 fourth graders. One of the groups was taught the words in either semantically related or semantically unrelated sets. The findings of the study indicated superior learning when using semantically unrelated sets based on measures of both accuracy and test completion times (latency). Finally, in another study, Tagashira, Kida, and Hoshino (2010) again confirmed the negative effects of semantically oriented grouping but did so while also revealing that the degree of the interference-related (negative) effects of semantically oriented grouping depended upon degree of L1 familiarity of the target L2 words in question.

As is often the case, not all studies in this area point in the same direction. In a study by Hippner-Page (2000), third-, fourth-, and fifth-grade students at the same level of instruction in English as a second language were presented with target words in thematically and semantically related groups. The results of the study indicated that both the semantic and thematic groups were beneficial with one group benefitting more from thematic grouping and the other benefitting more from semantic grouping. Among the possible explanations offered for the pattern of effects observed (in light of the negative effects of semantic groupings observed in other studies), Hippner-Page notes that "all words in a group were related under the same theme and not a random, meaningless mixture" (p. 41) and, with regard to the students' pre-existing vocabulary knowledge, that "if a student already knows some of the words in a semantic set, or theme, he was adding to a previous set instead of making a new set" (p. 42). These possibilities, along with other methodological provisions specific to Hippner-Page's study, may help to account for the apparent disparity between the results of this study and those of various previous studies revealing negative effects for semantic as compared to thematic sets.

Lexical networks, semantic relatedness, and lex-IP

Vocabulary acquisition is all about the creation and expansion of lexical networks and the various types of spreading activation that takes place within these networks. Whereas the TOPRA model posits that the formal, semantic, and mapping-oriented components within these networks are largely dissociable and independent, research on the effects of semantic versus thematic sets suggests that extensive focus on one particular set of semantic properties within the semantically oriented network can lead to an overload that increases the possibility of interference within the network and leads to less efficient lex-IP, at least if one is interested in L2 vocabulary gains as measured in the various studies reviewed above. Although the overload and interference in question may remain within the semantically oriented processing system as opposed to, for example, developing form- or mapping-oriented networks, a sufficiently complete and independent semantic representation of a given word needs to be activated in order for the form-meaning mapping process to ensue in an efficient manner. If the semantic space for multiple target words overlap, the mapping process can be impeded as, in essence, there is a better chance of "wires getting crossed" during the mapping process.

What might this phenomenon look like visually? From the perspective of a connectionist simulation, the negative effects of semantic grouping might be represented by a series of single nodes for a particular semantic feature being shared by more than one target word form. In this case, when a learner initiates the mapping process, the overlapping nodes are activated in a short period of time. In this way overall lex-IP, in particular with regard to the activation of sufficiently viable semantic space for each target word form, is slower, leading to less efficient L2 vocabulary learning. Figure 11.1 presents a visual representation of this phenomenon with regard to the amount of space of overlapping nodes within the semantic space of each of three target words that are related semantically. The middle area of the figure depicts semantic feature nodes shared by all three words. The overlapping areas between two words only depict areas in which nodes are shared by two of the three words. Finally, the remaining space for each target word depicts space for which the semantic feature nodes are independent and separate from the semantic feature nodes of the other two words. The more semantically related the words in question, the more the words in question will overlap in their semantic space and the corresponding number of semantic feature nodes that they share. In the visual representation, the three circles would be even closer, overlapping to a greater degree, in such a case.

From this standpoint, the overloading and "tripping" of the developing system/network is due to an incomplete independent activation of all of the nodes in the target semantic representation for the target word in question. It makes sense that this type of overloading and tripping would occur (in this case, within the lexical network on the semantic front) during lex-IP when target words share a high degree of semantic space. The overload in turn leads to less efficient lex-IP (based on less efficient utilization of overall processing resources) when it comes to encoding and consolidating the mapping component of L2 vocabulary learning. The mapping-oriented nodes become overlapped as they "attempt" to connect with the semantic-feature nodes within the overall network.

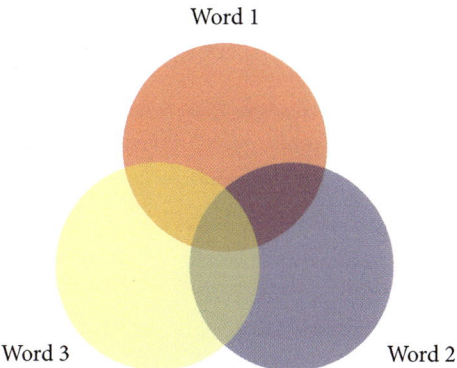

Figure 11.1 Visual depiction of the potential interference-oriented effects of activating semantic feature nodes that overlap in varying degrees (in this case, based on three target words).

Summary and implications

The data reviewed in this chapter remind us, critically, of the distributed nature of lexical knowledge and the distributed nature of all of the subcomponents of lexical knowledge, such as form, meaning, and mapping. The negative effects of semantic clustering on L2 vocabulary learning suggest that within the distributed representation of one subcomponent, in this case the semantic one, input that leads to excessive overlap among nodes that underlie the representation of one particular instance (based on one target lexical item) for one particular subcomponent can lead to less efficient processing and encoding as a particular subcomponent of word knowledge for a given target word is being processed in the input. As such, extant demonstrations of the negative effects of presenting target words in semantic sets also draw into question potential effects of presenting target words in form-oriented sets. Would presenting words in form-oriented sets such as *fine, find, dine, nine, dime, mind, lend, line,* etc. lead to overload and interference? Following what we have described for high degrees of overlap on the semantic front, logic suggests that it might.

Lastly, from an instructional standpoint, research findings on the detrimental effects of presenting target vocabulary in semantic sets suggest that excessive overlap in the activation of different components of lexical space, including the formal, semantic, and mapping-oriented components, can become overloaded by similarity among target words being presented as lex-INPUT. As such, instructors, language program directors, and developers of instructional materials should rethink suppositions about any supposed benefits of presenting target words that are highly similar in this regard. Whereas the use of semantically oriented sets of target words necessarily implies all of the challenges and inefficient engagement of lex-IP outlined in this chapter, the use of thematically oriented sets does not. Therefore, instead of continuing the practice of presenting target vocabulary in semantic sets in L2 textbooks and other instructional materials, target vocabulary should be presented on a thematic basis or on some other basis that does not result in the presentation of sets of target vocabulary within the same semantic field. Change in this area is clearly warranted based on the increasing body of research that continues to reveal examples of the negative effects of grouping target words in semantically oriented sets.

CHAPTER 12

Effects of input enhancement

Input enhancement refers to techniques that cause certain items in the input, such as words or different types of lexical phrases, to stand out so that learners might pay more attention to them. In written input, for example, one may underline, bold, or increase the font size of target vocabulary in a text. In spoken input, one might enunciate certain items more slowly, in higher amplitude, or in some other manner intended to draw attention to these items. Research on input enhancement for L2 grammar acquisition has tested and demonstrated somewhat limited, notwithstanding positive effects for techniques of this nature, including increasing noticing and some accelerated learning for targeted L2 grammatical forms (see Wong, 2005, for a review of these studies on L2 [morpho]syntax). This chapter reviews research on the effects of a wide variety of types of input enhancement on L2 vocabulary learning and, in doing so, analyzes the relationship between the potential attention-drawing properties of these techniques, varying degrees of lex-IP, and vocabulary learning.

What counts as input enhancement for L2 vocabulary learning?

To begin, consider the wide range of possible ways in which one might enhance target vocabulary in the input. Where one draws the line between what can be considered "enhancement" per se to promote L2 vocabulary learning (or to promote grammar learning for that matter) is debatable. One can enhance target vocabulary in written input by underlining, bolding, shadowing, increasing font size, changing font, changing color, or some other type of type of textual manipulation in an attempt to enhance target vocabulary in the written mode. In the spoken mode one could increase the amplitude of target words, slow down when pronouncing target words, or use an exaggerated form of stress when producing target words. As is the case, one can also modify the input itself, but then it becomes questionable whether this type of technique can be considered input "enhancement" only. For example, could provision of explicit grammar rules about a particular target morphosyntactic feature be considered only input "enhancement" when it comes to trying to promote the acquisition of the target structure in question or would that go beyond the confines of what could truly be considered "enhancement"? The decision to enhance a form in this way would fall under what Doughty and

Williams (1998) described as a "proactive" (as opposed to "reactive") stance when it comes to focus on form, that is, "selecting *in advance* an aspect of the target to focus on (also see Doughty & Williams, 1998, for more on what may constitute enhancement with regard to grammar teaching). What about the use of marginal glosses to clarify the meaning of target words in a text? Clearly, this technique would fall under the category of proactive, but should it be considered input enhancement, input modification, or both?

At the end of the day, one alters the physical properties of input when enhancing, such as when changing the print on a page in some way or altering the nature of sound waves in the air, but if one goes further than altering the physical properties of a target item, we enter territory that some might not label as "enhancement" only. In the rest of this chapter we cast a wide net and include techniques such as marginal glosses in our discussion and analysis of the effects or non-effects of different types of spoken and written enhancement. In so doing, it is important to note and reflect upon the extent to which the techniques discussed can appropriately be called "input enhancement" and how the cognitive mechanisms underlying the effects of one technique may differ from another. In the next chapter (Chapter 13), we then zero in on one particular type of input enhancement related to how novel vocabulary is presented in spoken input: *acoustic variability*, or the degree to which target words are varied acoustically based upon sources such as the number of talkers, speaking styles, or speaking rates used to produce the target words. In light of the increasing body of research on acoustic variability, vocabulary learning, and lexical processing, we conclude that chapter by presenting a model of the role of phonetically relevant acoustic variability across the lifespan. The model accounts for a unique pattern of effects of different sources of acoustic variability on (a) the initial stages of the development of lexical representations and (b) speech processing for lexical items at much later stages.

Why might input enhancement lead to better L2 vocabulary learning?

The potential benefits of input enhancement on L2 vocabulary learning may concern, for one, the amount of attention that a learner pays to a particular word. This *attention-drawing potential* of input enhancement may be more pronounced, at least in some circumstances, in contexts of incidental vocabulary learning than in intentional contexts. Whereas in intentional vocabulary learning contexts a learner is already, by definition, paying attention to one or more target words, in incidental contexts, the primary focus of the learner's attention may be on the meaning of the discourse-level input (disc-INPUT) being provided. Barcroft (2009), for example, considered the potential attention-drawing potential of an L1 synonym generation, which is a task that goes beyond input enhancement alone, in both intentional and incidental contexts of L2 vocabulary learning during reading and found that, despite the attention-drawing potential of this task, its *resource-depleting potential* in the semantic direction and away from the form and mapping directions lead to decreased L2 word form learning. This finding does not deny the attention-drawing potential of a semantically oriented task such as synonym generation in incidental contexts of vocabulary learning, however. It simply did not manifest to the degree that the resource-depleting potential of synonym generation did under the particular circumstances of incidental L2 vocabulary learning in the study in question.

Different types of spoken- and written-mode input enhancement can carry attention-drawing potential as well, and this potential may be more utilizable and pronounced in incidental contexts of L2 vocabulary learning. For example, if a learner is reading a text for meaning in a digital format and not instructed to attempt to learn any novel words in the text (an incidental, not intentional context of L2 vocabulary learning), the learner may be more likely to pay attention to a particular word if that word is flashing within the text while all of the other words in the text are not flashing. In this case, the enhancement technique of having the word flash carries attention-drawing potential that may lead to the learner paying more attention to the word in question whereas otherwise it might have been skipped over or not focused on to a sufficient degree. As such, the attention-drawing potential of this enhancement technique may increase the likelihood that the enhanced word will be learned, and the same could hold true for a set of three or four target words flashing within in a digital text.

Relatedly, going back to the attention-drawing potential of the synonym-generation task examined by Barcroft (2009), note that in the partial replication study by Burfoot (2010) no statistically significant negative effect of the synonym-generation task was observed. The lack of statistically significant negative effect in the latter study may have been due to the attention-drawing potential of the synonym-generation task for some reason being more pronounced as compared to the resource-depleting potential of this task in the later study. In other words, both the attention-drawing potential and the resource-depleting potential of the task were present in both studies, but in the later study the attention-drawing potential was greater, cancelling out and making less observable the potential negative effects of the task due to resource depletion. Interestingly, one reason the synonym-generation task in the later study may have involved more attention drawing could be related to what might be considered a particular type of input enhancement in the later study that was not present in the earlier study: *contrasting scripts* at the point at which each target word in the text was translated. In the earlier study, L2 English words were translated to L1 Spanish, which involved using only Roman script whereas in the later study, L2 English words were translated using *hanzi* script. Therefore, the contrasting scripts, which could be viewed as a particular type of input enhancement (textual enhancement in this case) in the later study may have increased overall attention-drawing potential and in this way made the potential negative effects of resource depletion less observable.

A key issue here is the role of distinctiveness in input enhancement. Whereas the presence of parenthetical translations and lines on which to write synonyms in Barcroft's (2009) study could be viewed as a form of textual enhancement that could potentially have drawn attention to the target words, it seems that in Burfoot's (2010) the attention-drawing potential of this same type of textual enhancement was increased by the use of two different types of script. The role of distinctiveness is important when it comes to input enhancement not only in incidental contexts but also in intentional contexts of L2 vocabulary learning, as the findings of a study reported in the next section should elucidate.

In addition to the attention-drawing potential of input enhancement, certain types of enhancement can also affect the quality of developing lexical representations during the initial stages of word learning. Whereas simply paying more attention to a target word can be associated with increases in the overall quantity of lex-IP that takes place for a particular word or set of words, some types of input enhancement also may affect the quality of developing lexical representations. Imagine, for example, a situation in which each time a given word appears in a text it appears in a different font, different font size, and so forth. As the perceptual system of the learner makes adjustments for each variant instance (exemplar) of the word in question, the quality of the developing representation might be influenced, possibly resulting in a qualitatively different formal representation of the word in question when compared to what would have been the case if only one font and one font size had been used. To date, there is little if any direct evidence of such potential differences in the quality of lexical representations after lex-IP for words presented with this type of graphemic variability, but there is strong evidence for it with regard to the effects of acoustic variability, as discussed in detail in the next chapter.

Research on input enhancement and L2 vocabulary learning

Beginning with research on *textual enhancement*, or input enhancement in the written mode by means of techniques such as underlining, **bolding**, writing TARGET WORDS in all capital letters, changing the fonts of *words*, and so forth, in one study, Barcroft (2003a) investigated the role of *distinctiveness*, defined as "the degree to which an item in the input diverges from the form in which other items in the input are presented" (p. 133), as it relates to textual enhancement during intentional L2 vocabulary learning. In the study, English-speaking learners of L2 Spanish were instructed to study lists of 24 new Spanish words. Each target word appeared with its L1 English translation. In the first experiment, one list appeared with 9 of the 24 words enhanced in that they were bolded and appeared in a larger font (enhanced version). Another list appeared with none of the 24 words enhanced (unenhanced version). In a second experiment, one list appeared with only 3 of the 24 words enhanced (enhanced version) in that they were bolded and appeared in larger font in the same way that they were in the first experiment, and again, none of the 24 were enhanced in another list (unenhanced version). Immediate and delayed posttests based L1-to-L2 and L2-to-L1 cued recall were then administered.

The results of Experiment 1 with the less distinctive type of enhancement (9 of 24 items enhanced) indicated no significant effect for enhancement. However, the results of Experiment 2 with the more distinctive type of enhancement (3 out of 24 items enhanced) revealed a positive effect for enhancement. These findings point to the important role of distinctiveness when predicting the potential effects of textual enhancement. It appears that increasing the degree of distinctiveness used when enhancing target words increases the attention-drawing potential of textual enhancement. Interestingly, in the study in question, the benefits of sufficiently distinctive textual enhancement emerged in an intentional context of L2 vocabulary learning. As such, the findings are particularly telling when it comes to the potential benefits of textual enhancement because the participants were clearly already focused on all 24 target words and attempting to learn them. Nevertheless, the three textually enhanced target words in Experiment 2 were enhanced with a sufficient degree of distinctiveness so as to draw learners' attention to these three words and to learn them better when compared to the other 21 words being studied.

In research on textual enhancement in more incidentally oriented contexts of L2 vocabulary learning, numerous studies have demonstrated the benefits of glossing words during reading (see Azari, 2012, for one review). For example, in one study that included a variety of manipulations of text-based factors, Hulstijn, Hollander and Greidanus (1996) found positive effects on vocabulary learning during reading for the following manipulations: (a) increasing the number of times that a word appears in a text; (b) allowing students to use a bilingual dictionary (as compared to a control group); and (c) including definitions of words in marginal glosses (as compared to the dictionary use group). Other studies have compared the effects of different types of multiple-choice glosses. Hulstijn (1992), for example, found multiple-choice glosses to be more effective than single glosses and L1 glosses to be more effective than L2 glosses. Rott, Williams, and Cameron (2002) also demonstrated benefits of multiple-choice over regular glosses. Other research by Goudarzi and Moini (2012) also demonstrated that L1 glossing can increase the incidental learning of collocations during reading. Webb and Boers (2013) found the same effect using target collocations such as *cut corners, lose touch,* and *face the fact.*

Another body of research has focused on different options for text manipulation and multimedia annotations when learners read in digital formats. Folse and Chien (2003, p. 6 on online version) offered the following four points based on a review of early studies (through approximately 2003) in this area:

> (1) picture annotations and video annotations should not be considered together as "visual annotations" but rather should be treated as two separate features; (2) learners have better retention of L2 vocabulary when they have access to multiple simultaneous modes of annotation; (3) video annotations, though certainly more complex than simple pictures, have not been shown to be consistently more effective than simple pictures or even text annotations; and (4) textual clues presented in L1 (i.e., translations) produce better L2 vocabulary learning than textual clues presented in the L2, at least at the lower proficiency levels and possibly at all levels.

Of course more recent research continues to advance our understanding in this area. One more recent study by Chun and Plass (2011) speaks strongly to the potential of certain types of multimedia annotations for increasing incidental vocabulary learning, demonstrating gains of 25% in accuracy on production tests and 77% on recognition tests and confirming that words annotated with pictures + text lead to higher scores as compared to words annotated with video + text or text only. Explaining this benefit of pictures + text over video + text is another story, however, particularly in light of other findings that point in the opposite direction, such as those of Al-Seghayer (2001), who found the use of video clips to be more effective than a still picture. Careful attention needs to be paid to variables such as time spent focusing on a target word, time spent focusing on the video and not the target word form, and so forth, when attempting to account for the effects of different types of multimedia annotations of this nature.

Research on more "traditional" techniques of textual enhancement – the type that do not involve additions to a text (as in the case with glosses in general) or task performance on the part of readers (as in the case of multiple-choice glosses) – is not as convincing when it comes to potentially improving incidental L2 vocabulary learning during reading. Kim (2006), for example, examined the effects of explicit lexical elaboration (each target word followed by *which means* and synonym or a definition) and implicit lexical elaboration (each target word followed by an appositive explanation only) as well as typographical enhancement on the incidental vocabulary learning of 297 Korean learners of L2 English. The typographical enhancement was to present each target word in bold face. The results of the study revealed no benefit for typographical enhancement, even when combined with one of the two types of lexical elaborations. On the other hand, both explicit and implicit lexical elaboration, which involve further modification of a text with focus on target words, improved meaning recognition of target words.

The relationship between input enhancement and lex-IP

There are multiple ways in which enhancing a target word can affect lex-IP and, as a consequence, L2 vocabulary learning. In contexts of incidental L2 vocabulary learning, it may be that the attention-drawing potential of an enhancement technique simply increases the amount of time that a learner focuses on a given word, allowing more time for lex-IP to proceed and in this way positively affecting L2 vocabulary learning. In cases of glossing, which ultimately should perhaps not be considered an input "enhancement" technique per se (given how it involves more extensive alteration of a text), the causal factors go further: a learner is provided with a definition or an opportunity to work with a word meaning to which the learner otherwise might not have had access. As such, the learner is able to map the novel word form onto its meaning, which would not be the case if the learner did not have such ready access to the meaning (single-definition gloss, multiple-choice gloss, or otherwise). In cases in which basic types of textual enhancement facilitate intentional L2 vocabulary learning, as was the case in the study by Barcroft (2003a), the benefits of enhancement may still be due to learners simply spending more time focused on the enhanced words, allowing more time for lex-IP to ensue and in this way positively affecting overall rates (proportional or otherwise) of intentional L2 vocabulary learning.

There are other cases in which input enhancement may affect lex-IP differently, however, and these cases go beyond the benefits of additional time focusing on target word. In such cases, a learner may spend the same amount of time focused on target words in both enhanced and unenhanced conditions, but the enhanced condition affects the quality of lex-IP and, as a consequence, the developing lexical representation for each target word in question. The case of presenting target words in more (as opposed to less) acoustically varied formats is one good example of input enhancement of this nature. As is explained and analyzed in detail in the next chapter, presenting target words in spoken input in phonetically relevant acoustically varied formats seems to produce a more robust or distributed developing lexical representation for the target words in question.

Summary and implications

The research reviewed in this chapter suggests that input enhancement can positively affect L2 vocabulary learning, at least under some circumstances, in both intentional and incidental learning contexts. More extensive alterations of a text, such as providing marginal glosses, picture and text annotations, and so forth, have been found to be effective at promoting incidental vocabulary learning whereas simple typographical enhancements have been found not to have significant effects. As such, our expectations for textual enhancement in the traditional sense, based on techniques such as bolding, should be limited. Nevertheless, the demonstration that sufficiently distinctive forms of textual enhancement (such as when bolding and enlarging only 3 out of 24 target words) can facilitate L2 word learning even in intentional learning contexts speaks to potential of more traditional techniques of input enhancement.

From a theoretical perspective, much of the existing research on input enhancement and L2 vocabulary learning concerns (a) the amount of time one spends focusing on target words, (b) the ability of learners to learn more words when they are given more ready access to the meanings of the words, and most likely in many cases, (c) some combination of both (a) and (b). As such, this research does not say much about the act of lex-IP itself other than what is inherent in (a), (b), and (c). All else being equal, the more time that is allocated for lex-IP of a given word, the more it is processed as lex-INPUT and the better it is learned; and the more one is provided with access to both the form and the meaning of a word, the more easily lex-IP can proceed, in particular with regard to the mapping component of L2 vocabulary learning. There are cases in which input enhancement may lead to qualitatively different developing lexical representations, however. Presenting target words in an acoustically varied manner, which is a prime example of such a case, is discussed at length in the next chapter.

From a pedagogical perspective, research findings in this area have clear and important implications. If instructors, language program directors, and developers of instructional materials want to promote incidental L2 vocabulary during reading, they should include the type of glossing techniques (e.g., multiple-choice glosses) found to be most effective in this area, regardless of whether these techniques should be considered only "input enhancement" (as opposed to something else, such as "text addition" or "other types of text manipulation"). For texts presented in digital formats, annotations that include both text and pictures should help learners to learn target vocabulary as well. Finally, even in contexts of intentional L2 vocabulary learning, textual enhancement techniques such as bolding and enlarging target words may lead to increased vocabulary learning for the enhanced items in question. More research is needed in this area to refine our understanding of exactly which types of enhancement may be most useful in different contexts and for different components of vocabulary learning and to clarify the underlying causes of any benefits observed, but on the whole, the limited amount of research available today on the effects of different types of input enhancement still weighs, overall, on the side of utilizing different input enhancement techniques when presenting target vocabulary.

CHAPTER 13

Effects of acoustically varied input

In addition to the enhancement techniques discussed thus far, another particularly effective method of modifying input concerns the degree to which it is acoustically varied. When presenting spoken input, one can increase the number of talkers, speaking styles, or speaking rates used to produce the input segment in question. Manipulations of this nature increase *acoustic variability*, which refers to any variation(s) in the dimensions of speech that do not alter linguistic content. When presenting a word as input for a total of six repetitions, for example, the degree of acoustic variability is increased when the target word is spoken by three talkers for two repetitions each or six talkers for one repetition each as compared to using a single recording of one talker six times. In this case, the type of acoustic variability that is increased is *talker variability*, but acoustic variability can also be increased if the word in question is spoken in different speaking styles (*speaking style variability*), different speaking rates (*speaking rate variability*), different amplitude levels (*amplitude variability*), and different levels of fundamental frequency (F0) (*F0 variability*). These types of variations in nonlinguistic features correspond to what can be referred to as *indexical*, in contrast to linguistic, features of speech (see, e.g., Abercrombie, 1967).

What is the effect of increased acoustic variability on vocabulary learning? A number of studies conducted within the past decade (Barcroft & Sommers, 2005, 2014b; Sommers & Barcroft, 2007, 2011; Sommers, Barcroft, & Mulqueeny, 2008) have indicated that some but not all sources of acoustic variability produce positive and graded effects on L2 vocabulary and that at least one type of acoustic variability, talker variability, produces positive and graded effects on L1 vocabulary learning. These findings have direct implications for L2 vocabulary instruction (increase acoustic variability using sources such as multiple talkers, multiple speaking styles, and multiple speaking rates when presenting target vocabulary in spoken input) and, from a theoretical standpoint, suggest that appropriately acoustically varied input leads to qualitatively different developing lexical representations than those produced by acoustically consistent input. Not all sources of variability have been found to produce positive effects on vocabulary learning, however. Amplitude variability has been found to produce no effect whereas F0 variability has been found to produce null effects, except for speakers of a tone language (Zapotec in this case) (Barcroft & Sommers, 2014b; Sommers & Barcroft, 2007).

There is a larger and even more interesting story, however, when it comes to the relationship between different sources of acoustic variability, lexical learning, and lexical processing. It begins with research on the effects of different sources of acoustic variability on speech processing in L1 (e.g., Mullenix, Pisoni & Martin, 1989; Sommers & Barcroft, 2006; Sommers, Nygaard & Pisoni, 1994), the findings of which indicate that some but not all sources of variability negatively affect speech processing in L1 as measured by performance on L1 word identification in noise. Interestingly, the same three sources found to negatively affect L1 word identification performance – talker, speaking style, and speaking rate – are the same three sources found to positively affect L2 vocabulary learning (and L1 vocabulary learning, at least in the case of talker) whereas amplitude and F0 variability have been found to produce null effects on both L1 word identification and vocabulary learning. F0 variability is unique in that it has produced null effects on both L1 word identification and null effects on L2 vocabulary learning for English speakers, but it also has been found to produce positive effects on L2 vocabulary learning among speakers of a tone language (Zapotec) while the effect of F0 variability on L1 word identification among speakers of a tone language has yet to be investigated.

Sommers and Barcroft (2007) first accounted for this overall pattern of effects by proposing the *extended phonetic relevance hypothesis* (EPRH), expanding upon what Sommers, Nygaard, and Pisoni (1994) had proposed (the *phonetic relevance hypothesis*) regarding why talker but not amplitude variability negatively affected L1 word identification. Before providing more details about the EPRH and what research findings in this area imply about lex-IP, we first review in more detail research on (a) the effects of different sources of acoustic variability on L1 speech processing (based on L1 word identification performance), (b) the effects of talker variability on learning L2 phonemic contrasts, and (c) the effects of different sources of acoustic variability on vocabulary learning (primarily L2 vocabulary learning but also one study on L1 vocabulary learning). After this review, we summarize the overall pattern of effects of different sources of variability on both vocabulary learning and L1 word identification and present and discuss a model proposed by Barcroft and Sommers (2014a) regarding the effects of phonetically relevant acoustic variability across the lifespan and review the key implications of research in this area for lex-IP.

Acoustic variability and L1 speech processing

Since the 1980s, studies have investigated the effects of different sources of acoustic variability (and in particular, talker variability) on L1 speech processing. A number of these studies have demonstrated negative effects for talker variability based on measures such as L1 vowel perception (Assmann, Nearey & Hogan, 1982), word recognition (Mullennix, Pisoni & Martin, 1989; Ryalls & Pisoni, 1997), and word naming (Mullennix, Pisoni & Martin, 1989). Negative effects of speaking-rate variability on L1 have also been demonstrated by Sommers, Nygaard, and Pisoni (1994) and Sommers and Barcroft (2006), the latter of whom also found (in different experiment) that variability in speaking style produced negative effects on L1 word identification. The speaking styles (or voice types) used in this experiment were normal, excited, denasalized, elongated, child-like, and whispered. All of these were produced by a single talker. In the variability condition, participants were exposed to either all six of these speaking styles when attempting to identify L1 words in noise, and in the variability condition, they were exposed to only one of the speaking styles (each speaking style being rotated across an equal number of participants). Figure 13.1 depicts the results of the study. All of these findings suggest that the sources of acoustic variability in question (talker, speaking rate, speaking style) pose a cost to L1 speech processing, as measured by performance on L1 word identification.

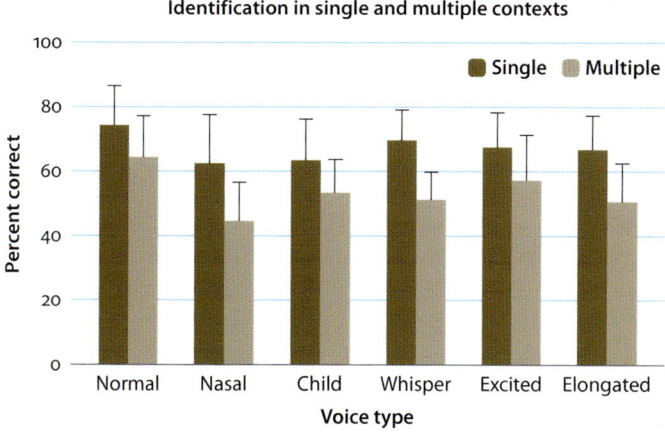

Figure 13.1 Effects of variability in speaking style (voice type) on L1 word identification in noise.

Nonetheless, other sources of acoustic variability have been found to have no effect on L1 word identification. Sommers, Nygaard, and Pisoni (1994), for example, found that variability in amplitude had little or no effect on performance of this task. To explain this finding they proposed the phonetic relevance hypothesis, which posited that only variability in sources that are relevant to phonetic perception will produce the type of cognitive costs that impair L1 word identification. In other words, talker variability had been found to produce negative effects because it was phonetically relevant whereas amplitude variability had been found to produce no negative effect because it was not phonetically relevant. Sommers and Barcroft (2006) provided further evidence for the phonetic relevance hypothesis by demonstrating that F0 variability had no significant effect on the L1 word identification performance of English speakers. Given that F0 is not phonetically relevant for English speakers in the sense that Sommers, Nygaard, and Pisoni had described, the null findings for F0 are consistent with what the researchers had proposed previously.

Acoustic variability and learning L2 phonemic contrasts

Interestingly, in contrast to the negative effects of phonetically relevant sources of variability (such as talker variability) observed for tasks related to L1 speech processing, other research on talker variability has demonstrated that acoustic variability can be useful when training L2 learners on a challenging L2 phonemic contrast. In particular, a number of studies have demonstrated that it is useful when training Japanese speakers to distinguish between the English liquid consonants /r/ and /l/, as in the minimal pair *rake-lake* (Logan, Lively, & Pisoni, 1991; Lively, Logan, Pisoni, 1993; Lively, Pisoni, Yamada, Tokura, et al., 1994; Bradlow, Pisoni, Akahane-Yamada & Tokura, 1997; see also Hardison, 2003). In contrast to negative effects of variability with regard to L1 word identification, these findings suggest that variability may be useful when processing and learning novel L2 forms. More specifically, Logan, Lively, and Pisoni argued that acoustic variability can help L2 learners to develop "stable and robust phonetic categories" and that these phonetic categories "show perceptual constancy across different environments" (p. 876). Clearly, the processes in play when one processes phonetically relevant acoustically varied input containing novel L2 form differs substantially from when one is processing known word forms that were previously acquired in an attempt to identify them.

Acoustic variability and vocabulary learning

The potential benefits of acoustic variability with regard to learning novel L2 forms are even more striking when one considers research on its effects on vocabulary learning. To date, a series of studies have investigated the effects of five sources of acoustic variability – talker, speaking style (voice type), speaking rate, amplitude, and F0 – on L2 vocabulary learning (Barcroft & Sommers, 2005, 2014b; Sommers & Barcroft, 2007) and, for talker variability, on L1 vocabulary learning (Sommers, Barcroft & Mulqueeny, 2008). The findings of these studies indicate that variability in talker, speaking style, or speaking rate produces strong positive effects on vocabulary learning whereas variability in amplitude and F0 do not, at least for English speakers. F0 variability has been found to positively affect L2 vocabulary learning among speakers of a tone language, however (Barcroft & Sommers, 2014b). These findings are consistent with the proposal that input with phonetically relevant acoustic variability leads to more robust developing lexical representations and in this way facilitates vocabulary learning. When combined with previously discussed findings regarding the cognitive costs of attending to phonetically relevant acoustically varied input during L1 speech processing, they are also consistent with a model proposed by Barcroft and Sommers (2014a) regarding the effects of phonetically relevant acoustic variability over extended periods of time. Before discussing these theoretical proposals in more detail, we should first begin to review the existing research on different sources of acoustic variability and vocabulary learning.

To begin, in one study, Barcroft and Sommers (2005) assessed the effects of talker variability and within-speaker voice type variability. Participants in their study were English speakers attempting to learn 24 new words in Spanish. All of the participants were presented with each target word 6 times for the same amount of time. During the learning phase, the participants were exposed to 8 of the words in each of three different learning conditions: no variability, moderate variability, and high variability. In the no-variability conditions, all 6 repetitions of each word was spoken by the same talker or in the same voice type. In the moderate-variability conditions, 2 repetitions of each word were spoken by 3 different talkers or in 3 different voice types. In the high-variability conditions, 1 repetition of each word were spoken by 6 different talkers or in 6 different voice types. The six different voice types used were neutral, nasal, whispered, excited, elongated, and pitch-shifted, all of which were based on the productions of the same speaker (and digital manipulations thereof for some voice types). After the learning phase, the participants were tested on picture-to-Spanish cued recall and Spanish-to-English cued as measures of vocabulary learning. Both their accuracy and latency, or reaction time (in milliseconds), were measured.

When single voice types or single talkers were rotated in the no-variability and moderate-variability conditions (in Experiments 2 and 3), the results revealed positive graded effects for both voice-type and talker variability. Vocabulary learning scores were higher and reaction times were faster with increasing amounts of acoustic variability. Figure 13.2 depicts the accuracy results of Experiment 3 for talker variability. Figure 13.3 depicts the accuracy results of Experiment 2 for within-speaker voice-type variability. The researchers interpreted these findings based on the idea that greater acoustic variability in the input can facilitate L2 vocabulary learning by producing more robust or more distributed representations of the L2 words in the mind.

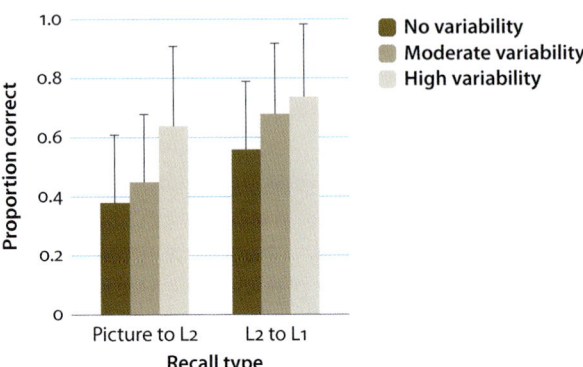

Figure 13.2 Effects of talker variability on L2 vocabulary learning based on picture-to-L2 and L2-to-L1 recall combined (error bars = standard deviations of the mean). Reprinted with permission.

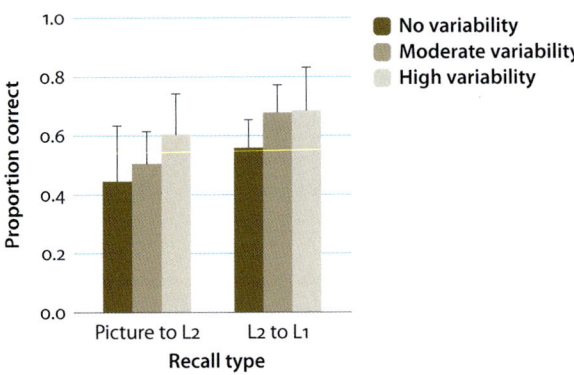

Figure 13.3 Effects of within-speaker voice-type variability on L2 vocabulary learning based on picture-to-L2 and L2-to-L1 recall combined (error bars = standard deviations of the mean). Reprinted with permission.

Figure 13.4 presents a visual model of how acoustically varied input may lead to more robust representations of new words. In terms of instruction, these findings suggest that presenting new L2 words in the voice of multiple talkers or in different voice types of a single talker positively affects our ability to learn new L2 words, at least during the early stages. Six repetitions by the same talker of the identical acoustic variety of a word on the left side of the figure leads to a pronounced but not very distributed representation of the target word form in question. However, in the moderate variability conditions, two repetitions each from three different talkers leads to a more distributed or robust representation, and in the high variability condition, one repetition each from six different talkers leads to an even more distributed or robust representation. In turn, when it comes time to attempt to retrieve a target word form, the additional mental "hooks" associated with the

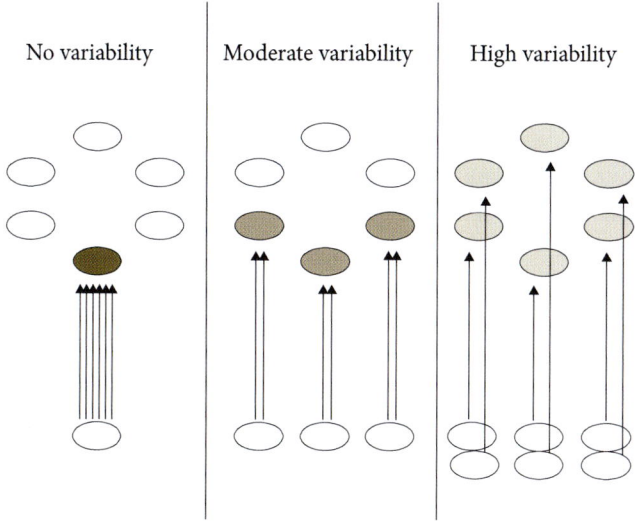

Figure 13.4 Model of acoustically varied input and lexical representation (bottom layer = input; arrows = repetitions of word; top layer = lexical representation). Reprinted with permission.

more robust representations lead to better recall performance. This theoretical proposal is discussed further later in the chapter.

In another study, Sommers and Barcroft (2007) found that acoustic variability based on within-speaker variations speaking rate also produced positive effects on L2 vocabulary learning (again with high variability leading to more learning than both moderate and low and moderate leading to more learning than low) but that acoustic variability based on variations in overall amplitude and acoustic variability based on variations in overall fundamental frequency (F0) had no significant effect on L2 vocabulary learning, at least for the English speakers in the study. These findings suggest that speaking rate is another source of variability that may be manipulated to produce more robust lexical representations and to improve L2 vocabulary learning effectiveness whereas overall amplitude and overall F0 are not. According to the researchers' interpretation, these findings emerged due to how talker, voice type, and speaking rate affect phonetically relevant properties of speech whereas overall amplitude and overall F0 do not, again, at least for the English speakers who were the participants in the study. Based on these findings and previous findings on acoustic variability and speech processing, the researchers proposed that only sources of variability that affect phonetically relevant properties will produce positive effects on vocabulary learning and pose costs to speech processing, which, again, we refer to as the *extended phonetic relevance hypothesis* (EPRH).

Sommers, Barcroft, and Mulqueeny (2008) also investigated whether the benefits of talker variability, one phonetically relevant source of acoustic variability, would extend to a context of L1 vocabulary learning. In this study, adult speakers of English attempted to learn 24 very low frequency concrete nouns in English (e.g., *stummel*, which refers to a particular part of a pipe). The procedures were largely similar to those used by Barcroft and Sommers (2005) (including three levels of talker variability in a within-subject design) except that all of the words were novel L1 (instead of L2 words) and no L2-to-L1 posttest was included. The results of the study demonstrated that, again, talker variability positively affected vocabulary learning. Vocabulary learning scores were highest in the high variability condition and lowest in the low variability condition, suggesting that phonetically relevant acoustic variability plays an important part in lexical development not only in L2 vocabulary learning but in L1 as well.

Before considering a visual model designed to account for the effects of phonetically relevant acoustic variability across the lifetime, let us consider another study that tested the EPRH in a new manner. In this study, Barcroft and Sommers (2014b) tested the EPRH by assessing the effects of overall F0 variability on L2 vocabulary in two groups. (1) The first group was composed of bilingual speakers of Spanish and Zapotec, the second of which is a tone language (that contrasts using not only tonal contours but also pure tones). The second group was composed of Spanish speakers with substantial knowledge of L2 English, but neither Spanish nor English is a tone language. Therefore, F0 should be phonetically relevant at the lexical level for the first group (who spoke Zapotec) but not for those in the second group (who did not speak Zapotec). All of the participants attempted to learn 24 Russian concrete nouns while hearing words and viewing pictures of the referents of the words in each of three levels of F0 variability: (a) no variability, or 1 F0 for 6 repetitions of a word; (b) moderate variability, 3 F0s x 2 repetitions; or (c) high variability, or 6 F0s x 1 repetition. The results of the study revealed that L2 vocabulary learning scores were significantly higher in the high F0 variability than in the moderate and no variability condition (and higher in moderate than in no variability) for speakers of the tone language (Zapotec) only whereas no null effects were observed for F0 in the other group (who did not speak a tone language). These results provide strong evidence in favor of the EPRH given that, as predicted, only the participants for whom F0 was phonetically relevant (at the lexical level) benefitted from the presence of F0 variability in the input.

Summary of research findings in support of EPRH

Table 13.1 summarizes the findings of research on the effects of five different sources of acoustic variability on L1 word identification and L2 word learning. As can be seen clearly in the table, a unique pattern of findings has emerged with regard to the relationship between whether a source of variability is relevant to a group of learners and the impact that it has on L1 word identification and L2 word learning. The pattern is wholly consistent with the EPRH. If a source is phonetically relevant, it produces negative effects (cognitive costs) on L1 word identification and positive effects on L2 word learning. If a source of variability is not phonetically relevant, however, it produces no effect (null effects) on both L1 word identification and L2 word learning. In the case of F0 variability, because this source is not phonetically relevant (at the lexical level) to non-tone language speakers, it produces no effect on both fronts for learners who do not speak a tone language. Because F0 is a phonetically relevant source for tone language speakers, on the other hand, it produces positive effects on L2 word learning for learners who are also tone language speakers. To date, no study has been conducted on the effect of F0 variability on L1 word identification among tone-language speakers, but following the EPRH, the hypothesis would be that F0 variability should result in negative effects on L1 word identification for tone language speakers. Hopefully, a study of this nature can be carried out in the near future in order to provide an additional test of the EPRH. Although we find the results of Barcroft and Sommers (2014b) demonstrating positive effects of F0 variability on L2 vocabulary learning for tone language speakers, an additional study on the effects of F0 variability in this context is definitely warranted.

Table 13.1 Effects of five sources of acoustic variability on L1 word identification and L2 word learning.

Source of variability	Phonetically relevant?	L1 word identification	L2 word learning
Talker	Yes	Negative[1]	Positive[5]
Speaking style	Yes	Negative[2]	Positive[5]
Speaking rate	Yes	Negative[3]	Positive[6]
Amplitude	No	Null[2]	Null[6]
F0 for tone language speakers	Yes	?	Positive[7]
F0 for non-tone language speakers	No	Null[4]	Null[6,7]

[1]Mullennix et al. (1989); [2]Sommers & Barcroft (2006); [3]Sommers, Nygaard & Pisoni (1994); Sommers & Barcroft (2006); [4]Sommers & Barcroft (2006); [5]Barcroft & Sommers (2005); also Sommers, Barcroft, & Mulqueeny, 2008 for talker and L1 vocabulary learning; [6]Sommers & Barcroft (2007); [7]Barcroft & Sommers (2014b).

A visual model of the effects of acoustic variability across the lifespan

Figure 13.5 depicts a visual model proposed by Barcroft and Sommers (2014a) to explain how phonetically relevant acoustic variability produces the pattern of effects we observe in the research findings summarized in Table 13.1. A primary assumption of the model is that the source of variability in question is phonetically relevant to the listeners/language learners who are exposed to it. On the left side of the model (Word Learning), the relative size of the three circles represent the degree to which a word form is distributed (or robust) in the mental lexicon. Referring back to Figure 13.4, less distributed representations result from acoustically consistent input whereas more distributed representations result from acoustically varied input.

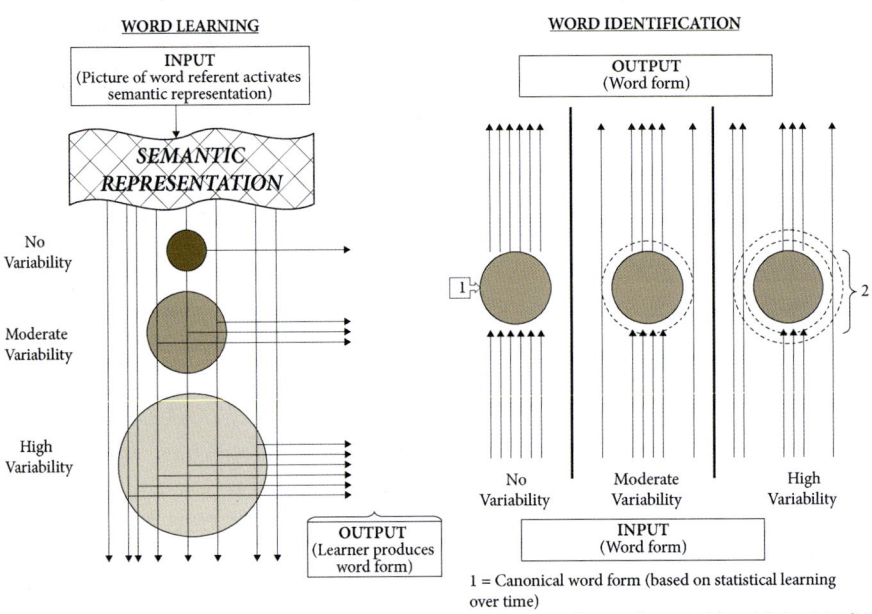

1 = Canonical word form (based on statistical learning over time)
2 = Ongoing reshaping of canonical form (albeit minimal) from new less canonical input in moderate and high variability conditions

Figure 13.5 Model of the effects of phonetically relevant acoustic variability across the lifespan.

With this in mind, what the left side of the model depicts are cognitive procedures during a posttest phase when a participant is viewing a picture of the referent of a target word and attempting to retrieve the target word form for it. In such a situation, the picture activates the semantic representation for the word, which is portrayed by the arrow that goes from the input box to the semantic representation box. Processing then ensues from the semantic representation, which is already distributed, in the direction(s) of the target word form, which is distributed to one degree or another based on how acoustically varied it was when presented in the input. For example, for an L2 learner of Spanish, a picture of a pair of scissors activates the semantic space for that item, which in turn leads to a "search" for the appropriate word form, which is the Spanish word *tijeras*. The multiple (in this case six) lines that stream downward and which are not spread across the semantic box uniformly represent the distributed nature of this search. Looking at the figure, one can see clearly why words learned with more acoustically varied input are more likely to be retrieved. Because they are more distributed, they cast wider nets (in this case depicted by bigger circles), and one of the "search" arrows extending from the semantic space is more likely to come into contact with them. Following the model, a word learned using no variability makes contact only once; a word learned using moderate variability makes contact three times; and a word learned using high variability makes contact six times. Each successful contact is associated with a successful retrieval of the target word form and more successful production of the target word.

The right side of the model, on the other hand, illustrates how phonetically relevant acoustic variability affects word identification and the ongoing development of word form representations in the mental lexicon. It depicts cognitive operations that take place during word identification well after the target word in question was acquired. In this case, the input is pictured on the bottom and output on the top (although the entire model could be inverted and still depict the same operations in question). The three circles (on the right side of the model) represent the spoken form of any previously acquired word. The lines with arrows going upward assume the role of instances in which the target word form in question is spoken as part of the input to which the listener is exposed. When one of these lines makes contact with the solid area of a circle, a word is correctly identified (successful word identification). When one these lines misses the solid area of a circle, a word is not correctly identified (unsuccessful word identification).

Importantly, the degree to which the upward-moving lines are dispersed reflects the extent to which the listener is being exposed to acoustically consistent versus acoustically varied samples of the word in question. The more spread apart the lines, the more acoustically varied the sample. For no variability, the six lines are close together, reflecting lack of acoustic variability in the input, and all six lines make contact with the solid circle, leading to six successful cases of word retrieval and, consequently, word identification. For moderate variability, the six lines are more spread out, reflecting a greater degree of acoustic variability in the input, which leads to making fewer contacts with the solid circle and fewer successful cases of retrieval and word identification. For high variability, the six lines are even more spread out, reflecting an even greater degree of acoustic variability in the input, which leads to making even fewer contacts with the solid circle and fewer successful cases of retrieval and word identification. It is in this way that the model illustrates how progressive increases in phonetically relevant acoustic variability lead to progressively worse word identification performance.

Given that all language users function as language learners as well as they continue to process linguistic input over extended periods of time, the right side of the model also demonstrates how words presented with increased acoustic variability affect the developing canonical representations of word forms, which in the model are represented by three circles with solid centers and dotted-circle exteriors. As listeners are exposed to acoustically varied input that is not consistent with the most central aspects of the current canonical representation of the word form, the inconsistencies are registered and the canonical form can gradually change over time, even if the changes are largely or completely imperceptible based on a limited number of exposures to the acoustically "inconsistent" input. The manner in which the circles in the model can change over time reflects this process. The dotted outer circles reflect the degree to which the exemplar of a word is inconsistent with the current canonical form: the more outer circles, the more inconsistent the exemplar (high variability being the most inconsistent here), the fewer outer circles, the less inconsistent the exemplar with respect to the current canonical form (no variability being the least inconsistent here). The canonical spoken form of a word can evolve over time in this manner, as is often notably reflected in cases of accommodation when a speaker of one variety of a language relocates and comes into contact with another variety of the same language.

Although more fine-grained testable models of this nature are needed, one of the key benefits of the proposed model is that it accounts for the role of acoustic variability in both the development of spoken word form representations and the use and extended development of spoken word form representations over time. It depicts how the processing of indexical features of speech are beneficial during the early stages of word learning by creating more robust developing lexical representations and pose costs well after a spoken word form has been acquired due to inconsistencies between canonical word forms and acoustically varied exemplars to which a listener-learner is exposed.

Acoustic variability, vocabulary learning, and lex-IP

What are the most important theoretical implications of research on acoustic variability and vocabulary with regard to our understanding of lex-IP? Perhaps the most central implication is that language learners do not ignore or discard indexical features of speech when they process novel lexical items as input. To the contrary, they attend to, encode, and retain these features and make use of them to facilitate the retrieval of word forms in an impressive manner. Our current theoretical proposal, which asserts that the processing of phonetically relevant acoustic variability in the input leads to more distributed (or robust) developing lexical representations, is a key observation to be stated with regard to lex-IP.

Additional research may be warranted to assess the proposal further, but to date, the evidence is consistent with it. In a study not discussed thus far, for example, Sommers and Barcroft (2011) provided evidence from several angles that favored the distributed-representation proposals over an alternative proposal favoring increased overall cognitive effort as an account for the benefits of acoustic variability. One of the experiments reported in this study required participants to learn target L2 words produced in a denasalized ("nasal-sounding") voice as compared to normal voice, the former condition being associated with increased overall cognitive effort. The results indicated better vocabulary learning in the normal-voice condition, as is consistent with the proposal of a more distributed developing lexical representation. These results, in addition to other data presented in the study, provide strong support against cognitive effort alone as a viable explanation of the benefits of increased acoustic variability.

Also pertinent to our understanding of lex-IP is the observation that learners only seem to make use of indexical features of speech that are phonetically relevant to them based on their linguistic experience in life up to that point. Acoustic variability based on indexical information related to talker, speaking style, and speaking rate produce substantial vocabulary learning gains, which appears to be due to how these sources of acoustic variability are phonetically relevant across the board. Amplitude, on the other hand, does not seem to be phonetically relevant in any language and has not, at least to date, been found to produce any vocabulary learning gains. Finally, F0 variability has been found to produce no effect on vocabulary learning for speakers of languages in which tone is not contrastive (at least at the word level) and positive effects on vocabulary learning for speakers of at least one language (Zapotec) in which tone is contrastive at the word level.

This last finding is particularly critical when it comes to understanding lex-IP because it suggests that learners process lex-INPUT in different ways based on their own particular linguistic backgrounds. Therefore, lex-IP is not something that all learners engage in starting off with a clean slate. In this case of Zapotec speakers, knowledge of Zapotec, a tone language, oriented them toward attending to and encoding F0 as an indexical feature whereas research indicates that speakers of English and Spanish do not. This type of predisposition based on previous linguistic experience is also an important observation to note and to research further among other observations and assertions that can be made in the study of lex-IP.

Acoustic variability and vocabulary instruction

Finally, when it comes to language instruction, the implications of research on acoustic variability are numerous and, to a large extent, straightforward: *use more talker variability, speaking-style (voice-type) variability, and speaking-rate variability when presenting target vocabulary to learners. Also, for speakers of tone languages, use more F0 or tone variability when presenting target vocabulary to learners.*

Developers of instructional materials, language program directors, course coordinators, and instructors alike all can take advantage of the benefits of these different types of acoustic variability. Those who develop instructional materials, for example, can incorporate appropriate sources of acoustic variability in audio materials used for vocabulary instruction, such as computer-based audio materials. Language program directors and course coordinators can plan different ways of making sure that target vocabulary are presented in acoustically varied formats in order to facilitate vocabulary acquisition, including interacting with developers of course materials and asking that appropriate sources of acoustic variability be incorporated in the materials purchased for different language courses. Lastly, individual instructors can make efforts to take advantage of the benefits of acoustic variability by varying their own speaking styles and speaking rates in a thoughtful manner when presenting target vocabulary in spoken input in the classroom.

UNIT 4

Conclusions and future research

CHAPTER 14

Summary of theoretical and instructional implications

To date, a sizeable body of research has provided information about the nature of lex-IP, its role as one of many different levels of input processing, and a variety of interesting phenomena related to lex-IP. Much of this research was designed to focus specifically on issues related to lex-IP whereas another portion of it has been conducted with a primary focus elsewhere but while still providing data that are useful to our understanding of particular aspects of lex-IP. What we know largely stems from the implications of studies on the effects of different types of tasks (Unit 2) and different ways of presenting vocabulary as input (Unit 3). In this chapter we (a) isolate and discuss central theoretical implications of this research by identifying a series of observations that can be made at this point about lex-IP and vocabulary learning and (b) summarize key pedagogical implications of the same existing body of research. These summaries and analyses are followed by a discussion of future directions for research in the next and final chapter.

Summary of theoretical implications

Beginning with theory, recall that *lexical input processing* (lex-IP) refers to the cognitive processes by which learners allocate processing resources when they are exposed to a new word lexical phrase as input. As such, inquiry about lex-IP inherently crosses the borders of the study of language acquisition and psychology and finds itself situated among the study of other levels of input processing, such as sentence-level input processing, as part of a larger research program on multilevel input processing, which is still in its infancy. As should be clear from the previous chapters in this book, some of the key theoretical developments in the study of lex-IP within the past two decades concern the need to investigate multilevel input processing and to situate lex-IP appropriately within it; the importance of specifying different types of processing related to specific subcomponents of vocabulary learning (form, meaning, mapping) and the relative impact of any one type of processing on other types of processing and their corresponding learning counterparts; the potential for one type of processing (such as semantic) to decrease other types of processing (such as form and mapping) in both intentional and incidental contexts of vocabulary learning; the role of partial word form learning as a natural part of the incremental process of vocabulary learning and patterns that can be observed in partial word form learning; the potential for semantically oriented sets to interfere and detract from successful lex-IP and vocabulary learning; and the potential of different types of input enhancement to increase time dedicated to lex-IP and to affect the quality of developing lexical representations, such as when the presentation of target words in phonetically relevant acoustically varied formats leads to more robust or distributed developing lexical representations during the initial stages of vocabulary learning.

In order to highlight these theoretical developments and others, in the next section we summarize a number of key observations that currently can be made about lex-IP. The observations have been broken down into categories or groups based on issues in the area of research to which they pertain: (1) lex-IP within multilevel input processing; (2) basics about vocabulary learning and lex-IP; (3) specificity in type of processing; (4) processing resource allocation for subcomponents of vocabulary learning; (5) attention-drawing and resource-depleting potential of tasks in incidental contexts; (6) output with versus without access to meaning; (7) partial word form learning; (8) increased and spaced exposure; (9) semantic processing, lex-IP, and vocabulary learning; and (10) input enhancement, lex-IP, and vocabulary learning. Each group of observations constitutes a sub-area of inquiry in which we have observed pivotal theoretical advances related to lex-IP.

Thirty observations about lex-IP and vocabulary learning

The following thirty observations, grouped into ten sets, summarize key points about the nature of lex-IP is and specific phenomena related to lex-IP and L2 vocabulary learning based on theoretical developments and research findings in this area to date.

1. *Lex-IP within multilevel input processing*
    a. Lex-IP is one of many levels of input processing.
    b. Processing resource availability for lex-IP is tied to other levels of IP (and vice versa).
    c. Lex-IP takes place with isolated lexical items or sentence- and discourse-level input.
2. *Basics about vocabulary learning and lex-IP*
    a. Vocabulary learning concerns encoding, storage, and retrieval within mental networks.
    b. Lex-IP and vocabulary learning involve subcomponents: form, meaning, and mapping.
    c. Lex-IP and vocabulary learning occur in both intentional and incidental contexts.

3. *Specificity in type of processing*
   a. Different tasks result in increases and decreases in different types of processing.
   b. Semantic and structural processing are (at least largely) dissociable.
   c. Semantic and mapping-oriented processing are (at least largely) dissociable.
   d. Structural and mapping-oriented processing are (at least largely) dissociable.
4. *Processing resource allocation for subcomponents of vocabulary learning*
   a. Processing for one subcomponent of vocabulary learning exhausts processing resources.
   b. Increased processing for one subcomponent can increase learning for that subcomponent.
   c. Increased processing for one subcomponent can decrease processing/learning for others.
5. *Attention-drawing and resource-depleting potential of tasks in incidental contexts*
   a. Tasks increase different types of processing in incidental contexts.
   b. Tasks have both attention-drawing and resource-depleting potential in these contexts.
   c. Resource depletion from semantic tasks can decrease word form processing and learning.
6. *Output with versus without access to meaning*
   a. Output with and without access to meaning affect lex-IP differently.
   b. Output without access to meaning can detract from lex-IP and vocabulary learning.
   c. Output with access to meaning (retrieval) increases vocabulary learning.
7. *Partial word form learning*
   a. Word forms are processed and learned incrementally in segments.
   b. Word-initial and word-final segments are privileged over word-medial segments.
   c. Word-initial privileging is more pronounced in shorter words than in longer words.
8. *Increased and spaced exposure*
   a. Increased exposure to vocabulary increases lex-IP and vocabulary learning.
   b. Spaced (over massed) exposure to vocabulary increases lex-IP and vocabulary learning.
9. *Semantic processing, lex-IP, and vocabulary learning*
   a. Semantic properties of words are processed and learned incrementally.
   b. Semantic properties learned for L1 words transfer to novel L2 words.
   c. Excessive overlap in the semantic properties can cause interference during lex-IP and vocabulary learning.

10. *Input enhancement (IE), lex-IP, and vocabulary learning*
    a. Sufficiently distinctive IE can increase focus on and processing/learning of vocabulary.
    b. Some types of IE increase focus and time allocated to lex-IP.
    c. Some types of IE (e.g., acoustic variability) affect the quality of lexical representations.

To a large extent, the observations within the first group (*lex-IP within multilevel input processing*) are tied conceptual work presented in Chapter 2 about the nature of linguistic input, different levels of input and input processing, and how processing resource allocation must take place with respect to all of the different levels at which input can be processed. Recall the discussion of how a single sentence or a given segment of discourse provide information at multiple levels of linguistic analysis and some type of executive control, regardless of how distributed in nature it may be, ultimately must allocate processing resources to different levels of input processing, such as phon-IP, lex-IP, morph-IP, syn-IP, prag-IP, and soc-IP. We also viewed specific examples of how processing resource allocation may be divided between lex-IP and syn-IP and among d.morph-IP, i.morph-IP, and syn-IP in different hypothetical situations.

The second group of observations (*basics about vocabulary learning and lex-IP*) concerns issues also discussed in Chapter 2. Beyond these particular three observations, we reviewed where lexical knowledge fits with regard to two distinct systems of human memory (declarative and procedural) and how the meaning of "explicit" instruction differs when it comes to lex-IP and lexical learning as compared to syn-IP and the learning of syntax. The distinct meaning of *intake* for lex-IP refers to the multiple bits and pieces of word form and the multiple bits and pieces of semantic information associated with word forms that is attended to in the input and made available to the developing lexicosemantic system. Additionally, we clarified that lex-IP must take place for lexical learning to occur, regardless of whether it occurs in an intentional or a more incidentally oriented context.

The seven observations that appear in the third group (*specificity in type of processing*) and the fourth group (*processing resource allocation for subcomponents of vocabulary learning*) are tied to the predictions of the TOPRA model, which posits that different types of processing that are (at least largely) dissociable can impact upon one another in predictable ways when overall processing demands are sufficiently high. Increases in semantic processing invoked by a semantic task such as sentence writing or addressing questions about word meaning can decrease available processing resources for other types of processing, such as form processing, mapping-oriented processing, or both, and in this way decrease learning for these other subcomponents of L2 word knowledge. In Chapter 5, we reviewed a study that provided convincing evidence in favor of the predictions of the TOPRA model. It revealed a double dissociation between the effects of a semantic task and a structural task on free recall in a known language versus a new language. For the known language, the semantic task resulted in higher free recall than did the structural task, demonstrating a levels-of-processing effect, whereas in the new language the structural task resulted in higher free recall than did the semantic task, demonstrating an inverse levels-of-processing effect. This pattern of effects is precisely what the TOPRA model predicts.

In Chapter 6 we also reviewed a series of demonstrations of the strong negative impacts that a semantic task like sentence writing can have in intentional contexts of L2 vocabulary, negative effects that can become even more pronounced when word forms (and script) are more dissimilar to word forms in the L1 of the learners in question. Finally, a study in which Japanese learners of L2 English attempted to map secondary meanings of homographs onto previously acquired L2 word forms provided support for the predictions of the TOPRA model from a new angle. The findings of the study indicated that both a semantic task and a structural task decreased learning performance on making the new mappings in question, again demonstrating how increases in processing for one subcomponent of vocabulary (the semantic or structural subcomponent in this case) can decrease processing and learning for another subcomponent (the mapping subcomponent in this case).

Evidence for the fifth group of observations (*attention-drawing and resource-depleting potential of tasks in incidental contexts*) was also presented in Chapter 6 based on studies demonstrating the resource-depleting potential of semantically oriented tasks in incidental contexts of L2 vocabulary learning. On some occasions, however, the attention-drawing potential of a semantic task may make its resource-depleting potential less observable. These two potential effects of a given task in the context of incidental presents a challenge to future research in this area, but the predictions of the TOPRA model with regard to the dissociability of different types of processing for different subcomponents of vocabulary learning in no way disappear simply because one changes from an intentional to an incidental vocabulary learning context.

The sixth group of observations (*output with versus without access to meaning*) concerns the very different impacts of two tasks that at first blush may look very similar. The first is *output without access to meaning*, which refers to output of a parroting nature, whereas the second is *output with access to meaning*, which refers to output that involves retrieval of previously encoded information. In the case of vocabulary learning, examples of output without access to meaning are tasks such as copying target words, copying segments of target words, or choral repetition. As reviewed in Chapter 7, tasks of this nature have not been found to positively affect

L2 word learning and, at least in the case of word copying and fragment writing, can be deleterious. On the other hand, output with access to meaning at the lexical level involves attempting to retrieve target words to which one has been previously exposed. In contrast to findings on output without access to meaning, research on output with access to meaning (retrieval opportunities) has consistently indicated positive effects on L2 vocabulary learning, and, importantly, these positive effects have been demonstrated in both intentional and incidental contexts of L2 vocabulary learning.

The seventh group of observations (*partial word form learning*) is based on studies reviewed in Chapter 9 in which learners were instructed to produce partial word forms for words that they were able to produce completely. These studies indicate that learners produce fragments for many of the target words under such conditions, in fact, more so than they produce complete target word forms. The findings in this area indicated that 1-letter segments were produced more than longer segments, that word-initial segments are privileged in processing with shorter words whereas with longer words privileging of word-final segments becomes more prevalent.

The two observations in the eighth group (*increased and spaced exposure*) are connected to the long history of research on the memorial benefits of increasing the number of exposures to target stimuli and of spacing exposures, instead of massing them, over time. As discussed in Chapter 10, one study demonstrated that the goal of *effectiveness* (amount learned within the same amount of time) is best achieved when it comes to presenting target vocabulary in the input (during intentional learning) by increasing repetitions of target words at the cost of exposure interval, at least to the point of 3-second intervals per word. Other studies demonstrated the *spacing effect* with regard to L2 vocabulary learning, including in one longitudinal study on L2 vocabulary learning that tested retention up to five years after an extensive study phase.

The three observations in the ninth group (*semantic processing, lex-IP, and vocabulary learning*) are based on an area of research initiated in the 1990s on whether vocabulary is best learned in semantically related or semantically unrelated sets. The majority of the research suggests that semantically *unrelated* sets work better due to how large amounts of overlapping semantic information (overlapping nodes in semantic space) can cause interference within lexical networks. A simple visual model of what this type of overlap may look like was presented in Chapter 11.

Finally, the tenth group of observations (*input enhancement, lex-IP, and vocabulary learning*) bear upon research on different types of input enhancement in the written mode (textual enhancement) and in the spoken mode on L2 vocabulary learning, as discussed in Chapter 12. Here the issue of what counts as input "enhancement" becomes pertinent, as a number of studies have demonstrated benefits for providing different types of glosses and multimedia annotations, but these involve text manipulations that go beyond other techniques such as underlining, bolding, or changing the font of target vocabulary that appears in written input. The interpretation of observed benefits for the more simple techniques is that enhancement can cause learners to pay more attention and dedicate more time to enhanced items and in this way increase lex-IP and corresponding amounts of L2 vocabulary learning.

Chapter 13 then reviewed research on the use of acoustically varied input, which has been found to be a particularly effective type of input enhancement when it comes to vocabulary learning. As was pointed out, the phonetic relevance of a source of variability predicts whether or not it will have an effect on vocabulary learning, and when it does, the effect is positive and substantial. Phonetic relevance also predicts whether the same source of variability should pose costs during speech processing, as evidenced by the negative effects of certain sources of variability on word identification performance. At the end of Chapter 13, we also presented a model of how phonetically relevant sources of variability affect developing lexical representations at the initial stages of vocabulary learning and how they affect speech processing and canonical representations of spoken word forms later on.

Summary of instructional implications

On the pedagogical side, theoretical advances and research findings on lex-IP have numerous implications for language instruction. The central implications of research and theoretical developments in this area have been incorporated within the principles of *input-based incremental* (IBI) vocabulary instruction (Barcroft, 2012), which appear in Appendix A. While some of these principles concern logical features to include within an overall approach to L2 vocabulary instruction, the following six principles are the ones that are tied most directly to research findings and theoretical developments related to lex-IP:

- Present new words frequently and repeatedly in the input.
- Use meaning-bearing comprehensible input when presenting new words.
- Present new words in an enhanced manner.
- Limit forced output without access to meaning during the initial stages.
- Limit forced semantic elaboration during the initial stages.
- Progress from less demanding to more demanding activities over time.

Each of these principles is tied to some particular aspect or aspects of the research reviewed and theoretical issues discussed in this book.

Without drawing a series of connections in a belabored manner, let us consider one telling example of how the principles are related to theory and research on lex-IP. Some years ago, the principle *limit forced semantic elaboration during the initial stages* would have been considered highly counter-intuitive given the tendency of so many researchers and instructors to apply ideas about levels of processing, and in particular the benefits of semantically oriented "deeper" processing, to L2 vocabulary learning in an unqualified manner. However, numerous research findings on lex-IP, as reviewed in Chapters 5 and 6, now substantiate that unqualified applications of levels of processing in the realm of L2 vocabulary learning do not work because of the particular nature of L2 words as novel stimuli. Additionally, what previously may have seemed as a counterintuitive principle is now visually depicted by the TOPRA model in a manner in which it should be able to be viewed as intuitive.

Details about how to implement the IBI approach to vocabulary instruction are spelled out and exemplified in fourteen sample lessons in a book by Barcroft (2012). The lessons are designed for upper-level learners of L2 English but can be translated with appropriate modifications to teach vocabulary in any L2. As the name of the approach indicates, it emphasizes the presentation of target words in the input (*input-based*) and the gradual build-up of lexical knowledge and increasingly productive use of target vocabulary (*incremental*) over time. The approach also emphasizes the incorporation of effective vocabulary learning techniques within larger contexts of communicative, task-based, and content-oriented language learning. Increased repetition of target vocabulary can be achieved, for example, while students and instructor are focused on any given communicative task, information-exchange activity, or content. Additionally, when it comes to reading, the approach advocates promoting input-based learning of target vocabulary prior to being exposed to the same vocabulary within a reading, which should in turn increase comprehension of the text in question and increase the likelihood of further incidental vocabulary learning while reading the text for meaning.

CHAPTER 15

Directions for future research

New research is needed on a wide variety of issues related to lex-IP in order to continue to advance our understanding in this area. Whereas most research on lex-IP to date has been behavioral in nature, the inclusion of both behavioral and more neurologically oriented (electrophysiological, neuroimaging, etc.) studies in the future is likely to be of particular benefit when it comes to improving our understanding of the wide range of issues related to lex-IP. In this final chapter we present a list of key issues related to lex-IP that can be addressed by future studies. The list is clearly incomplete, but well-conceived future research in each of these areas should improve our understanding of lex-IP in general, the relationship between lex-IP and other levels of input processing, and connections between different aspects of lex-IP and successful L2 vocabulary learning. The areas of investigation in question are the following: understanding multilevel input processing; quantifying predictions of the TOPRA model; assessing tasks in incidental contexts; advancing our understanding of dissociable types of processing; evaluating different input-retrieval patterns; isolating benefits of input enhancement; and appraising qualitative effects of acoustic variability.

Understanding multilevel input processing

To begin, research on the relationship between different levels of input processing basically does not yet exist in the research literature. While this book has offered conceptual work and basic theoretical premises regarding multilevel input processing, virtually no research has been conducted in this area to date. Among the questions needing to be addressed are the following: How are (limited) processing resources allocated to different levels of input processing, such as lex-IP, d.morph-IP, i.morph-IP, and syn-IP over time? To what extent are (limited) processing resources allocated to one particular level as compared to multiple levels at any given point of time? To what extent are different levels of input processing dissociable? Fully or only partially? If only partially, to what extent? Whereas to date the bulk of research on input processing has focused on i.morph-IP and syn-IP at the sentence level, new behavioral and neurological research on multilevel input processing appears to be an area of new inquiry that is likely to be rich and fruitful although we acknowledge the steep methodological challenges to be addressed in the process.

Quantifying predictions of the TOPRA model

To date, the findings of a number of studies have provided strong support for multiple predictions of the TOPRA model (Barcroft, 2002a) in intentional contexts of L2 vocabulary learning, including demonstrations of strong negative effects of sentence writing (Barcroft, 2004a; Wong & Pyun, 2012) and negative effects of other semantic tasks, such as addressing questions about word meaning (Barcroft, 2003b). In one of the most telling studies to test predictions of the TOPRA model to date, Sommers and Barcroft (2013) found that increased referent token variability, a non-form oriented task, decreased L2 word learning in varying degrees: high referent token variability resulted in less L2 word learning than did moderate and no referent token variability, and moderate token variability resulted in less L2 word learning than did no referent token variability, revealing the graded negative effect of this non-form oriented manner of presenting target words and their corresponding referents in the input.

Future studies in this area can assess the extent to which increases in one type of processing results in decreases in processing in another type of processing (or other types of processing) in a more quantifiable manner. When two or more types of processing are dissociable and overall processing demands are sufficiently high, to what extent can the movement of the internal bars in the TOPRA model predict resultant processing and learning outcomes in a quantifiable manner? In a learning context in which only semantic and structural processing are in play, for example, do proportional increases in one of the two types of processing (based on whatever processing-specific tasks or otherwise are used to invoke the type of processing in question) result in an equally proportional decreases in the other type of processing? Considering the movement of internal bars in the TOPRA model, the predictions of the model would be that increases in one type would result in similarly proportional decreases in the other type of processing (and learning counterpart) in question. As such, one can test the predictions of the TOPRA model in a more quantifiable manner.

If the proportions of increase and decrease do not turn out to be comparable, then one might consider the underlying reasons for the pattern of effects observed. In that case, why do the TOPRA predictions not pan out? Are more than two types of dissociable processing (and learning counterparts) involved? If the proportions of increase and decrease turn out to be comparable, these findings would provide very strong new support for the TOPRA model. To date, the most convincing evidence for the predictions of the TOPRA model in a more specifically quantifiable sense are found in the demonstration of the graded negative effects of referent token variability, a manner of presenting target words as input that increases semantic and non-form oriented processing, on L2 word learning. Clearly, electrophysiological measures and neuroimaging would also be telling in research on this issue.

Assessing tasks in incidental contexts

One of the challenges of assessing the effects of different types of tasks in contexts of incidental L2 vocabulary learning concerns the extent to which we can and cannot isolate the extent to which a given task is invoking a particular type of processing at different points in time during the overall period of time in question, be it during a reading for meaning or some other context of potential incidental vocabulary learning. To date we have considered both the attention-drawing and resource-depleting potential of requiring learners to perform tasks in contexts of potential incidental vocabulary learning during reading, but are there ways of isolating the attention-drawing potential from the resource-depleting potential of a given task?

In particular, it would be useful to find a means of tracking the effects of a semantic task such as synonym generation with regard to different types of processing over time as learners read a text and attend in varying degree to novel words in the text and other aspects of the text. Perhaps the inclusion of some type of input enhancement and the use of eye-tracking as a research methodology could be useful in this regard. One could replicate the study by Barcroft (2009) and the study by Burfoot (2010), for example, in order to assess whether the contrasting scripts in the later study might have constituted a form of input enhancement (textual enhancement in this case) and in this way increased the attention-drawing potential of the synonym-generation task in the later study.

Advancing our understanding of dissociable types of processing

We have reviewed a substantial amount of evidence (in Chapters 5 and 6) suggesting that the formal, semantic, and mapping components of vocabulary learning are at least largely dissociable. This evidence is also consistent with other research on L1 vocabulary learning, including neural evidence. Gupta (2012), for example, discussed and reviewed neural evidence that favors viewing word learning as a "confluence of memory systems," one in which (a) semantic representations are connected to but separate from (b) phonological word form representations (and their corresponding input and output phonology for word form representations) (see Figure 8.2 in Gupta's chapter). This view (of the independence of the phonological and semantic components of word learning) is consistent with what we have seen from research on the TOPRA model regarding the effects of different semantic and structural tasks on intentional L2 word learning (e.g., Barcroft, 2002a) and, in some cases, on incidental L2 word learning (e.g., Kida, 2010). Questions that remain to be addressed, however, are the following: (1) To what extent can presently specified subprocesses in vocabulary learning (formal, semantic, mapping) be broken down further into more fine-grained subprocesses? (2) To what extent are these more fine-grained subprocesses dissociable and independent from other more fine-grained types of processing? (3) If more fine-grained subprocesses are dissociable from another, can increases in more fine-grained Processing Type A lead to decreases in Processing Types B, C, ... and their learning counterparts, as the TOPRA model would predict?

Future research on more fine-grained dissociable subprocesses might involve, for example, distinguishing between (a) processing and learning novel phonemes (such as L2 phonemes that do not exist in a learner's L1) and (b) processing and learning phonemic sequences composed of known phonemes. Might these two subprocesses be dissociable during vocabulary learning? If so, might increases in processing for one of these two subprocesses decrease available processing resources for the other? On the semantic front, might a more fine-grained distinction between learning the denotative versus connotative meanings of words be valid, such as when a child acquiring L1 English gradually learns both the referential and connotative meanings of a word such as *heart*? Might focusing heavily on denotative meanings (how the heart differs from other organs in the body) necessarily restrict possible amounts of concurrent processing and learning of the connotative meanings (ways in which we associate *heart* with affection and love), and vice versa? If this is the case, it would imply that a denotative-meaning-focused task should not be expected to increase connotative-meaning learning, and vice versa. These are just two examples of ways in which to explore the potential dissociability between more fine-grained types of processing as they relate to more fine-grained subcomponents of vocabulary knowledge and continue to make use of the predictions of the TOPRA model for different potentially dissociable (and independent) types of processing and their learning counterparts. Research on some possible dissociations is likely to be more fruitful than research on others when it comes to advancing theory and practice. The theoretical and pedagogical value of identifying different dissociable and potentially competing types of processing depends upon a variety of factors, including how clearly dissociable the types of processing in question do or do not seem to be prior to investigation. While the two examples provided here may seem fairly obvious and intuitive, others may be much less so and therefore of unique potential when it comes to advancing our understanding of the numerous subprocesses involved in vocabulary learning.

Evaluating different input-retrieval patterns

With regard to the positive effects of providing learners with retrieval opportunities, as demonstrated to date in intentional vocabulary learning studies by Royer (1973), McNamara and Healy (1995), and Barcroft (2007a) and in incidental vocabulary learning studies by Barcroft (2013, 2015), future studies in this area might continue to discern what is most effective when it comes to different possible input-retrieval patterns in both intentional and incidental contexts of vocabulary learning. The findings of Barcroft (2013), for example, suggest that simply allowing learners to continue to retrieve target words is not more effective than allowing them to view target words again after retrieval during incidentally oriented vocabulary learning during reading. Future studies that assess a number of other potential input-retrieval patterns in this context could help to advance our understanding substantially in this area, both with regard to theory and instruction.

Isolating benefits of input enhancement

Existing research on the effects of different types of input enhancement on L2 vocabulary learning has yielded somewhat mixed results, at least if we put aside the benefits of different types of glossing and multimedia annotations and the pronounced positive effects of acoustic variability. There are a number of studies that point to the potential of certain types of input enhancement to facilitate noticing and acquisition of target (morpho)syntactic structures, but it would be helpful to isolate further how different possible types of input enhancement affect L2 vocabulary learning. With regard to intentional L2 vocabulary learning, what are the boundaries of what can be considered a sufficiently distinctive form of input enhancement? With regard to incidental L2 vocabulary learning, why have more constrained techniques such as simple bolding of words not lead to increased L2 vocabulary learning? Can enhancement techniques of this nature ever lead to improved learning of target words? If not, why not? A study utilizing eye-tracking might be a useful research methodology in this area as well.

Appraising the qualitative effects of acoustic variability

Finally, although the effects of phonetically relevant acoustic variability may be the most well documented and theoretically accounted for of all of the areas of research discussed in this chapter, both in terms of its effects on developing lexical representations and speech processing, future research in this area can be very informative, particularly if it involves more neurologically oriented measures of the effects of phonetically relevant acoustic variability. Can the qualitative differences brought about by (phonetically relevant) acoustic variability proposed by Barcroft and Sommers (2005) be observed, for example, using more neurologically oriented measures? Relatedly, can the benefits of phonetically relevant types of variability on vocabulary learning and the corresponding costs on speech processing be documented in an electrophysiological or neuroimaging study? If so, future studies on these issues would undoubtedly help to advance our understanding in this area in a decisive manner.

Concluding remarks

The suggestions discussed here regarding future research on lex-IP are, of course, only a small subset of what might be done to advance our understanding of lex-IP and its relationship to vocabulary learning. The centrality of lex-IP as an area of inquiry within the larger study of multilevel input processing should speak for itself. Also, in and of itself, the study of multilevel input processing should be a target for inquiring minds interested in conducting new research in this area. One of the most intriguing aspects of research on lex-IP is that it examines the place at which form meets meaning in language and in memory. As such, new research findings and theoretical developments in this area should continue to be of interest to psychologists, language scientists, language instructors, and anyone else interested in the nature of how we encode and retain form-meaning connections at this fundamental level.

References

Abbs, B., Gupta, P., & Khetarpal, N. (2008). Is overt repetition critical to expressive word learning? The role of overt repetition in word learning with and without semantics. *Applied Psycholinguistics*, 29(4), 627–667. DOI: 10.1017/S0142716408080272

Abercrombie, D. (1967). *Elements of general phonetics*. Chicago, IL: Aldine.

Ahmed, M. O. (1989). Vocabulary learning strategies. In P. Meara (Ed.), *Beyond words*. London: British Association for Applied Linguistics in association with Centre for Information on Language Teaching and Research.

Aitchison, J. (1994). *Words in the mind: An introduction to the mental lexicon*, 2nd edn. Oxford: Blackwell.

Aitchison, J. & Straf, M. (1982). Lexical storage and retrieval: A developing skill? In A. Cutler (Ed.), *Slips of the tongue and language production* (pp. 197–241). Berlin: Mouton de Gruyter.

Al-Seghayer, K. (2001). The effect of multimedia annotation modes on L2 vocabulary acquisition: A comparative study. *Language Learning & Technology*, 5(1), 202–232.

Amer, A. A. (1986). Semantic field theory and vocabulary teaching. *English Teaching Forum*, 24(1), 30–31.

Anderson, J. R. (2000). *Learning and memory: An integrated approach*, 2nd edn. Hoboken, NJ: John Wiley & Sons.

Assmann, P. F., Nearey, T. M., & Hogan, J. (1982). Vowel identification: Orthographic, perceptual, and acoustic aspects, *Journal of the Acoustic Society of America*, 71, 975–989. DOI: 10.1121/1.387579

Atkinson, R. C., & Raugh, M. R. (1975). An application of the mnemonic keyword method to the acquisition of a Russian vocabulary. *Journal of Experimental Psychology: Human Learning and Memory*, 104, 126–133. DOI: 10.1037/0278-7393.1.2.126

Azari, F. (2012). Review of effects of textual glosses on incidental vocabulary learning. *International Journal of Innovative Ideas*, 12(2), 13–24.

Baese-Berk, M. M., & Samuel, A. G. (in press). Listeners beware: Speech production may be bad for learning speech sounds. *Journal of Memory and Language*.

Bahrick, H. P. (1979). Maintenance of knowledge: Questions about memory we forgot to ask. *Journal of Experimental Psychology: General*, 108|(3), 296–308. DOI: 10.1037/0096-3445.108.3.296

Bahrick, H. P., Bahrick, L. E., Bahrick, A. S., & Bahrick, P. E. (1993). Maintenance of foreign language vocabulary and the spacing effect. *Psychological Science*, 4, 316–321. DOI: 10.1111/j.1467-9280.1993.tb00571.x

Barcroft, J. (1998a, October). L2 vocabulary learning: Do sentence writing and oral repetition help? Poster presentation at the *Second Language Research Forum*, Honolulu, Hawai'i.

Barcroft, J. (1998b, April). The Effects of Three Processing Conditions on L2 Vocabulary Learning. *Applied Linguistics Colloquium*, Department of Spanish, Italian and Portuguese, University of Illinois at Urbana-Champaign.

Barcroft, J. (2000a). *The effects of sentence writing as semantic elaboration on the allocation of processing resources and second language lexical acquisition*. Unpublished Doctoral Dissertation, University of Illinois at Urbana-Champaign, Urbana, IL.

Barcroft, J. (2000b). The nature of partial word form learning. Presentation on November 18, 2000 at *Fourth Hispanic Linguistics Symposium*, Bloomington, IN.

Barcroft, J. (2002a). Semantic and structural elaboration in L2 lexical acquisition. *Language Learning*, 52(2), 323–363. DOI: 10.1111/0023-8333.00186

Barcroft, J. (2002b). Strategies and performance on an immediate lexical learning task. Poster presented at the *Second Language Research Forum*, Toronto, Canada, October.

Barcroft, J. (2003a). Distinctiveness and bidirectional effects in input enhancement for vocabulary learning. *Applied Language Learning*, 13, 133–159.

Barcroft, J. (2003b). Effects of questions about word meaning during L2 lexical learning. *The Modern Language Journal*, 87(4), 546–561. DOI: 10.1111/1540-4781.00207

Barcroft, J. (2004a). Effects of sentence writing in L2 lexical acquisition. *Second Language Research*, 20(4), 303–334. DOI: 10.1191/0267658304sr233oa

Barcroft, J. (2004b). Second language vocabulary acquisition: A lexical input processing approach. *Foreign Language Annals*, 37(2), 200–208. DOI: 10.1111/j.1944-9720.2004.tb02193.x

Barcroft, J. (2004c). Theoretical and methodological issues in research on semantic and structural elaboration in lexical acquisition. In B. VanPatten, J. Williams, S. Rott, & M. Overstreet (Eds.), *Form-meaning connections in second language acquisition* (pp. 219–234). Mahwah, NJ: Lawrence Erlbaum Associates.

Barcroft, J. (2005). La enseñanza del vocabulario en español como segunda lengua [Vocabulary instruction in Spanish as a second language]. *Hispania*, 88(3), 568–583. DOI: 10.2307/20063160

Barcroft, J. (2006). Can writing a new word detract from learning it? More negative effects of forced output during vocabulary learning. *Second Language Research*, 22(4), 487–497. DOI: 10.1191/0267658306sr276oa

Barcroft, J. (2007a). Effects of opportunities for word retrieval during second language vocabulary learning. *Language Learning*, 57(1), 35–56. DOI: 10.1111/j.1467-9922.2007.00398.x

Barcroft, J. (2007b). Effects of word and fragment writing during L2 vocabulary learning. *Foreign Language Annals*, 40(4), 713–726. DOI: 10.1111/j.1944-9720.2007.tb02889.x

Barcroft, J. (2008). Second language partial word form learning in the written mode. *Estudios de Lingüística Aplicada*, 47, 53–72.

Barcroft, J. (2009). Effects of synonym generation in incidental and intentional vocabulary learning during second language reading. *TESOL Quarterly*, 43(1), 79–103.

Barcroft, J. (2012). *Input-based incremental vocabulary instruction*. Arlington, VA: TESOL International.

Barcroft, J. (2013). Four input retrieval patterns and incidentally oriented vocabulary learning during reading. Presentation on December 20, 2013 at *Vocab@Vic Conference* at Victoria University of Wellington, New Zealand.

Barcroft, J. (2015). Can Retrieval Opportunities Increase Vocabulary Learning During Reading? *Foreign Language Annals*, 48, 2, 236–249.

Barcroft, J., & Rott, S. (2010). Partial word form learning in the written mode in L2 German and Spanish. *Applied Linguistics*, 31(5), 623–650. DOI: 10.1093/applin/amq017

Barcroft, J., & Sommers, M. S. (2005). Effects of acoustic variability on second language vocabulary learning. *Studies in Second Language Acquisition*, 27(3), 387–414. DOI: 10.1017/S0272263105050175

Barcroft, J., & Sommers. M. (2014a). A theoretical account of the effects of acoustic variability on word learning and speech processing. In V. Torrens & L. Escobar (Eds.), *The processing of lexicon and morphosyntax* (pp. 7–24). Newcastle-upon-Tyne: Cambridge Scholars.

Barcroft, J., & Sommers, M. (2014b). Effects of variability in fundamental frequency on L2 vocabulary learning: A comparison between learners who do and do not speak a tone language. *Studies in Second Language Acquisition*, 36(3), 423–449. DOI: 10.1017/S0272263113000582

Barcroft, J., Sommers, M., & Sunderman, G. (2011). Some costs of fooling Mother Nature: A priming study on the keyword method and the quality of developing L2 lexical representation. In P. Trofimovic & K. McDonough (Eds.), *Applying priming research to L2 learning and teaching: Insights from psycholinguistics* (pp. 49–72). Amsterdam: John Benjamins. DOI: 10.1075/lllt.30.07bar

Basi, R. K., Thomas, M. H., & Wang, A. Y. (1997). Bilingual generation effect: Variations in participant type and list type. *Journal of General Psychology*, 124(2), 216–222. DOI: 10.1080/00221309709595519

Begg, I., & Snider, A. (1987). The generation effect: Evidence for generalized inhibition. *Journal of Experimental Psychology: Learning, Memory, & Cognition*, 13, 553–563. DOI: 10.1037/0278-7393.13.4.553

Bogaards, P. (2001). Lexical units and the learning of foreign language vocabulary learning. *Studies in Second Language Acquisition*, 23(3), 321–343. DOI: 10.1017/S0272263101003011

Bjork, R. R. (1975). Retrieval as a memory modifier. In R. Solso (Ed.), *Information processing and cognition: The Loyola symposium* (pp. 123–144). Hillsdale, NJ: Lawrence Erlbaum Associates.

Bloom, K. C., & Shuell, T. J. (1981). Effects of massed and distributed practice on the learning and retention of second-language vocabulary. *Journal of Educational Research*, 74, 245–248. DOI: 10.1080/00220671.1981.10885317

Bradlow, A. R., Pisoni, D. B, Akahane-Yamada, R., & Tohkura, Y. (1997). Training Japanese listeners to identify English /r/ and /l/: IV. Some effects of perceptual learning on speech production. *Journal of the Acoustical Society of America*, 101, 2299–2310. DOI: 10.1121/1.418276

Brown, R., & McNeill, D. (1966). The "tip of the tongue" phenomenon. *Journal of Verbal Learning and Verbal Behavior*, 8, 325–337. DOI: 10.1016/S0022-5371(66)80040-3

Brown, T., & Perry, F. Jr. (1991). A comparison of three learning strategies for ESL vocabulary acquisition. *TESOL Quarterly*, 25, 655–670. DOI: 10.2307/3587081

Burfoot, S. (2010). Effects of synonym generation on incidental and intentionalL2 vocabulary learning during reading: A replication of Barcroft (2009). Academia.edu: <http://www.academia.edu/669738/The_Effects_of_Synonym_Generation_on_L2_Vocabulary_Recall>

Cassagne, J. M. (1995). *101 Spanish idioms. Understanding Spanish language and culture through popular phrases*. Lincolnwood, IL: Passport Books.

Channell, J. (1988). Psycholinguistic considerations in the study of L2 vocabulary acquisition. In R. Carter & M. McCarthy (Eds.), *Vocabulary and language teaching* (pp. 83–96). London: Longman.

Chen-Chun, C. L. (2013). Partial word knowledge: Insights from an analysis of word learnability. Poster presentation at the *Vocab@Vic Conference* in Wellington, New Zealand, December.

Chun, D., & Plass, J. L. (2011). Effects of multimedia annotations on vocabulary acquisition. *The Modern Language Journal*, 80, 183–198. DOI: 10.1111/j.1540-4781.1996.tb01159.x

Coady, J. (1997). L2 vocabulary acquisition: A synthesis of research. In J. Coady & T. Huckin (Eds.), *Second language vocabulary acquisition* (pp. 273–290). Amsterdam: John Benjamins. DOI: 10.1017/cbo9781139524643.020

Coomber, J. E., Ramstad, D. A., & Sheets, D. R. (1986). Elaboration in vocabulary learning: A comparison of three rehearsal methods. *Research in the Teaching of English*, 20, 281–293.

Craik, F. I. M., & Lockhart, R. S. (1972). Levels of processing: A framework for memory research. *Journal of Verbal Learning and Verbal Behavior*, 11, 671–684. DOI: 10.1016/S0022-5371(72)80001-X

Craik, F. I. M., & Tulving, E. (1975). Depth of processing and the retention of words in episodic memory research. *Journal of Experimental Psychology: General*, 104, 268–294. DOI: 10.1037/0096-3445.104.3.268

Crutcher, R. J., & Healy, A. F. (1989). Cognitive operations and the generation effect. *Journal of Experimental Psychology: Learning Memory, and Cognition*, 15, 669–675. DOI: 10.1037/0278-7393.15.4.669

DeKeyser R., Salaberry, R., Robinson, P., & Harrington, M. (2002). What gets processed in processing instruction? A commentary on Bill VanPatten's "processing instruction: An update". *Language Learning*, 52, 805–823. DOI: 10.1111/1467-9922.00204

Dempster, F. N. (1987). Effects of variable encoding and spaced presentations on vocabulary learning. *Journal of Education Psychology*, 79, 162–170. DOI: 10.1037/0022-0663.79.2.162

Doughty, C., & Williams, J. (1998). Pedagogical choices in focus on form. In C. Doughty & J. Williams (Eds.), *Focus on form in classroom second language acquisition* (pp. 197–202). Cambridge: Cambridge University Press.

Dunbar, S. (1992). Developing vocabulary by integrating language and context. *TESL Canada Journal*, 9(2), 73–79.

Ebbinghaus, H. (1885). *Über das Gedächtnis. Untersuchungen zur experimentellen Psychologie* [Memory: A Contribution to Experimental Psychology] (in German). Trans. Henry A. Ruger & Clara E. Bussenius. Leipzig, Germany: Duncker & Humblot. See also English version online: <http://psychclassics.yorku.ca/Ebbinghaus/index.htm>

Ellis, N. (1994). Vocabulary acquisition: The implicit ins and outs of explicit cognitive mediation. In N. Ellis (Ed.), *Implicit and explicit learning of languages*. San Diego, CA: Academic Press.

Ellis, N., & Beaton, A. (1993). Factors affecting the learning of foreign language vocabulary: Imagery keyword mediators and phonological short-term memory. *Quarterly Journal of Experimental Psychology*, 46A, 533–558. DOI: 10.1080/14640749308401062

Ellis, N., & Beaton, A. (1995). Psycholinguistic determinants of foreign language vocabulary learning. In B. Harley (Ed.), *Lexical issues in language learning* (pp. 107–165). Amsterdam: John Benjamins. DOI: 10.1111/j.1467-1770.1993.tb00627.x

Erten, I. H., & Tekin, M. (2008). Effects on vocabulary acquisition of presenting new words in semantic sets versus semantically unrelated sets. *System: An International Journal of Educational Technology and Applied Linguistics*, 36(3), 407–422. DOI: 10.1016/j.system.2008.02.005

Eysenck, M. W. (1979). Depth, elaboration, and distinctiveness. In S. Laird, I. Cermak, & M. Fergus (Eds.), *Levels of processing in human memory* (pp. 189–215). Hillsdale, NJ: Lawrence Erlbaum Associates.

Finkbeiner, M., & Nicol, J. (2003). Semantic category effects in second language word learning. *Applied Psycholinguistics*, 24, 369–383. DOI: 10.1017/S0142716403000195

Fitzpatrick, T., Barfield, A. (Eds.). (2009). *Lexical processing in second language learners: Papers and perspectives in honour of Paul Meara*. Bristol, UK: Multilingual Matters.

Folse, K. (2006). The effect of type of written exercise on L2 vocabulary retention. *TESOL Quarterly*, 40(2), 273–293. DOI: 10.2307/40264523

Folse, K., & Chien, Y. (2003). Using L2 research on multimedia annotations to evaluate CALL vocabulary materials. *Sunshine State TESOL Journal*, 2, 25–37.

Gass, S. (1997). *Input, interaction, and the second language learner.* Mahwah, NJ: Lawrence Erlbaum Associates.
Gass, S. (1999). Discussion: Incidental vocabulary learning. *Studies in Second Language Acquisition, 21,* 319–333.
Gates, A. I. (1917). Recitation as a factor in memorizing. *Archives of Psychology, 6*(40).
Gardiner, J. M., Craik, F. I., & Bleasdale, F. A. (1973). Retrieval difficulty and subsequent recall. *Memory & Cognition, 1*(3), 213–216. DOI: 10.3758/BF03198098
Gardiner, J. M., & Rowley, J. M. (1984). A generation effect with numbers rather than words. *Memory & Cognition, 12,* 443–445. DOI: 10.3758/BF03198305
Gholami, J., & Khezrlou, S. (2013/2014). Semantic and thematic list learning of Second language vocabulary. *The CATESOL Journal, 25*(1), 151–162.
Glover, J. A. (1989). The "testing" phenomenon: Not gone but nearly forgotten. *Journal of Educational Psychology, 81,* 392–399. DOI: 10.1037/0022-0663.81.3.392
Goudarzi, Z., & Moini, M. R. (2012). The effect of input enhancement of collocations in reading on collocation learning and retention of EFL learners. *International Education Studies, 5*(3), 247–258. <http://dx.doi.org/10.5539/ies.v5n3p247> DOI: 10.5539/ies.v5n3p247
Greene, R. L. (1988). Generation effects in frequency judgment. *Journal of Experimental Psychology: Learning, Memory and Cognition, 14,* 298–304. DOI: 10.1037/0278-7393.14.2.298
Greene, R. L. (1989). Spacing effects in memory: Evidence for a two-process account. *Journal of Experimental Psychology: Learning, Memory, & Cognition, 15,* 371–377. DOI: 10.1037/0278-7393.15.3.371
Greene, R. L. (1992). *Human memory. Paradigms and paradoxes.* Hillsdale, NJ: Lawrence Erlbaum Associates.
Griffith, D. (1976). The attentional demands of mnemonic control processes. *Memory & Cognition, 4,* 103–108. DOI: 10.3758/BF03213261
Gupta, P. (2012). Word learning as the confluence of memory mechanisms: Computational and neural evidence. In M. Faust (Ed.), *The handbook of the neuropsychology of language,* Volume 1 (pp. 146–163). Chichester, England: Wiley-Blackwell. DOI: 10.1002/9781118432501.ch8
Hardison, D. M. (2003). Acquisition of second-language speech: Effects of visual cues, context, and talker variability. *Applied Psycholinguistics, 24,* 495–522. DOI: 10.1017/S0142716403000250
Harrington, M. & Jiang, W. (2013). Focus on the forms: From recognition practice in Chinese vocabulary learning. *Australian Review of Applied Linguistics, 36,* 132–145.
Hatch, E., & Brown, C. (1995). *Vocabulary, semantics, and language education.* Cambridge: Cambridge University Press.
Haynes, M. (1998, March). Word form, attention and vocabulary development through reading. Paper presented at the American Association for Applied Linguistics conference. Seattle, WA.
Hintzman, D. L. (1974). Theoretical implications of the spacing effect. In R. L. Solso (Ed.), *Theories in Cognitive Psychology: The Loyola Symposium* (pp. 77–99). Hillsdale, NJ: Lawrence Erlbaum Associates.
Hintzman, D. L., & Block, R. A. (1971). Repetition and memory: Evidence for a multiple-trace hypothesis. *Journal of Experimental Psychology, 88,* 297–306. DOI: 10.1037/h0030907
Hippner-Page, T. (2000), Semantic clustering versus thematic clustering of English vocabulary words for second language instruction: Which method is more effective? <http://files.eric.ed.gov/fulltext/ED445550.pdf> (23 October, 2014).
Hirshman, E., & Bjork, R. R. (1988). The generation effect: Support for a two-factor theory. *Journal of Experimental Psychology: Learning, Memory & Cognition, 14,* 484–494. DOI: 10.1037/0278-7393.14.3.484

Hogan, R. M., & Kintsch, W. (1971). Different effects of study and test trials on long-term recognition and recall. *Journal of Verbal Learning and Verbal Behavior*, 10, 562–567. DOI: 10.1016/S0022-5371(71)80029-4

Hudson, G. (2000). *Essential introductory linguistics*. Malden, MA: Blackwell.

Hulstijn, J. H. (1992). Retention of inferred and given word meanings: Experiments in incidental learning. In P. J. L. Arnaud & H. Béjoint (Eds.), *Vocabulary and applied linguistics* (pp. 113–125). London: Macmillan.

Hulstijn, J. H., Hollander, M., & Greidanus, T. (1996). Incidental vocabulary learning by advanced foreign language students: The influence of marginal glosses, dictionary use, and recurrence of unknown words. *Modern Language Journal*, 80, 327–339. DOI: 10.1111/j.1540-4781.1996.tb01614.x

Hulstijn, J. H., & Laufer, B. (2001). Some empirical evidence for the involvement load hypothesis in vocabulary acquisition. *Language Learning*, 51, 539–558. DOI: 10.1111/0023-8333.00164

Hyde, T. S., & Jenkins, J. J. (1969). The differential effects of incidental tasks on the organization of recall of a list of highly associated words. *Journal of Experimental Psychology*, 82, 472–481. DOI: 10.1037/h0028372

Johns, E. E., & Swanson, L. G. (1988). The generation effect with nonwords. *Journal of Experimental Psychology: Learning, Memory, and Cognition*, 14(1), 180–190. DOI: 10.1037/0278-7393.14.1.180

Johnson-Laird, P. N., Gibbs, G., & de Mowbray, J. (1978). Meaning, amount of processing, and memory for words. *Memory and Cognition*, 6, 372–375. DOI: 10.3758/BF03197468

Johnson, D. D., & Pearson, P. D. (1978). *Teaching reading vocabulary*. New York, NY: Holt, Rinehart, & Winston.

Johnson, D. D., & Pearson, P. D. (1984). *Teaching reading vocabulary*, 2nd edn. New York, NY: Holt, Rinehart, & Winston.

Kida, S. (2010a). The role of processing-resource allocation in incidental L2 vocabulary learning through reading. *Annual Review of English Language Education in Japan*, 21, 171–180. <http://ci.nii.ac.jp/naid/110008512407>

Kida, S. (2010). The role of quality and quantity of vocabulary processing in incidental L2 vocabulary acquisition through reading. Paper presented on March 7, 2010 at the *Annual Conference of the American Association of Applied Linguistics* in Atlanta, GA.

Kida, S., & Barcroft, J. (2014). Effects of increased semantic and structural processing on mapping meanings onto homographs in L2. Presentation on August 12, 2014 at *International Association of Applied Linguistics World Congress* at Brisbane, Australia.

Kim, Y. (2006). Effects of input elaboration on vocabulary acquisition through reading by Korean learners of English as a foreign language. *TESOL Quarterly*, 40(2), 341–373. DOI: 10.2307/40264526

Kole, J. A. (2007). *The retrieval process in mediated learning: Using priming effects to test the direct access and covert mediation models*. Unpublished Doctoral dissertation, University of Colorado, Boulder.

Kondo, H. (2007). The effects of semantic elaboration on L2 vocabulary learning. *Research Journal of Jin-Ai University*, 6, 71–78.

Krashen, S. (1981). *Second language acquisition and second language learning*. Oxford: Pergamon.

Krashen, S. (1982). *Principles and practice in second language acquisition*. New York NY: Pergamon.

Krashen, S. (1985). *The input hypothesis: Issues and implications*. New York NY: Longman.

Krashen, S. (1989). We acquire vocabulary and spelling by reading: Additional evidence for the input hypothesis. *Modern Language Journal*, 73, 440–464. DOI: 10.1111/j.1540-4781.1989.tb05325.x

Krashen, S. (2008). The comprehension hypothesis extended. In T. Piske & M. Young-Scholten (Eds.), *Input matters in SLA* (pp. 81–94). Bristol, UK: Multilingual Matters.

Kroll, J. F., Michael, E., Tokowicz, N., & Dufour, R. (2002). The development of lexical fluency in a second language. *Second Language Research*, 18, 137–171. DOI: 10.1191/0267658302sr201oa

Kroll, J. F., & Sunderman, G. (2003). Cognitive proceses in second language learners and bilinguals: The development of lexical and conceptual representations. In C. Doughty & M. Long (Eds.), *Handbook of second language acquisition* (pp. 104–129). Cambridge, MA: Blackwell. DOI: 10.1002/9780470756492.ch5

Lakoff, G. (1987). *Women, fire, and dangerous things: What categories reveal about the mind*. Chicago, IL: University of Chicago. DOI: 10.7208/chicago/9780226471013.001.0001

Landauer, T. K., & Bjork, R. A. (1978). Optimum rehearsal patterns and name learning. In Gruneberg, M. M., Morris, P. E., & Sykes, R. N. (Eds.). *Practical aspects of memory* (pp. 625–632). London: Academic Press.

Laufer, B. (1997). The lexical plight in second language reading: Words you don't know, words you think you know, and words you can't guess. In J. Coady & T. Huckin (Eds.), *Second language vocabulary acquisition* (pp. 20–34). Amsterdam: John Benjamins. DOI: 10.1017/cbo9781139524643.004

Laufer, B., & Hulstijn, J. H. (2001). Incidental vocabulary acquisition in a second language: The construct of task-induced involvement. *Applied Linguistics*, 22(1), 1–26. DOI: 10.1093/applin/22.1.1

Leach, L., & Samuel, A. G. (2007). Lexical configuration and lexical engagement: When adults learn new words. *Cognitive Psychology*, 55(4), 306–353. DOI: 10.1016/j.cogpsych.2007.01.001

Lee, J., & Van Patten, B. (2003). *Making communicative language happen*. New York, NY: McGraw Hill.

Lively, S. E., Logan, J. S., & Pisoni, D. B. (1993). Training Japanese listeners to identify English /r/ and /l/: II. The role of phonetic environment and talker variability in learning new perceptual categories. *Journal of the Acoustical Society of America*, 94, 1242–1255. DOI: 10.1121/1.408177

Lively, S. E., Pisoni, D. B., Yamada, R. A., & Tohkura, et al. (1994). Training Japanese listeners to identify English /r/ and /l/: III. Long-term retention of new phonetic categories. *Journal of the Acoustical Society of America*, 96, 2076–2087. DOI: 10.1121/1.410149

Liu, N., & Nation, I. S. P. (1985). Factors affecting guessing in context. *RELC Journal*, 16, 33–42. DOI: 10.1177/003368828501600103

Logan, J. S., Lively, S. E., & Pisoni, D. B. (1991). Training Japanese listeners to identify English /r/ and /l/: A first report. *Journal of the Acoustical Society of America*, 89, 874–886. DOI: 10.1121/1.1894649

Marton, W. (1977). Foreign vocabulary learning as problem number one of foreign language teaching at the advanced level. *Interlanguage Studies Bulletin*, 2, 33–47.

Mastin, L. (2010). Declarative (Explicit) & Procedural (Implicit) Memory. Online: http://www.human-memory.net/types_declarative.html

McCarthy, M. (1990). *Vocabulary*. Oxford: Oxford University Press.

McDaniel, M. A. (1984). The role of elaborative and schema processing in story memory. *Memory and Cognition*, 12, 46–51. DOI: 10.3758/BF03196996

McDaniel, M. A., Waddill, P. J., & Einstein, G. O. (1988). A contextual account of the generation effect: A three-factor theory. *Journal of Memory & Language*, 27, 521–536. DOI: 10.1016/0749-596X(88)90023-X

McElroy, L. A., & Slamecka, N. J. (1982). Memorial consequences of generating nonwords: Implications for semantic-memory interpretations of the generation effect. *Journal of Verbal Learning and Verbal Behavior*, 21, 249–259. DOI: 10.1016/S0022-5371(82)90593-X

McNamara, D. S., & Healy, A. F. (1995a). A procedural explanation of the generation effect: The use of an operand retrieval strategy for multiplication and addition problems. *Journal of Memory and Language*, 43, 652–679. DOI: 10.1006/jmla.2000.2720

McNamara, D. S., & Healy, A. F. (1995b). A generation advantage for multiplication skill training and nonword vocabulary acquisition. In A. F. Healy & L. E. Bourne, Jr. (Eds.), *Learning and memory of knowledge and skills: Durability and specificity* (pp. 132–169). Thousand Oaks, CA: Sage. DOI: 10.4135/9781483326887.n5

Melka, F. (1997). Receptive vs. productive aspects of vocabulary. In N. Schmitt & M. McCarthy (Eds.), *Vocabulary: Description, acquisition, and pedagogy* (pp. 84–102). Cambridge: Cambridge University Press.

Meyer, A., & Bock, K. (1992). The tip-of-the-tongue phenomenon: Blocking or partial activation? *Memory & Cognition*, 20(6), 715–726. DOI: 10.3758/BF03202721

Machalias, R. (1991). Semantic networks in vocabulary teaching and their application in the foreign language classroom. *Journal of the Australian Modern Language Teachers' Association*, 26(3), 19–24.

Michnick Golinkoff, R., & Hirsh-Pasek, K. (2000). Word learning: Icon, index, or symbol? In R. Michnick Golinkoff, K. Hirsh-Pasek, L. Bloom, L. B. Smith, A. L. Woodward, N. Akhtar, M. Tomasello, & G. Hollich, *Becoming a word learner: A debate on lexical acquisition*. Oxford: Oxford University Press. DOI: 10.1093/acprof:oso/9780195130324.001.0001

Miozzo, M., Costa, A., Hernandez, M., & Rapp, B. (2010), Lexical processing in the bilingual brain: Evidence from grammatical/morphological deficits. *Aphasiology*, 24(2), 262–287. DOI: 10.1080/02687030902958381

Morris, C. D., Bransford, J. D., & Franks, J. J. (1977). Levels of processing versus transfer appropriate processing. *Journal of Verbal Learning and Verbal Behavior*, 16, 519–533. DOI: 10.1016/S0022-5371(77)80016-9

Mullennix, J. W., Pisoni, D. B., & Martin, C. S. (1989). Some effects of talker variability on spoken word recognition. *Journal of the Acoustical Society of America*, 85, 365–378. DOI: 10.1121/1.397688

Nagy, W. (1997). On the role of context in first- and second-language vocabulary learning. In N. Schmitt & M. McCarthy (Eds.), *Vocabulary: Description, acquisition, and pedagogy* (pp. 64–83). Cambridge: Cambridge University Press.

Nagy, W., Anderson, R., & Herman, P. (1987). Learning words from context during normal reading. *American Research Journal*, 24, 237–270.

Nagy, W., Herman, P., & Anderson, R. (1985) Learning words from context. *Reading Research Quarterly*, 20, 233–253. DOI: 10.2307/747758

Nairne, J. S., & Widner, R. L. Jr. (1988). Familiarity and lexicality as determinants of the generation effect. *Journal of Experimental Psychology: Learning Memory, and Cognition*, 14, 694–699. DOI: 10.1037/0278-7393.14.4.694

Nation, I. S. P. (2001). *Learning vocabulary in another language*. Cambridge: Cambridge University Press. DOI: 10.1017/CBO9781139524759

Nation, I. S. P., & Waring. (1997). Vocabulary size, text coverage and word lists. In N. Schmitt & M. McCarthy (Eds.), *Vocabulary: Description, acquisition and pedagogy* (pp. 238–254). Cambridge: Cambridge University Press.

Neumann, O. (1996). Theories of attention. In O. Neumann, & A. F. Sanders (Eds.), *Handbook of perception and action* (pp. 389 – 446). San Diego, CA: Academic Press.

O'Neill, W., Roy, L., & Tremblay, R. (1993). A translation-based generation effect in bilingual recall and recognition. *Memory & Cognition*, 21(4), 488–495. DOI: 10.3758/BF03197180

Paribakht, T. S., & Wesche, M. (1997). Vocabulary enhancement activities and reading for meaning in second language vocabulary acquisition. In J. Coady & T. Huckin (Eds.), *Second language vocabulary acquisition* (pp. 174–200). Amsterdam: John Benjamins. DOI: 10.1017/cbo9781139524643.013

Paribakht, T. S., & Wesche, M. (1999). Reading and "incidental" L2 vocabulary acquisition: An introspective study of lexical inferencing. *Studies in Second Language Acquisition*, 21(2), 195–24. DOI: 10.1017/S027226319900203X

Payne, D. G., Neely, J. H., & Burns, D. J. (1986). The generation effect: Further tests of the lexical activation hypothesis. *Memory & Cognition*, 14, 246–252. DOI: 10.3758/BF03197700

Peters, A. M. (1985). Language segmentation: Operating principles for the perception and analysis of language. In D. I. Slobin, *The cross-linguistic study of language acquisition, Vol. 2: Theoretical issues* (pp. 1029–1067). Hillsdale, NJ: Lawrence Erlbaum Associates.

Poeppel, D., & Embick, D. (2005). Defining the relation between linguistics and neuroscience. In Cultler, A. (Ed.). *Twenty-first century psychologinguistics: Four cornerstones* (pp. 103–120). Mahwah, NJ: Lawrence Erlbaum Associates.

Potter, M., So, K., Von Eckardt, B., & Feldman, L. (1984). Lexical and conceptual representation in beginning and proficient bilinguals. *Journal of Verbal Learning and Verbal Behavior*, 23, 23–38. DOI: 10.1016/S0022-5371(84)90489-4

Prince, P. (1996). Second language vocabulary learning: The role of context versus translations as a function of proficiency. *The Modern Language Journal*, 80, 478–493. DOI: 10.1111/j.1540-4781.1996.tb05468.x

Pulido, D. (2003). Modeling of the role of second language proficiency and topic familiarity in L2 incidental vocabulary acquisition through reading. *Language Learning*, 53, 233–284. DOI: 10.1111/1467-9922.00217

Robinson, P. (2008). Attention and Memory during SLA. In C. J. Doughty, & M. H. Long (Eds.), *The handbook of second language acquisition*. Oxford: Blackwell.

Roediger, R. (2009). The critical role of retrieval in enhancing long-term memory: From the laboratory to the classroom. Keynote Address on November 19, 2009 at the *50th Annual Meeting of the Psychonomic Society*, Boston, MA. <http://www.psychonomic.org/meetingvids.html>

Roediger, H. L., & Guynn, M. J. (1996). Retrieval processes. In E. L. Bjork & R. A. Bjork (Eds.), *Memory* (pp. 197–236). San Diego, CA: Academic Press. DOI: 10.1016/B978-012102570-0/50009-4

Rott, S. (1999). The effect of exposure frequency on intermediate language learners' incidental vocabulary acquisition and retention through reading. *Studies in Second Language Acquisition*, 21, 589–619. DOI: 10.1017/S0272263199004039

Rott, S. (2007). The effect of frequency of input-enhancements on word learning and text comprehension. *Language Learning*, 57(2), 165–19. DOI: 10.1111/j.1467-9922.2007.00406.x

Rott, S., Williams, J., & Cameron, R. (2002). The effect of multiple-choice L1 glosses and input-output cycles on lexical acquisition and retention. *Language Teaching Research*, 6(3), 183–222. DOI: 10.1191/1362168802lr108oa

Royer, J. M. (1973). Memory effects for test-like events during acquisition of foreign language vocabulary. *Psychological Reports*, 32, 195–198. DOI: 10.2466/pr0.1973.32.1.195

Ryalls, B. O., & Pisoni, D. B. (1997). The effect of talker variability on word recognition in preschool children. *Developmental Psychology*, 33(3), 441–452. DOI: 10.1037/0012-1649.33.3.441

Sagarra, N., & Alba, M. (2006). The key is in the keyword: L2 vocabulary learning methods with beginning learners of Spanish. *Modern Language Journal*, 90, 228–243. DOI: 10.1111/j.1540-4781.2006.00394.x

San Mateo Valdehíta, A. (2013). El efecto de tres actividades centradas en las formas [Focus on forms, fonfs]: La selección de definiciones, la selección de ejemplos y la escritura de oraciones, en el aprendizaje de vocabulario de segundas lenguas. *Revista Electrónica de Lingüística Aplicada*, 12, 17–36.

Schulman, A. I. (1971). Recognition memory for targets from a scanned word list. *British Journal of Psychology*, 62, 335–346. DOI: 10.1111/j.2044-8295.1971.tb02044.x

Schmidt, S. R. (1985). Encoding and retrieval processes in the memory for conceptually distinctive events. *Journal of Experimental Psychology: Learning Memory and Cognition*, 11, 565–578. DOI: 10.1037/0278-7393.11.3.565

Schmidt, S. R. (1990). A test of resource-allocation explanations of the generation effect. *Bulletin of the Psychonomic Society*, 28, 2, 93–96. DOI: 10.3758/BF03337658

Schmidt, S. R., & Cherry, K. (1989). The negative generation effect: Delineation of a phenomenon. *Memory & Cognition*, 17, 359–369. DOI: 10.3758/BF03198475

Schmitt, N. (1997). Vocabulary learning strategies. In N. Schmitt & M. McCarthy (Eds.), *Vocabulary: Description, acquisition, and pedagogy* (pp. 199–227). Cambridge: Cambridge University Press.

Seal, B. D. (1991). Vocabulary learning and teaching. In M. Celce-Murcia (Ed.), *Teaching English as a second or foreign language* (pp. 296–311). Boston, MA: Heinle & Heinle.

Seibert, L. (1927). An experiment in learning French vocabulary. *The Journal of Educational Psychology*. 18, 5, 294–309. DOI: 10.1037/h0074206

Siegel, M., & Misselt, A. (1984). Adaptive feedback and review paradigm for computer-based drills. *Journal of Educational Psychology*, 75(2), 310–317. DOI: 10.1037/0022-0663.76.2.310

Slamecka, N. J., & Fevreiski, J. (1983). The generation effect when generation fails. *Journal of Verbal Learning and Verbal Behavior*, 22, 153–163. DOI: 10.1016/S0022-5371(83)90112-3

Slamecka, N. J., & Graf, P. (1978). The generation effect: Delineation of a phenomenon. *Journal of Experimental Psychology*, 4(6), 592–604.

Slamecka, N. J., & Katsaiti, L. T. (1987). The generation as an artifact of selective displaced rehearsal. *Journal of Memory & Language*, 26, 589–607. DOI: 10.1016/0749-596X(87)90104-5

Smith, R. W., & Healy, A. F. (1998). The time-course of the generation effect. *Memory & Cognition*, 26(1), 135–142. DOI: 10.3758/BF03211376

Sommers, M. S., & Barcroft, J. (2006). Stimulus variability and the phonetic relevance hypothesis: Effects of variability in speaking style, fundamental frequency, and speaking rate on spoken word identification. *Journal of the American Acoustical Society* 119(4), 2406–2416. DOI: 10.1121/1.2171836

Sommers, M., & Barcroft, J. (2007). An integrated account of the effects of acoustic variability in L1 and L2: Evidence from amplitude, fundamental frequency, and speaking rate variability. *Applied Psycholinguistics*, 28(2), 231–249. DOI: 10.1017/S0142716407070129

Sommers, M., & Barcroft, J. (2011). Indexical information. Encoding difficulty, and second language vocabulary learning. *Applied Psycholinguistics*, 32(2), 417–434. DOI: 10.1017/S0142716410000469

Sommers, M., & Barcroft, J. (2013). Effects of referent token variability on L2 vocabulary learning. *Language Learning*, 63(2), 186–210.
Sommers, M. S., Barcroft, J., & Mulqueeny, K. (2008). Further studies of acoustic variability and vocabulary. Paper presented at the *49th Annual Meeting of the Psychonomic Society*, Chicago, November.
Sommers, M. S., Nygaard, L. C., & Pisoni, D. B. (1994). Stimulus variability and spoken word recognition. I. Effects of variability in speaking rate and overall amplitude. *Journal of the Acoustical Society of America*, 96, 1314–1324. DOI: 10.1121/1.411453
Stahl, S., & Fairbanks, M. (1986). The effects of vocabulary instruction: A model-based meta-analysis. *Review of Educational Research*, 56, 72–110. DOI: 10.3102/00346543056001072
Stevenson, R. J. (1981). Depth of comprehension, effective elaboration, and memory for sentences. *Memory & Cognition*, 9, 169–176. DOI: 10.3758/BF03202332
Tagashira, K., Kida, S., & Hoshino, Y. (2010). Hot or gelid? The influence of L1 translation familiarity on the interference effects in foreign language vocabulary learning. *System*, 38(3), 412–421. DOI: 10.1016/j.system.2010.03.015
Thomas, M., & Dieter, J. N. (1987). The positive effects of writing practice on integration of foreign words in memory. *Journal of Educational Psychology*, 79(3), 249–253. DOI: 10.1037/0022-0663.79.3.249
Thompson, C. P., & Barnett, C. (1981). *Bulletin of the Psychonomic Society*, 18(5), 241–243. DOI: 10.3758/BF03333615
Tinkham, T. (1993). The effect of semantic clustering on the learning of second language vocabulary. *System*, 21(3), 371–380. DOI: 10.1016/0346-251X(93)90027-E
Tinkham, T. (1997). The effects of semantic and thematic clustering on the learning of second language vocabulary learning. *Second Language Research*, 13(2), 138–163. DOI: 10.1191/026765897672376469
Tresselt, M. E., & Mayzner, M. S. (1960). A study of incidental learning. *Journal of Psychology*, 50, 339–347. DOI: 10.1080/00223980.1960.9916451
Tulving, E. (1967). The effects of presentation and recall in free recall learning. *Journal of Verbal Learning and Verbal Behavior*, 6, 175–184. DOI: 10.1016/S0022-5371(67)80092-6
van Hell, J. G., & Mahn, A. C. (1997). Keyword mnemonics versus rote rehearsal: Learning concrete and abstract foreign words by experienced and inexperienced learners. *Language Learning*, 47, 3, 507–546. DOI: 10.1111/0023-8333.00018
Ullman, M. T. (2001). A neurocognitive perspective on language: The declarative/procedural model. *Nature Review Neuroscience*, 2, 717–726. DOI: 10.1038/35094573
Ullman, M. T. (2004). Contributions of memory circuits to language: The declarative/procedural model. *Cognition*, 92, 231–270. DOI: 10.1016/j.cognition.2003.10.008
Ullman, M. T. (2005). A cognitive neuroscience perspective on second language acquisition: The declarative/procedural model. In C. Sanz (ed), *Mind in context in adult second language acquisition: Methods, theory, and practice* (pp. 141–178). Washington, DC: Georgetown University Press.
VanPatten, B. (1996). *Input processing and grammar instruction: Theory and research*. Norwood, NJ: Ablex.
VanPatten, B. (2003). *From input to output: A teacher's guide to second language acquisition*. Boston, MA: McGraw-Hill.
Wajnryb, R. (1987). Vocabulary – consolidation through clusters. *English Teachers Journal*, 35, 67–70.

Wang, A. & Thomas, M. (1995). The effect of imagery-based mnemonics on the long-term retention of Chinese characters. In B. Harley (Ed.), *Lexical issues in language learning* (pp. 167–183). Amsterdam: John Benjamins.

Waring, Robert. (1997). *The negative effects of learning words in semantic sets: A replication. System*, 25(2), 261–274. DOI: 10.1016/S0346-251X(97)00013-4

Webb, S., & Boers, F. (2013). Do textual enhancement techniques increase incidental learning of collocation? Presentation on December 19, 2013 at *Vocab@Vic Conference* at Victoria University of Wellington, New Zealand.

Wesche, M., & Paribakht, T. S. (1999). Introduction. *Studies in Second Language Acquisition*, 21, 175–180. DOI: 10.1017/S0272263199002016

West, M. (1988). Catenizing. *ELT Journal*, 6, 147–151.

Wheeler, M. A., & Roediger, H. L. (1992). Disparate effects of repeated testing: Reconciling Ballard's (1913) and Bartlett's (1932) results. *Psychological Science*, 3, 240–245. DOI: 10.1111/j.1467-9280.1992.tb00036.x

Wickens, C. D. (1984). Processing resources in attention. In R. Parasuraman & D. Davies (Eds.), *Varieties of Attention* (pp. 63–102). New York NY: Academic Press.

Wickens, C. D. (1989). Attention and skilled performance. In D. Holding (Ed.), *Human Skills* (pp. 71–105). New York, NY: John Wiley & Sons.

Wong. W. (2005). *Input enhancement: From theory and research to the classroom*. New York, NY: McGraw-Hill.

Wong, W. & Barcroft, J. (2012). Repetez s'il vous plait, or not?: Choral repetition and L2 vocabulary learning. Presentation at on July 12, 2012 at *11th International Conference of the Association for Language Awareness* at Concordia University, Montreal.

Wong, W., & Pyun, D. O. (2012). The effects of sentence writing on L2 French and Korean lexical acquisition. *Canadian Modern Language Review*, 68, 164–189. DOI: 10.3138/cmlr.68.2.164

Appendix A

Ten principles of input-based incremental (IBI) vocabulary instruction

1. Develop and implement a vocabulary acquisition plan.
2. Present new words frequently and repeatedly in the input.
3. Promote both intentional and incidental vocabulary learning.
4. Use meaning-bearing comprehensible input when presenting new words.
5. Present new words in an enhanced manner.
6. Limit forced output without access to meaning during the initial stages.
7. Limit forced semantic elaboration during the initial stages.
8. Promote learning L2-specific word meanings and usage over time.
9. Progress from less demanding to more demanding activities over time.
10. Apply research findings with direct implications for vocabulary instruction.

Appendix B

Experimental words from Barcroft and Rott (2010) categorized according to language (German and Spanish), number of syllables (three and four) and number of letters

	Letters	German	Spanish
Two-syllable words	5	Kröte (frog)	borla (tassel)
	5	Erbse (pea)	balde (bucket)
	5	Ziege (goat)	pinza (clothespin)
	5	Kelle (soup spoon)	trompo (spinning top)
	5	Eimer (bucket)	naipe (playing card)
	5	Nelke (carnation)	gaita (bagpipe)
	6	Wurzel (root)	flecha (arrow)
	6	Felsen (rock)	gancho (hook)
	6	Büchse (can)	clavel (carnation)
	6	Glocke (bell)	choclo (corn)
	6	Quaste (tassel)	tuerca (nut)
	7	Rutsche (slide)	plancha (iron)
Three-syllable words	6	Kasuar (ostrich)	arroyo (stream)
	7	Matrose (sailor)	colibrí (hummingbird)
	7	Gebäude (building)	taladro (drill)
	7	Bulette (hamburger)	gorrión (sparrow)
	7	Gebirge (mountains)	volante (steering wheel)
	7	Kolibri (hummingbird)	tenazas (pliers)
	7	Gemälde (painting)	candado (lock)
	7	Perücke (wig)	clavija (plug)
	7	Patrone (cartridge)	serrote (saw)
	7	Forelle (trout)	toronja (grapefruit)
	8	Radierer (eraser)	chiringa (kite)
	9	Bedienung (waiter)	churrusco (caterpillar)

Index

A
acoustic variability 149–153, 155–162, 177
allomorphs 30
attention-drawing hypothesis 69, 83
attention-drawing potential 89–90, 140–143, 169

B
bathtub effect 119–122
bilingual mental lexicon 49
bound morphemes 30

C
choral repetition 96–98
collocational properties 32
collocations 32, 144
concept 33, 39–41
conceptual/semantic representations 33–34
conceptual/semantic space 22, 37
controlled presentation patterns 51
cued recall 65

D
declarative memory 18–19
Declarative-Procedural model 19
degree of partial word form learning 118
developing lexical system 23
direct instruction 25, 48
distinctiveness hypothesis 135
double dissociation 66

E
expanding rehearsal 129–130
extended phonetic relevance hypothesis 155

F
focused attention 51–53
free morphemes 30
free recall 65

G
generation effect 104–108

I
idiolect 33
incidental vocabulary learning 25–27
inferring word meanings 53
input enhancement 46–47, 139–142
input processing 1–2
input-based incremental (IBI) vocabulary instruction 171–172
input 1–2, 11–13
intake 1–2, 13–14, 23–24
intentional vocabulary learning 25–27, 39–40
interference theory 134–135
inverse levels-of-processing effect 66
involvement load hypothesis 87–88

K
Keyword method 47, 81–82

L
L2-specific meanings 37, 40–41
learning burden 41
lemma 30
lexeme 30
lexical phrases 11
lexical processing 43–44
lexical units 34
lexical-level bootstrapping 35

M
meaning-bearing input 11, 26
morphemes 30
morphosyntactic properties 31–32
multilevel input processing 12–13, 15–21

O
onomatopoeia 30
output with access to meaning 93–94
output without access to meaning 93–94

P
partial word form learning 115–118
phonemes 30
prefixes 30
procedural memory 18–19
processing resource allocation 58–59

R
receptive versus productive knowledge 50
recliner effect 121–123
referent token variability 70–71, 79–80
resource-depleting potential 141, 169, 175
resource-depletion hypothesis 69, 83
retrieval 104–112

S
semantic clustering 133–138
semantic elaboration 60–61
semantic set 133–135, 137–138
spacing effect 127–129
structural elaboration 60

T
testing effect   103–104
text-based factors   46–47
textual enhancement   142–147
thematic set   133–138
transfer-appropriate processing   27

Type of Processing – Resource Allocation (TOPRA) model   62–64

V
vocabulary learning strategies   47

W
word boundaries   36
word-based determinants of learnability   40, 49